THE ESSENTIAL LIBRARY FOR

❧ IRISH ❧ AMERICANS

BY MORGAN LLYWELYN
FROM TOM DOHERTY ASSOCIATES

FICTION

Bard
Brian Boru
The Elementals
Finn Mac Cool
Lion of Ireland
Pride of Lions
Strongbow
1916

NONFICTION

The Essential Library for Irish Americans

THE ESSENTIAL LIBRARY FOR

IRISH AMERICANS

MORGAN LLYWELYN

A TOM DOHERTY ASSOCIATES BOOK
NEW YORK

THE ESSENTIAL LIBRARY FOR IRISH AMERICANS

Copyright © 1999 by Morgan Llywelyn

All rights reserved, including the right to reproduce this book,
or portions thereof, in any form.

This book is printed on acid-free paper.

Edited by David G. Hartwell

A Forge Book
Published by Tom Doherty Associates, Inc.
175 Fifth Avenue
New York, NY 10010

Forge® is a registered trademark of Tom Doherty Associates, Inc.

Book design by Lisa Pifher

Library of Congress Cataloging-in-Publication Data

Llywelyn, Morgan.
    The essential library for Irish Americans / Morgan Llywelyn.—
1st ed.
        p.   cm.
    ISBN 0-312-86914-2
    1. Ireland—Bibliography.   2. Irish Americans—Books and
reading.
I. Title.
Z2031.L59   1999
[DA906]
016.9415—dc21   98-46785
                                                                  CIP

First Edition: March 1999

Printed in the United States of America

0   9   8   7   6   5   4   3   2   1

CONTENTS

INTRODUCTION

Ireland has an enviable reputation for literature. Long before Christianity introduced the written word, Ireland's Celtic bards were its living books. They were entrusted with the history and genealogy of their race, together with the wealth of folklore and mythology that had been handed down from generation to generation. Subsequent research in other orally transmitted cultures has gone a long way toward proving the astonishing accuracy of this method. Once grooved in the brain, words were ineradicable. An Irish bard memorized his particular share of tribal wisdom by rote. The process could take as long as twenty years. Because it contained the intellectual wealth of the race, language thus became sacred and its meaning imbued with mystical power. In Ireland today, it still is.

Ireland's special magic is an inexhaustible resource for creativity. In relation to the small size of the island, which is no larger than the state of Pennsylvania, Ireland's influence on the international writing community is immense. Drawing on their Irish heritage, four native sons of this land have won the Nobel Prize for Literature: William Butler Yeats, George Bernard Shaw, Samuel Beckett, and Séamus Heaney. In recent times such contemporary Irish writers as William Trevor and John Banville have continued to gain international recognition for their literary output.

A number of highly acclaimed American writers are also of Irish descent, utilizing talents they inherited with blood and bone. Writers as diverse as F. Scott Fitzgerald, James T. Farrell, Jimmy Breslin, Mary Gordon, and Tom Clancy have secured a permanent place in the hearts of millions of readers.

The books chosen for this collection represent many aspects of the written word. Some are classics; others are literally hot off the press. Every one will reward the American reader with insight into the Irish, and perhaps a surprise or two along the way. *The Essential Library* attempts to avoid perpetuating stereotypical clichés. During the last century, a form of crude "stage Irishman" was frequently depicted in burlesque theater and on the American stage. With his corny brogue and his big red nose, he was the brunt of outrageous slurs. The image may have originated with the political cartooning of the Irish by the British satirical magazine, *Punch. Punch* invariably depicted the Irish as filthy peasants, sly rogues and drunkards, the scum of the earth. Such ethnic insults were a part of nineteenth-century humor, but unfortunately the Irish caricature has remained fixed in some minds right down to the present day.

The Essential Library undertakes to present a more accurate portrait. There is much to discover about Ireland and the Irish that may come as a surprise. For example, the word "brogue" does not have that meaning in Ireland, where an Irish accent is simply called . . . an Irish accent; or, in the Irish language itself, *blas*. Whereas "brogue" means a type of shoe. The famous Irish shamrock is not a special, magical plant; merely a variety of common clover. The Irish do not say, "Faith and begorra," nor do they refer to their homeland as the Emerald Isle. And far from being the national drink, Irish coffee was invented on the spur of the moment to welcome the chilled, weary Americans who made the first passenger flights across the Atlantic. The Americans have been its greatest devotees ever since.

Ready for more? St. Patrick did not drive the snakes out of Ireland; thanks to the Ice Age nine thousand years ago, there were never any snakes here. And although it may disappoint tourists to hear this, there are no leprechauns either. The tiny scoundrel with his green jacket and pot of gold is a purely fictitious creation, a bit of storytelling fun—which is why a leprechaun tale or two may be found in this collection.

Having lived for many years in America, and for many years in Ireland, I am aware how much unites the two cultures—and how much separates them. Ireland is not a smaller, greener version of America. Although English is spoken in both countries, American/English and Irish/English are two vastly different languages.

The baked goods Americans call "cookies," the Irish call "sweet biscuits." An American "biscuit" is a "scone" in Ireland. American "soda pop" is Irish "minerals." In Ireland, "cute" means shrewd, cunning; "bold" means naughty. And as for "crack," in America it may be a sharp noise, a break in the surface, or a form of cocaine, but when spoken in

Ireland, the same word—written as *craic*—refers to lively conversation. When you cross the Atlantic, sentence structure changes as well. In an Irish/English sentence, for example, "Where are you after going?" translates as "Where did you go?", not "Where do you want to go?"

On St. Patrick's Day, it is said everyone claims to be Irish, but throughout the rest of the year a growing number of Americans are tracing their Irish roots and rediscovering their heritage. The books chosen for this library have been carefully selected for that readership, as well as for anyone who loves to read. Each of them in some way illuminates Ireland, Irish America, or the condition of being Irish.

Some well-known titles are conspicuous by their absence because they are too flawed in their representations of the land and its people. The writers whose works have been chosen genuinely *know* Ireland, although they may have widely differing opinions. Most of the books named here can be found in American bookstores, purchased over the Internet, or ordered from specialty bookshops. Of necessity, the list is not limited to recent publications. Books have a very short shelflife these days. A few of those that are absolute essentials for the well-read Irish-American are not currently in print; others were published only in Britain. Naturally, some of the best and most representative books about Ireland are from Irish sources.

Every book listed here can be acquired by readers in the United States at the time of writing. Those that cannot be purchased through commercial sources can be accessed through interlibrary loans or university libraries, or in some instances ordered direct from Irish booksellers. Addresses for a few suggested sources are given at the end of this book. For a comprehensive overview of Irish-American writing, I would suggest *The Irish Voice in America: Irish-American Fiction from the 1870's to the 1980's,* by Charles Fanning, which is published by the University Press of Kentucky (1991).

The Essential Library hopes to introduce you to many hours of enjoyable reading. There are a number of categories, each with something special to offer. Histories and reference works will provide much more than a basic education about Ireland. Crammed with fascinating tidbits, these are books that make you want to grab someone by the arm and say, "Just listen to this! Did you know that the Irish elk had antlers *twelve feet* wide? Did you know that the ancient Irish had ten degrees of marriage? Did you know . . . ?"

Biographical works examine the lives of men and women who represent Ireland and the Irish heritage in a variety of ways. Some are famous on the world stage and have had a major impact on society. Others are relatively unknown, yet worth knowing. Saint or sinner, each subject is unforgettable.

Readers who want well-written fiction will find the sort of books they enjoy as well. Adventure, family sagas, historical novels, tales of suspense and the supernatural, enough romance to satisfy the hungriest heart—it's all here. Unfortunately, space prevents the listing of many other fine novels, and more are being written all the time.

The library offers examples of Irish humor, too. Many centuries ago, the Irish developed satire to an art form, but contemporary writers tend to be either wry and sarcastic, or self-deprecating. Much of their wit is also very provincial and does not "travel well." One needs to be familiar with the people and events in order to appreciate the humor. However, that is not always the case, as the works cited here demonstrate.

Myth and folklore are strongly represented because mythology is a singularly formative influence in Ireland—both present and past. What is now perceived as mythology was once our religion, the mystical and spiritual soul of the Celtic people. The first Christian missionaries to Ireland did not attempt to expunge the earlier beliefs; instead, they cleverly grafted the "new" faith onto the old, appropriating pagan festivals and introducing many druidic concepts into Celtic Christianity. Irish mythology therefore occupies a similar position to Irish culture as the Jewish religion does to the Jewish culture.

Poetry is prominent here, too. No other literary form is more identified with Ireland, which has produced two Nobel Prize–winning poets. Irish poetry reaches direct to the soul: sometimes with the lyrical mythic imagery of Yeats, sometimes with the deceptively simple phrases of Heaney. There is no one form of Irish poetry. Yet there is a unifying thread that runs through all Irish poems: the underlying bardic voice, the true legacy of the Gael.

Then there are the travel and picture books that provide visual windows into the Irish world. Every year an astonishing number of new ones appear, testimony to the enduring allure of Ireland's charm. For certain breathtaking views, no written word will do. You have to drink this scenery with your eyes.

Some of Ireland's finest writing has been for the stage, but I have not included plays in this list because they really belong in a separate category. However, I would recommend that every Irish American be familiar with the work of such writers as John Millington Synge, Seán O'Casey, and Brian Friel. *The Playboy of the Western World* scandalized audiences at its first production in 1907, yet ultimately made Synge immortal. O'Casey's *The Shadow of a Gunman, Juno and the Paycock,* and *The Plough and the Stars* are not only great theater but powerful social commentary. Friel's *Dancing at Lughnasa* took America by storm in the 1990s for good reason. Beneath its zany depiction of Irish peasant life lie universal truths.

Choosing these books has been a challenge. For the most part I have limited selections to one volume (or one series) by each author. Biography is an exception because both Tim Pat Coogan and Richard Ellman have written definitive biographies of several major Irish figures. They have, and deserve, multiple entries, as does James Joyce.

Any recommended reading list is subjective. I personally have read every book on this list, and have selected the ones I would like to put in my guestroom for a visiting Irish American friend. Imagine them lined up on bookshelves and stacked on the bedside table, waiting to give you a broad-spectrum view of this land so many love.

Your bed is made up with fresh Irish linen and a plump duvet. There is a gentle turf fire glowing on the hearth and a good reading lamp close to hand. Settle in, make yourself comfortable . . . and begin.

AUTOBIOGRAPHY, BIOGRAPHY, AND MEMOIRS

ADAMS, GERRY

Before the Dawn

Brandon Press in association with William Heinemann, London, 1996; William Morrow, New York, 1997

The life and times of the leader of Sinn Féin told in his own words. Describing the making of an Irish republican and the activities of today's Irish Republican Army (IRA), *Before the Dawn* is essential reading for anyone with an interest in contemporary Ireland.

Gerry Adams is a classic product of the Catholic working class of Northern Ireland. His father was a building laborer, his mother a "doffing mistress" in a linen mill. When Gerry Adams was born in West Belfast in 1948, his parents were living with his mother's mother. Harsh poverty and chronic overcrowding were a way of life. Eventually Gerry would have nine siblings, but things never got any easier for the family. Yet their lives were little different from those around them.

Both sides of the family had strong backgrounds in republican and working-class politics. The year before Gerry Adams was born, his father had been released from prison after serving five years for republican activities—a sentence that began when the senior Adams was only sixteen years old. The dream of a united Ireland that had fueled the Easter Rising in 1916 was still alive, and nowhere more ardently supported than among the Irish Catholics in West Belfast. Since the six northern counties were partitioned off from the rest of Ireland by the Anglo-Irish Treaty of 1921, northern Catholics had known the pain of being an oppressed minority in their own land.

The late forties were a time of great change internationally as the postwar boom got underway; but Belfast was the exception—at least for Catholics. Former center of a thriving linen industry, Belfast was also home to Harland & Wolff, the shipbuilders who had once built the *Titanic* and supplied many ships to the war effort. But Protestants controlled the management positions; the best Catholics could hope for was menial labor. The province was sustained on the principle of inequality. Those in power, who profited from it, did not want to see that principle threatened.

Gerry Adams was a shy, scrawny child, who took his Catholicism seriously. But in other ways he was the usual fun-loving boy, full of mischief without malice. His autobiography paints a graphic, often engaging picture of a young man's rites of passage. Girls, sports, clowning around with his friends, peering anxiously into the mirror and counting his pimples—these were the staples of his boyhood.

The book is not without Irish humor, even in dark situations. The mothers of West Belfast often had to pawn items of their husbands' clothing to feed their families, and Adams recounts overhearing two women talking during a spell of changeable weather: "The weather can't make its mind up," one says. "One minute it's teeming with rain, the next the sun is splitting the trees."

"I know," replies the other. "You wouldn't know what to pawn, would you?"

But though his childhood seemed relatively normal, Adams was not growing up in a normal world. He tells us that for a long time he remained naive about sectarianism, partly because he did not encounter it in his everyday life, partly because he didn't recognize it when he did meet it. People from Catholic West Belfast shopped for bargains in the Protestant Shankill Road, where, as he says, "They didn't care what religion you were so long as you had the cash."

Then, in 1959, a man Adams describes as "a sectarian anti-Catholic demagogue named Ian Paisley" bellowed such a message of virulent religious hatred that a Protestant mob attacked a Catholic-owned fish-and-chip shop on the Shankill Road. Paisley's Ulster Protestant Association won control of the Shankill Unionist Association and vowed to keep Protestant and loyal workers in employment in preference to Catholic workers.

Again and again, Adams would witness the tragedy engendered by a society divided. As his body grew, so did his mind—and his sense of injustice. In school he found it strange that he and other students were taught only English history, as if Ireland did not exist. He asked questions but was denied answers, so his curious mind led him to attend educational classes conducted by Sinn Féin, the Irish republican political party whose name translates as "We Ourselves." There Gerry Adams read many books that had never been featured in his school curriculum. He began to feel an intense pride in the fact that he was Irish.

By the time he was seventeen the young man was restless in school, bored by an education that did not seem relevant to the life working-class Catholic men were destined to lead. Leaving school, he took a job as a barman in a public house, where he received a different form of education. In those pre-Troubles days, Protestant and Catholic sometimes met on equal footing in the bonhomie of the pub. Adams tells of singing a loyalist anthem one night with as much gusto as anyone else. In the pubs of Belfast he heard politics endlessly argued from all sides of the political spectrum.

Then Ian Paisley vowed to lead a march to tear down the Irish flag atop the Sinn Féin office, on the grounds that the flying of a "foreign" flag was illegal in the province. Fifty members of the Royal Ulster Constabulary burst into the office with sledgehammers and ripped down the flag. The largely Catholic Falls Road area was soon embroiled in a riot.

Within weeks, Gerry Adams officially joined the Sinn Féin party.

The year 1966 marked the fiftieth anniversary of the Easter Rising and was commemorated all over Ireland, north and south. Ian Paisley retaliated by launching the *Protestant Telegraph*, a weekly paper devoted to anti-Catholic tirades. Within a short time Paisley had so stirred up sectarian feelings that violence erupted, to which the government of Northern Ireland reacted with alarm. Arrests, beatings, internment . . . the British authorities had a large arsenal of weapons to use against any people so foolish as to demand their civil rights.

Adams describes the Orange Parade in Derry which set off what was called "The Battle of the Bogside." Orange parades through Catholic areas were blatantly triumphalist, celebrating the victory of the Protestant William of Orange over the Catholic James Stuart three hundred years earlier. At the edge of the area known as the Bogside, young Catholic nationalists clashed with loyalists in an effort to prevent the Orangemen from marching through their streets. The event turned into a siege. On the second day, seven hundred members of the Royal Ulster

Constabulary, backed by loyalist mobs, undertook to force their way into the Bogside behind a cloud of poison gas. People were clubbed with batons; petrol bombs were thrown; the innocent suffered along with the guilty. The Troubles had begun.

From the moment Adams joined Sinn Féin, his life has been in almost constant danger. He describes himself as being gripped by contradictory feelings in the early years. He had the youthful, exciting conviction that a revolution was happening and he was going to be a part of it. But he speaks now with chagrin of the sense of naïveté, of innocence almost, of his peers, who thought that the demands they were making were so reasonable, the other side must surely understand and give in.

They were wrong, of course; tragically so. The dead and dying were adding up on both sides, victims of a hatred that fed upon itself like cancer.

Before the Dawn is primarily an examination of the tragedy that is Northern Ireland, and the lengths to which that tragedy drives people on both sides of the divide. Adams is disarmingly frank about his own thoughts, while being careful to shield his wife and children from the dangerous glare of the spotlight. His courtship and marriage to Colette McArdle, "with a war raging all around us," is touchingly told, however.

A strong sense of duty permeates the writing, yet there is none of the fanaticism one might expect. Depending upon their own political bias, reviewers have variously described Adams's book as courageous and incisive—or as manipulative and mawkish. But no one fails to have an opinion. Gerry Adams is someone about whom it is impossible to be neutral. He is a major presence on the current Irish scene, and whatever happens in the future, his influence will be felt for a long time to come.

Borstal Boy

Hutchinson, London, 1958; David R. Godine, New York, 1991

In Ireland, the late Brendan Behan is described as "rebel, rogue, and writer"—in that order. This may say something very revealing about what the Irish prize in a man's character.

Born in Dublin in 1923 in Holles Street Hospital (the name on his birth certificate is Francis, not Brendan), Brendan Behan spent his childhood under the stern eye of a tough, domineering grandmother. Known to one and all as "Granny English," she not only spoiled him dreadfully but also plied him with drink from an early age. Later he would claim he did not remember a time he had not been drinking.

He left school at the age of fourteen to follow his father's trade as a housepainter, but continued to receive an education at home through the traditional Irish medium of hearing ballads and stories from Irish history. Following the family's strongly republican tradition, young Behan joined the IRA in 1939. He was arrested in Liverpool for possessing explosives when he was only sixteen years old. *Borstal Boy* opens with that arrest.

The landlady shouted up the stairs: "Oh God, oh Jesus, oh Sacred Heart. Boy, there's two gentlemen to see you."

I knew by the screeches of her that these gentlemen were not calling to enquire after my health. I grabbed my suitcase,

containing potassium chloride, sulphuric acid, gelignite and det-
onators . . . and the rest of my Sinn Féin conjuror's outfit. . . .

But before Behan could escape, they seized him. He was arrested
and thrown into jail, an experience that he describes with almost clinical
detail. At first the contempt of his captors evoked a measured response.
He was articulate and polite, but they would have none of it. He began
to fear for his life, and imagined a republican martyr's death: "Drums
muffled, pipes draped, slow march. When but a lad of sixteen years a
felon's cap he wore."

Romantic imaginings were soon replaced by harsh reality. At his
trial, Behan asserted his Irish patriotism. The juvenile court magistrate
was not amused; he sentenced the boy to three years of detention in
Walton Borstal. A borstal is the roughest sort of reform school. Behan's
descriptions of the brutality to which he was subjected there make one
wonder how anything decent could ever be produced by such "reform-
ing." The world of the borstal was indifferent to simple humanity. On
the day Behan arrived, the warders welcomed him by shouting abuse
deriding both his name and his nationality. Behan tells us that he tried
to distract himself by imagining the mythic Irish hero Cuchulain with
all his enemies around him, standing with his back against a tree, calling
on "the gods of death and grandeur to hold him up till his last blood
flowed."

A warder struck young Behan again and again. Then he was thrown,
shivering, into a cubicle he describes as not even the size of a dwarf's
coffin, and ordered to strip. He soon learned that humiliation, pain, and
fear were calculated elements of the punishment meted out to juvenile
offenders—particularly if they were Irish.

Conditions in the borstal were primitive, violence always seething
just below the surface. Later, Behan would describe one of his captors
as saying, "I have him bitched, balloxed and bewildered, for there's a
system and a science in taking the piss out of a screw and I'm a well-
trained man at it." The other boys in the borstal were a mixed lot,
mostly from an impoverished background and many already hardened
to a life of crime. One was a Dubliner called Jerry Gildea, whom Brendan Behan knew well. Behan describes adventures the boys had once
shared. His writing perfectly captures the bawdy, cocksure conversation
of teenage boys together, and those moments of carefree youth provide

a stark counterpoint to the horrors the two subsequently endured in the borstal.

To his credit, amid all the hatred to which he was exposed, Brendan Behan found something positive: friendship, solidarity, and healing moments of kindness. He was a complex man, who spun gold out of the dross of his life. The story he tells in these pages is not self-pitying. One can read it with horror but not contempt. And sometimes one is seized with sheer admiration for Brehan's turn of phrase. Consider this: "The morning is always a good time. Till about eleven o'clock when it begins to feel its age."

Borstal Boy is not a complete autobiography but a memoir of one segment of a man's youth. Those years were enormously influential, however, and the rest of Behan's life must be considered in the light of his reform school experiences. The book ends with his release from the borstal. He was immediately sent back to Ireland, where he describes his first glimpse of the Dublin Mountains with unconcealed joy: "There they were, as if I'd never left them, in their sweet and stately order around the Bay."

Brendan Behan would live and die loving Ireland, but his was not an easy life. As the result of a shooting incident in which a policeman was wounded, he was later rearrested and imprisoned for fourteen years. During this he learned the Irish language, read omnivorously, and began to write. His books and plays brought him both success and money, but his life was marred by sexual ambivalence, a dysfunctional marriage to Beatrice ffrench-Salkeld, and above all by alcoholism. Perhaps he had been doomed from the day he entered the borstal . . . or that earlier day when Granny English bought him his first pint.

Brendan Behan is special to Americans partly because of the time he spent in New York in the 1950s, when his play *The Quare Fellow* was a hot ticket. Many people still remember his theatrical tantrums, his affair with Valerie Danby-Smith, Ernest Hemingway's assistant, and his gargantuan binges. Yet for all that, the *New York Times* wrote, "He has more than charm, he has instinctive kindness and charity, a verbal grace, an unforced assertion of a strong personality."

Behan died in 1964 of alcoholism and diabetes; he is buried in Dublin. His life was almost a textbook example of how not to foster and develop a talent, but his writing endures as the legacy of a tragic yet enormously gifted Irishman.

BULGER, WILLIAM M.

While the Music Lasts:
My Life in Politics

Houghton Mifflin, Boston, 1996

I rish Americans have made a deep impact on politics in the United
States. Everyone is familiar with John F. Kennedy and Thomas P.
"Tip" O'Neill, both of whose lives have been the subject of excellent
biographies. But other stories are equally interesting and perhaps more
typical. William Bulger, for example, is the embodiment of the "Irish-
American boy makes good." The Irish qualities of affability, quick wit,
and a deep sense of loyalty have contributed in no small measure to his
success.

From beginning to end, *While the Music Lasts* is the memoir of a
dedicated politician, reminiscent of Edwin O'Connor's great novel, *The
Last Hurrah* (see p. 239). The same smoke-filled rooms provide background atmosphere for both books, although they are set in different
eras. O'Connor's novel is ultimately tragic, however, while Bulger's life
so far has been something of a triumph. For seventeen years he served
as president of the Massachusetts Senate, and is currently president of
the University of Massachusetts.

Born in 1943, Bulger was very much a product of the working-class
Irish enclave of South Boston—"Southies." At the time of the Great
Famine, the influx of Irish immigrants into Boston far exceeded the
population of the city itself, leaving a legacy that remains to this day.

Bulger opens his story with a revealing view of Boston as he knew
it in his boyhood: "In the distance soared the pale towers of Yankee

Babylon, their alien frigidity made bearable by what we perceived as the warmth and color of the hanging garden of South Boston, where we lived. . . . Our roots ran deep. They kept us from being merely part of the whole. We valued our mélange of cultural traditions, and we had a shared sense of security. We were a *Neighborhood.*"

Irish Americans frequently have turned to politics as the road to the power and status their ancestors were denied. Bulger tells us that he was fascinated by politics from an early age. He trained as an attorney, but that profession was always subordinate to a larger dream. In many ways a traditional Boston "pol," an avowed admirer of James Curley, Bulger entered the political arena to advance the interests of ordinary people. "It was not a sense of power I felt, but a joyful exhilaration at being able to make things better. One learns in time that standing up for such values . . . can trigger savage attacks. But you don't think about that for long, nor very seriously. Not while you still hunger to make a difference. Not while you still think it's all possible. Not while you can still hear the music."

Step by step, Bulger takes the reader along the path he followed as he set out to fulfill those early dreams. He describes with clarity the frustrations of a political system that sometimes seemed determined to prevent all progress. But he persisted, working his way up through that system, learning how to play the game. He helped draft anti–child abuse bills, and although he supported desegregation, he opposed the forced busing plans that divided Boston in the early seventies.

William Bulger is outspoken and forthright and never loses command of his facts. In accordance with the best political tradition, he uses his autobiography to settle some old scores; but throughout the book his devotion to his family is obvious. In 1960 he had married Mary Foley, whose mother, Sarah, had come from Connemara. Mary was to prove an inspiration to her husband through the trials of life. She bore him nine children, and they still live in the same South Boston house they bought in 1966. They are very much part of "the Neighborhood."

Theoretically, no true biography is possible until the subject has died, putting an end to that person's story. As long as someone remains alive, their existence is mutable and their influence constantly changes the shape of the lives they touch. The linear sequence of any man's experience and behavior forms a significant pattern, a mosaic distributed in time rather than in space. Each experience making up the pattern is given its final meaning by virtue of its place in, and contribution to, the whole.

It is well to study the lives of living Irish Americans such as William Bulger therefore, in order to reach a deeper understanding of just what constitutes their culture, and the importance of the Irish-American contribution to the larger American scene.

COOGAN, TIM PAT

De Valera: Long Fellow, Long Shadow

Hutchinson, London, 1993; HarperCollins, New York, 1996

In writing of Eamon de Valera, the author tackles one of Ireland's icons. Although he died in 1975, de Valera remains a towering presence whose shadow still falls over Irish life. The history of Ireland for much of the twentieth century is, quite simply, the history of de Valera.

Eamon de Valera was born in 1882, in New York City. On December 3, he was christened as Edward de Valera, but apparently his birth was registered under the name of George. This was not corrected until he was sentenced to death by the British for his part in the 1916 Rising. Then his mother obtained a copy of his birth certificate in an effort to prove his American citizenship and thus save his life.

According to the biography written by Lord Longford and T. P. O'Neill, de Valera's mother was an Irish girl named Catherine Coll, an immigrant from County Limerick, and his father was Juan Vivion de Valera, a young Spaniard whom Kate Coll met the year she arrived in America. However, Tim Pat Coogan's investigations have led him to take a second look at young "Dev's" origins and to question some of the assertions made by others.

From remarks that de Valera himself wrote in the family Bible, we know that his father died in 1884 in either Minneapolis or Denver. Whatever caused the separation of his parents, Kate put her small son into the care of another Irish immigrant woman and went back to work. The arrangement was less than ideal. Eventually the little boy's uncle

Ned, returning to Ireland, took the child with him, back to the family farm. Thus Eamon de Valera grew up in the land with which his name would forever be connected.

Coogan's intensively researched study of de Valera's life and times focuses on the influences of those early years in some detail, maintaining that "essential to the de Valera saga were the violence and servility bred in the dark underside of colonial Irish peasant life." Coogan clearly feels that the rage of the people at being rendered servile, and their respect for anyone who would help alleviate that condition, resulted in much of de Valera's subsequent political popularity. De Valera himself never forgot those years on the farm. His early thoughts were so conditioned by its routine that when he was asked to write a school essay on "Making Hay While the Sun Shines," the only thing he could think to say was, "What other time would you make hay?"

Although as a boy he often heard the events of the day discussed around the family table, in his grammar school days de Valera saw politics as a phenomenon outside the reality of daily existence. But he was smart enough to realize that unless he applied himself to getting a higher education, he would spend his life digging potatoes or hauling stones out of muddy fields. His enrollment at Blackrock College in Dublin would prove to be a turning point in his life. There his exceptional intellect was recognized and encouraged, with the result that in 1899 he took honors in Greek, Latin, English, French, arithmetic, algebra, and Euclid, and qualified for Student of the Year. The last honor endowed him with increased stature and self-confidence as a public speaker.

The priesthood tempted de Valera for a time; but, as Coogan wonders, "Was it [that] the mighty ego could not completely subordinate itself to the dictates of a Church whose rule as a layman he dutifully followed?" At any rate, he entered the teaching profession instead. Then in 1908 he fell in love with Sinead Flanagan, a primary school teacher four years older than himself. They were married in 1910—the ceremony conducted in Irish. By 1912, they had two children, Vivion and Mairin. When separated from his family by an appointment as director of a summer school in Galway, de Valera wrote long, unabashedly sentimental letters home.

But the man also had a steely core. He joined the nationalist Gaelic League and in 1911 stood for election to the governing body of that organization, but was defeated. In a state of high indignation, he claimed

the voting had been rigged. But he had had his first taste of politics.
Two years later, he joined the Irish Volunteers. The Volunteers had
recently been founded at the suggestion of Professor Eoin MacNeill,
vice president of the Gaelic League, as a measure to counter the heavily
armed Ulster Volunteer Force (UVF) in the North. The UVF had
vowed to prevent Home Rule in Ireland by force of arms.

According to Coogan, at the time de Valera joined the Volunteers,
he did not know that the corps was in effect the military arm of the
Irish Republican Brotherhood (IRB). Founded in 1858, the IRB was a
secret organization pledged to overthrow British rule and create an independent Irish republic. Heavily subsidized by Irish-American sup-
porters, the IRB had earlier infiltrated a number of nationalist
movements such as the Gaelic League, and was soon quietly in control
of the Volunteers as well. With the outbreak of World War I, its governing council began planning the Easter Rising to take advantage of
Britain's distraction.

When de Valera learned of the IRB connection with the Volunteers,
he does not seem to have been troubled by it. He had already cast his
lot firmly with the republican movement. In the Easter Rising he served
as a battalion commandant, endearing himself to his men by means of
a clever ruse to deflect British fire from his headquarters at Boland's
Mills. De Valera and his troops were taken prisoner at the end of Easter
Week, when the rebel forces surrendered to save Dublin and its citizens
from further bloodshed.

De Valera was fortunate to escape the executions that took the lives
of the republican leaders such as Patrick Henry Pearse and James Connolly. He was originally sentenced to death, but that sentence was com-
muted to penal servitude for life . . . after he had written touching
farewell notes to his friends and family, which Coogan quotes.

In Lincoln Prison, de Valera assumed a mantle of leadership he was
never to put aside. Coogan also tells us, "His strong religious faith was
of course a central reason why he was able to bear up against prison life
so well." De Valera's faith—though not necessarily in the Almighty—
was well founded. On February 3, 1919, Michael Collins and Harry
Boland organized his escape. De Valera, dressed as a woman in a fur
coat, and Boland lost themselves among courting couples from a nearby
military hospital.

The Volunteers reorganized and the first Dáil, or Irish republican parliament, was formed in defiance of Britain. On April 1, 1919, Eamon de Valera was elected as the first president of Dáil Éireann. He determined to go to America to seek aid for the cause. His goal was to have America speak out on behalf of Irish independence at the Paris Peace Conference.

As with every aspect of de Valera's career during those turbulent years, the story here is filled with plots and counterplots, subterfuges and spies. But thanks to the Irish Americans, in America he enjoyed the comforts of a room at the Waldorf-Astoria. There on June 23 he held his first American press conference and fired a shot across the bows of the American president, Woodrow Wilson: "We shall fight for a real democratic League of Nations, not the present unholy alliance which does not fulfil the purposes for which the democracies of the world went to war. I am going to ask the American people to give us . . . a League of Nations that will include Ireland."

Although he did not get that demand, de Valera firmly established himself as a towering presence on the Irish-American scene. He also proved to be an adept political animal, supporting candidates for office who would in turn support the Irish republican cause.

It was this gift for political maneuvering that would differentiate him from his erstwhile ally, Michael Collins. Collins successfully led the Irish forces in the War for Independence from Britain; but in the negotiations that followed, de Valera succeeded in placing Collins in the invidious position of having to negotiate the Anglo-Irish Treaty—a treaty that could not possibly give the Irish the republic they wanted. Coogan follows the machinations step by step, illuminating de Valera's thought processes as well as those of other major figures on the political scene.

When the treaty was signed in 1921, partitioning the island and maintaining six northern counties within the United Kingdom while creating an Irish Free State in the other twenty-six, civil war followed. At its conclusion, Collins was dead by an assassin's hand. The Irish Free State had been established, but Eamon de Valera was firmly ensconced as the symbol of the denied republic. Many held him personally responsible for the civil war.

De Valera sheds a clear, uncompromising light on the power struggles that followed. The civil war left scars on the Irish psyche that are still evident to this day. The republican movement looked to de Valera, not to the Free State Dáil, as the fountainhead of authority. In 1923, de Valera told a rally in Ennis, County Clare, that he remained unalterably opposed to partition and had entered politics to further that view. For him there could be only one Ireland: united. When he crossed the border to make a speech to that effect in Newry, he was promptly arrested and served with an exclusion order—thus reaping a windfall of publicity that helped polarize the Irish people around him.

Throughout his long career, de Valera showed a great flair for leadership, exploiting political tradition to instill in the people a pride in their Irishness. He also knew how to manipulate emotion. "Add in a few black cloaks, white horses and torchlight processions," says Coogan, "and the Eamon de Valera Show was a very tough act for his adversaries to follow."

In 1921, de Valera was chosen to be the first president of the Irish Free State. Then at seventy-six years of age, he had the satisfaction of becoming president of the Republic of Ireland. He attended President Kennedy's funeral, and in 1964, at the age of eighty-one, addressed the Congress of the United States. His death in 1975 followed by eight months the death of his wife.

Coogan's well-rounded biography does not focus solely on politics, but also gives us a look at the private life of a very difficult man. In keeping with the Irish tradition of a sexually powerful chieftain, for a time there were rumors of infidelities, including an affair in America. But by dint of a constant, unyielding assertion of his Catholicism and high moral code, de Valera managed to silence the gossip. Eventually most Irish people would consider it unthinkable for "the Chief" ever to have been less than a saint. Perhaps, Coogan suggests, Eamon de Valera was fortunate that he presided over a more innocent age.

His vision of Ireland became the guiding image for the nation. During his lifetime de Valera *was* Ireland, in the same way that Franklin Delano Roosevelt *was* America, to millions. He both defined and divided the country, and was directly responsible for the creation of the Irish Constitution, the Fianna Fáil political party, and the Irish Press newspaper group. De Valera's legacy was a political church-state monolith with serious implications for Northern Ireland, the role of women in society, the Irish language, and the whole concept of an Irish nation. Some people today still revere him as a near saint; others blame him for all of Ireland's ills. Neither is a true picture of the man.

In this thoughtful and often controversial study, Tim Pat Coogan argues that de Valera was a world figure who remade Ireland with the noblest intentions, while at the same time attempting to confine the Irish people to the narrowest of cultural and intellectual horizons. For good or ill we have been what he made us. Only today, as societal change is creating a new, European Ireland, can we look back and realize how far we have come out from under that tall man's shadow.

Michael Collins

Roberts, Rinehart, New York, 1992; Hutchinson, London, 1993

Hero of a 1990s major motion picture starring Liam Neeson, Michael Collins is one of the most colorful figures in the history of Ireland. Affectionately nicknamed "the Big Fellow," he was born in rural West Cork in 1890, the son of a farmer. The boy had a keen mind and little taste for farming, but for someone from his background there was no other work. So at sixteen, Collins, like many other Irishmen seeking opportunity denied them at home, went to London. There he found employment as a clerk, first in the Post Office and then with a firm of stockbrokers. Both aspects of this education in business practices were to serve him in good stead later.

While in London, Collins joined the Irish Republican Brotherhood, the secret society dedicated to winning Irish independence. He returned to Ireland and joined the republican militia, the Irish Volunteers, in time to take part in the Easter Rising of 1916. He was among those assigned to the General Post Office, where the Volunteers set up their military headquarters. The men who had signed the Proclamation—Ireland's Declaration of Independence—were executed by the British when the rising was put down, but Michael Collins was merely imprisoned and later released. Coogan makes plain that the British considered him a very minor player in the "Irish rebellion." That may have been true during Easter Week, but the authorities would later have reason to regret their decision to set him free.

From being a soldier, Collins became a political activist. The Easter Rising had had some positive results; British policy in regard to the governing of Ireland was changing. In hopes of avoiding another rebellion, the Irish were being allowed some token power in their own country. After the victory of the republican Sinn Féin party in the 1918 general election and the establishment of a new Irish parliament, Michael Collins was named minister of home affairs; later he became minister for finance. Beneath this highly respectable front, however, Collins was hard at work setting up an intelligence network. He used knowledge acquired during his time in London to outmaneuver the British at their own intelligence game.

When the War for Independence broke out in 1919, Michael Collins came into his own. He organized the supply of weapons and ammunition to rearm the Volunteers and demonstrated his leadership ability as commander in chief of the Irish Army. His men loved him. Collins proved a formidable opponent for the British, who in spite of their superior numbers and firepower could not outwit him. He wheeled around Dublin on his bicycle, unrecognized, sabotaging their every move.

Along with Collins's other talents went great physical energy, courage, and an irresistible charm that won the hearts of a number of women. His romances, some with married women, were a matter for much speculation. His love affair with Kitty Kiernan was moving toward marriage when Collins became a member of the delegation that went to London in 1921 to negotiate the Anglo-Irish Treaty. It looked as if Michael Collins had won the war.

The treaty proved to be a disaster. Led by the wily British prime minister, David Lloyd George, the British delegation would only agree to certain conditions. There would be no republic. Ireland could become a Free State with Dominion status within the British Commonwealth of Nations—but only on the condition that the island was partitioned and six counties remained part of the United Kingdom. Collins and the other members of the Irish party ultimately gave in, in order to gain freedom for the remaining twenty-six counties. Though he was convinced it was the best deal the Irish could get at the time, Collins remarked that in signing the treaty he had signed his own death warrant.

His words proved prophetic. The partitioning of Ireland caused enormous bitterness. Civil war broke out between pro-treaty forces, known as Free Staters, and Eamon de Valera's republicans, who wanted nothing less than a free and united Ireland. Michael Collins became commander in chief of the Free State forces. His ambush and murder in August 1922, almost on the eve of his wedding, is an enduring mystery. Arguments as to who shot Michael Collins will probably continue as long as Ireland itself. Meanwhile, the political divide between republicans and Free Staters, which resulted in the political parties of Fianna Fáil and Fine Gael, has shaped the Irish political scene ever since.

Tim Pat Coogan is one of the best known figures in Irish journalism, and a sharp-eyed observer of the political scene. Author, broadcaster, and former editor of the *Irish Press*, he has written several books, including a definitive work entitled *The IRA*. Coogan has a gift for uncovering long-hidden facts and piecing them together to make a coherent linear narrative that is as enjoyable as it is thorough.

His voice is never intrusive but always adds to the whole. To conclude with an example: "One of the continuing accusations against Collins is that he drank too much. But to paraphrase Lincoln's remark when Grant's drinking was reported to him, I would seriously advocate that the cadets in the Irish Army staff college be instructed to partake of a few glass of [Collins's] favorite whiskey each night, because the amount of work he got through was phenomenal."

COOKE, DENNIS

Persecuting Zeal:
A Portrait of Ian Paisley

Brandon Books, Dingle, Co. Kerry, Ireland, 1996

In contemporary Ireland, no one has better exemplified the interlocking of the twin powers of politics and religion than Ian Paisley. The lethal variety of Ulster sectarianism that nurtured and still sustains Paisley and those who follow him has no counterpoint south of the border. A number of religions are freely practiced in the Irish Republic today. While the largest denomination is still Roman Catholic, there are Anglicans, Baptists, Methodists, Presbyterians, Baptists, Quakers, Mormons, Unitarians, Seventh-Day Adventists—the list is long. Dublin contains both mosques and synagogues and has had two Jewish lord mayors. No one is discriminated against on grounds of religion.

It's different in the North.

Dennis Cooke explains that what he calls "Paisleyism" has its roots in both the ethnic and the religious aspects of Irish history. He elaborates with a thumbnail sketch of the development of Christianity, including its split during the Reformation and the rise of Protestantism. By detailing the different philosophies of republicans—those who espouse a united Irish republic—and Orangemen—those who are still celebrating the triumph of the Protestants over the Catholics in Ireland three hundred years ago—Cooke puts the political situation in perspective. Then he sets out to fit Ian Paisley into the background that created him.

Ian Richard Kyle Paisley was born in 1926 in the small cathedral city of Armagh—where the greatest of Ireland's High Kings, Brian

Bóru, was buried in 1014. Paisley was the second son of James Kyle Paisley, a Baptist pastor, and his wife Isabella. The Paisleys traced their origins to the settlers who had come from the lowlands of Scotland early in the seventeenth century. They were beneficiaries of the policy we know today as "ethnic cleansing," by which Oliver Cromwell had driven the native Irish off their lands to turn the property over to those who swore to be loyal to the English crown.

In the years before World War I, Paisley's father had been one of the hundred thousand men who joined the Ulster Volunteer Force (UVF), taking up arms in grim determination to resist Home Rule for Ireland. He subsequently instilled in his sons the fears and concerns that had led him to join the UVF. To quote Ian Paisley, "He taught my brother and me the principles of true patriotism and the principles of civil and religious liberty. He loved this country, he loved this land, and he wanted to see this land free from the power of Rome by the power of the Gospel."

Paisley's father, who was known as Kyle, served as pastor of the Hill Street Baptist Church in Ballymena, a largely Presbyterian town, from 1928 to 1933. During this period there was a major split in the congregation. Older members resented their new pastor's strongly fundamentalist tendencies. Eventually Kyle Paisley withdrew from Hill Street and took up a new ministry on Waveney Road, where he remained for thirty-three years. As time passed, he moved farther and farther into the realm of the reformers and evangelicals.

Ian Paisley always took a deep interest in his father's work. When he was sixteen, he was accepted for a year's training at the Barry School of Evangelism, a fundamentalist college in Wales. There the young Paisley became absolutely convinced that God was calling him to be a preacher. Kyle Paisley's preference was for his son to continue his studies in the Reformed Presbyterian Church, whose beliefs were now closer to his own. Paisley threw himself into his studies with the energy that was to characterize everything he did. A contemporary is quoted as saying, "He was a man of considerable physical presence. He seemed rather loud and uncouth for a cleric. Most working-class Protestants were not into high-profile teachers, were not into extravagant, embarrassing religious evangelism." But Ian Paisley was.

"As a Protestant I could not accept that the Church of Rome is a Christian Church," he wrote in 1986. "Recognising the Church of Rome as revealed in Scripture as the 'mother of harlots and abominations of the earth' we maintain our total resistance to every attempt to accept that system as a Christian church." Upon this rock he set out to build a reputation for himself in Northern Ireland, which had always regarded its Catholic minority with mixed feelings comprised of guilt and contempt. Even when they were tolerated, they were "not like us." And they had the Irish Republic to the south, waiting like Big Brother to wrench them free from the grip of Britain—or so the Protestant Orangemen feared.

Ian Paisley has learned to play on those fears with consummate skill. But there is little doubt that his own feelings are quite genuine. No one could preach hatred unrelentingly, for so long, without actually hating. Furthermore, he enjoys the fight for its own sake. Cooke writes that "Protests against the Roman Catholic Church are a great source of amusement to Paisley and his colleagues."

For more than two thousand years, Ireland has been a tribal society. Inheritors of the tradition of a warrior aristocracy, the Irish defined themselves in battle until at last they were—somewhat—subdued by England. The "plantation" of English loyalists in the North to hold the country for the crown did not eliminate those tribal feelings; indeed, it exacerbated them. The love of battle for its own sake infected the newcomers as well. Ian Paisley is a classic example.

Paisley found the platform he sought by founding the Free Presbyterian Church of Ulster in 1951, when he was still only twenty-five years old. The church was first constituted in Crossgar, County Down— on St. Patrick's Day. The Free Presbyterians were as separate and distinct from the original Presbyterian Church as Ian Paisley was unlike moderate Protestantism. His followers in the new church were people who shared his hatreds and fears.

As with anything involving Ian Paisley, the founding of the Free Presbyterians is shrouded in a mist of schism and contention. But one thing is clear, Cooke insists: hatred is a fundamental doctrine, seen as a natural characteristic of the true Christian. In Paisley's own words, "This hatred is of the loyal servant who hates everything and everyone who hates his Lord." Paisleyites hate everyone who disagrees with them, all who are guilty of what they see as "apostasy." Both Pope John Paul II and Billy Graham fall under this heading.

Since founding the Free Presbyterians, Ian Paisley has become an increasingly political animal. He sees himself—and relishes the picture—as a true defender of the faith, using every tool at his disposal, including the British Parliament and the European Parliament, to achieve his ends. Time has not mellowed him, it has only made him more convinced than ever. The IRA has often played into his hands by presenting him with the violence he has always accredited to "Papists." But there is just as much blood on his hands. Paisley's diatribes have sent Ulster paramilitaries out to shoot and bomb and kill an equal number. And he has followers eager to take up his mantle in future. While his wife Eileen remains in the background, little more than a supportive figure, it is obvious Paisley is grooming his son Ian to follow in his footsteps.

To people abroad, much of what happens in Northern Ireland is incomprehensible. The tragedy spills over in newspapers and on television until it seems to encompass the entire island. Ireland is perceived as having two diametrically opposed images: one is that of a welcoming green land full of friendly people; the other is of a war zone replete with bombs and bullets and sudden, senseless violence. Which is the real Ireland? Where does the truth lie?

As politicians attempt to move along the torturous road to a peaceful settlement in the North, it is important that everyone with an interest in Ireland understand the background of today's problems. Without understanding, there can be no hope for the future. A major step can be taken by exploring the forces that motivate Ian Paisley.

COOTE, STEPHEN

W. B. Yeats: A Life

Hodder & Stoughton, London, 1997

I n the latest of many biographies on the famous Nobel Prize–winning poet, Stephen Coote focuses on the life of the man rather than his work. This is a wise choice, for all poetry is to some extent personal and the writing of poetry is inextricable from the life of the poet.

William Butler Yeats was born in Dublin in 1865, the eldest son of John Butler Yeats. Shortly after his birth the family moved to London, where they remained until 1880. Young Willie spent his holidays in County Sligo, Ireland, however, with his grandparents the Pollexfens, who were millers and shipowners. Those early experiences of the west of Ireland would remain with him all his life, leading him back again and again.

When the family returned to Dublin, Willie's father wished him to enroll in Trinity College, but the boy refused because he was afraid he could not meet the school's stringent entrance exams. Instead, he studied at the Metropolitan School of Art, where he became friends with George Russell—better known as the poet "A. E."—and a group of enthusiastic amateur "mystics."

From the age of seventeen, Yeats had been writing plays and po-etry in imitation of Spenser and Shelley. About 1886 he decided to abandon art and devote himself to writing. Shortly thereafter he met Standish O'Grady, whose influence caused him to "turn my back on foreign themes and decide that the race was more important than the individual." From then on, his writing would focus on Ireland and the Irish.

Yeats joined Madame Blavatsky's Theosophists in 1887 and the Order of the Golden Dawn in 1890. He met most of the poets of his generation at the Rhymers Club, which he helped found, and in 1891 he began the Irish Literary Society of London. But undoubtedly one of the most important connections he made was with Isabella Augusta, Lady Gregory, who was to become his patron and friend and provide much of the sustenance for the Celtic Revival.

The Celtic melancholy so common to Irish people was a powerful factor in Yeats's personality. In reading Coote's excellent biography, one must conclude that Yeats deliberately, if unconsciously, sought out those very circumstances that would cause him grief. His passion for the fabled beauty, Maud Gonne, is the most outstanding example. Writing later of their meeting in 1889, Yeats described the occasion as the moment when "all the troubles of my life began." That may be true, but around his long-unrequited love for the headstrong and often heartless Maud he constructed a wealth of unforgettable poetry. There are few love stories in literature more exquisitely painful, or frustrating, than that of Yeats and Maud Gonne.

She was not only beautiful, but a headstrong, and ardent, Irish nationalist. Under her influence, Yeats joined the Irish Republican Brotherhood and played a prominent part in the celebrations of the centenary for the Rising of 1798. Then, in 1891, he proposed marriage to Maud Gonne, but was refused. Instead, she married John MacBride, who was executed by the British after the Easter Rising. Their son, Seán Mac-Bride, would one day win the Nobel Peace Prize.

Yet as long as W. B. Yeats and Maud Gonne lived, they maintained a relationship of sorts. Some of his greatest poetry was written to her. Who can forget, "When you are old and gray and full of sleep . . . remember . . . But one man loved the pilgrim soul in you."

Yeats lived a complicated inner life. He never seems to have come to terms with his demons, which may be true of most creative people. The urge to understand and explain oneself continues to be one of the great motivating powers for writers. In the case of W. B. Yeats, Coote tells us, that urge became an attempt to capture the whole soul of Ireland. He did not always succeed, yet it is his voice and his imagery that sums up his native land for many who will never visit its shores.

Together with Lady Gregory and Edward Martyn, Yeats founded the Irish Literary Theatre in 1898. Its first performance, in 1899, was his own play, *The Countess Cathleen*. In 1902, his *Cathleen Ni Houlihan*, starring Maud Gonne in the title role, electrified audiences. Then in 1904 the company moved into the Abbey Theatre (formerly the Mechanics' Theatre) and theatrical history was made. Synge, O'Casey, and the other great playwrights of the day had found a very special home for their work; a home whose artistic integrity Yeats fiercely defended.

But it is as a poet that William Butler Yeats is best remembered. Though he died in 1939, his poetry is as full of magic as on the day it was penned. To read "Innisfree" on a soft, gray morning beside a quiet stream is to be lost in Erin.

CRONIN, ANTHONY

Samuel Beckett: The Last Modernist

HarperCollins, London, 1996

S amuel Barclay Beckett was born in 1906 in Foxrock, an upper-class suburb of Dublin. Later he would claim to have been born on Good Friday, April 13. His birth certificate, however, shows him to have been born on May 13, which was a Sunday. His father, William, was a building contractor and property speculator. Beckett's privileged background provides an added dimension for the reader interested in twentieth-century social history.

Anthony Cronin's biography gives us a detailed picture of Beckett's youth and adolescence. Samuel's stormy relationship with his mother, May, obviously had much to do with his subsequent attitude toward women. She was temperamental and subject to acute depression; a mismatched mate for easygoing, jovial Willie Beckett.

Cronin also writes with great insight of Beckett's Irishness and the effect it had on his life and work. Moody, brilliant, intensely private, often sexually frustrated and ambivalent toward women, Beckett is depicted as the product of his environment just as much as he was the creature of his talent. By the time he was in university, a great gulf of misunderstanding had opened between the young man and his family. When he came home for weekends, there was no communication of any sort. Like most writers, Beckett would spend the rest of his life attempting to establish communication—if not with his family, then with the world.

At Trinity College, Beckett received first-class honors, taking a B.A. in modern languages; after attending the École Normale Supérieure in Paris, he returned to Trinity to lecture in French. He resigned to spend the 1930s between Dublin, London, and Paris. His career in writing fiction began with a book of interrelated short stories set in Dublin, entitled *More Pricks Than Kicks,* published in 1934. After writing a novel about the Irish Everyman, *Murphy,* in 1938, Beckett's prose took on a growing abstraction of language and character.

When World War II broke out, he returned to France and began to work for the Resistance, explaining that "the Nazis started coming after my Jewish friends." Over the next three years, Beckett and his wife Suzanne rarely stayed in one place for long, but he kept writing. His novel *Watt,* not published until 1953, is from this period. Beckett once described himself as the son of an affluent Irish family who fled to expatriate poverty in an effort to find the elements he required emotionally. Impoverishment and subtraction became his style.

Beckett's first and most famous play, *Waiting for Godot,* was first performed in Paris at the Theatre de Babylone in 1953. He had changed direction again, moving from abstract prose to a world of physical objects and tangible space that has been described as "a tragicomic zone of human suffering." A later play, *Not I,* was drawn from women he knew in Ireland "stumbling down the lanes, in the ditches beside the hedgerows."

Step by fascinating step, Cronin charts Beckett's evolution from one of several gifted literati in 1930s Dublin to winning the Nobel Prize for Literature in 1969. By adopting a personal slant, the author undercuts the myth of saintliness and nobility that came to surround Beckett toward the end of his life. A highly regarded writer himself, Cronin is able to enter fully into the mental and imaginative life of his subject. He strips away the veil of inaccessibility that the great playwright created for himself in his later years, to reveal both his humanness and his humanity.

We meet a sociable Sam Beckett, who in the 1960s frequented the Falstaff bar in the rue Montparnasse in Paris. There he and his friend, Dubliner Con Levanthal, put away numerous glasses of whiskey with "amazing sang-froid." Later they might go on to play billiards, a game Beckett approached with fierce zest and great skill. Cronin has an incisive feel for Parisian life and provides graphic descriptions of the pubs, brothels, and nocturnal wanderings that marked Beckett's life at that time. Thus the French years are as clearly delineated as the Irish years, illumining the character of a man who tried to be as elusive as his writing. By writing in the French language he only added to this mystique.

On July 17, 1989, Suzanne Beckett died. She and Sam had been together for over fifty years in a relationship of great intensity, if not absolute fidelity. With her death Beckett was free to marry his long-term lover Barbara, but the marriage, though discussed, never took place. Instead, Beckett began very obviously winding up his life.

Samuel Beckett died in Paris on December 22, 1989, of respiratory problems. He is buried beside his wife in Montparnasse Cemetery. The last word is Anthony Cronin's: "His characters live in confusion, and the possibility of an after-life is part of it. . . . Many are not fully at home in the world. Samuel Beckett was less at home than most. Yet he too had found some final partings difficult; and his work, like all great art, is in some sense a celebration of existence."

ELLMANN, RICHARD

James Joyce

Oxford University Press, New York, 1983

Described by Anthony Burgess as "the greatest literary biography of the century," this weighty and extensively footnoted tome still manages to be highly entertaining. Thanks to Richard Ellmann's considerable gifts as a biographer, not only James Joyce but also the milieu in which he lived spring to vivid life. Ellmann has gained access to a wealth of formerly unpublished material that sheds new light on the character of the man and his contemporaries. But he resists the temptation to be didactic; instead, he tells the life and times of James Joyce as a richly layered story in a way Joyce himself would have approved.

James Augustine Joyce was born in Dublin in 1882, into an era that produced a bumper crop of great writers. His father, John Stanislaus Joyce, was an official at the Tax Office. Although the young Joyce had to leave boarding school when his father lost his job, he subsequently attended Belvedere College and University College Dublin. There he studied languages and read St. Thomas Aquinas and Aristotle. His first published work was an essay on the playwright Ibsen, which appeared in the *Fortnightly Review* in 1900.

But family financial circumstances were always straitened. Upon graduating in 1902, Joyce went off to Paris on borrowed money and lived a life of near-destitution there. The death of his mother in 1903 brought him back to Dublin, where he met Oliver St. John Gogarty and consorted with the bohemian set of the day. Apart from occasional teaching, he failed to find a job. Yet he always wanted to be a writer, and continued to work at his craft. In *Portrait of the Artist as a Young Man* (1916), Joyce would have his hero say, "I go to forge in the smithy of my soul the uncreated conscience of my race."

Joyce's love affair with Galway-born Nora Barnacle as described by Ellmann is deeply touching. She was to become the model for his most famous female character, Molly Bloom. He also wrote for her such poems as "O Sweetheart, Hear You" and "I Would in That Sweet Bosom Be." In 1904, the pair eloped to Zurich. Joyce struggled to support the two of them by teaching English on the Continent. He returned to Ireland in 1909 and went into business, opening the Volta Cinema in Dublin. When this failed, he went back to Europe. But he was in Dublin once again in 1912 to discuss the publication of some of his short stories. The arguments he had with his publishers resulted in Joyce's leaving the country permanently. Yet he continued to draw upon Ireland—and particularly Dublin—for his inspiration.

Joyce's relationship with Nora Barnacle contained those seeds of domestic farce that he exploited so brilliantly in his writing. She bore Joyce two children and endured humiliating poverty, terrible arguments, and long separations. Although everyone knew Nora as his wife, Joyce did not actually make their marriage legal until 1931—and then only at the insistence of their daughter, Lucia. The man whose writing could so tellingly explore the human soul could also be curiously indifferent to the feelings of those around him.

The favorable attention which *Portrait of the Artist as a Young Man* received upon its publication in the United States in 1916 gave Joyce the encouragement he needed to proceed with his major project, *Ulysses*. His eyes had begun to trouble him, however. Between 1917 and 1930, he would endure twenty-five operations for iritis, glaucoma, and cataracts, and for brief periods he was completely blind.

In 1922, *Ulysses* was published by Sylvia Beach, who owned the bookshop in Paris called Shakespeare and Company. The book was banned in the United States and Great Britain for some years, but by 1936 was freely available in both countries.

In Paris, Joyce worked for seventeen years on the book that he himself considered his magnum opus, *Finnegan's Wake*. Published in 1939, it is a treasury of curious scholarship and has been described as "a philological divertissement." Even people who love *Ulysses* confess to having trouble reading *Finnegan's Wake*. The book begins with the end of a sentence left unfinished on the last page, to show that Joyce regarded history as a cycle. It is written in an amalgam of languages and packed with thousands of literary and historical allusions.

Like all good biographers, Ellmann is sympathetic to his subject but never hagiographic. The honest revelation of humanity is his purpose. He depicts James Joyce warts and all, piling up the myriad details of his life until the reader is presented with a complete, multifaceted individual.

Among Joyce's acquaintances were the luminaries of the day, and Ellmann draws extensively upon Joyce's correspondence to place his life in context. These are not archly "literary" letters, but the basic communications of a talented, troubled man trying to get through a life beset with difficulties.

The raffish quality of Joyce's personal lifestyle lends a curious charm to his biography, infusing it with a pungence made eloquent in his own writing. The creation of his acknowledged masterpiece, *Ulysses*, with its counterpoint of myth and fact, serves as metaphor for much of Joyce's life. The same may be said for his constant and exhaustive financial problems. In a subtle irony, the study of his work has now become a lucrative cottage industry for many.

Although his reputation rests on a novel about Ireland, James Joyce became and would remain one of Ireland's most famous expatriates. In 1940 he took his wife and two children, Georgio and Lucia, to Zurich, where he died in 1941 and is buried.

Every June, countless people come from abroad to help Ireland celebrate "Bloomsday," the re-creation of Leopold Bloom's one-day odyssey through Dublin. A large number of those visitors are Americans, eager to see the sights and smell the smells, linger in the pubs, laugh at the stories, and eat the fabled breakfast Bloom consumed that day (now served on June 16 in many Dublin restaurants). Wearing period dress has become a tradition. The streets are crowded with versions of James Joyce, Nora Barnacle, and Oliver St. John Gogarty.

Only a small percentage of these people actually have read *Ulysses*. Yet the novel has so entered the consciousness of English-speaking people that it has created its own world, one of great bohemian appeal. It is this which lures the visitors, and the best way to prepare for the pilgrimage would be to read Ellmann's biography.

ELLMANN, RICHARD

Oscar Wilde

Knopf, New York, 1988

Oscar Fingal O'Flahertie Wills Wilde was born in Dublin in 1854. His father, William Wilde, was a physician, an authority on diseases of the eye and ear, who was knighted in 1864. His mother, Jane Francesca Elgee, Lady Wilde, was a poet and ardent Irish nationalist who had adopted the pen name of Speranza. Her flamboyance was an early, powerful influence in Oscar's life.

He received his formal education at Portora Royal School in Enniskillen, Trinity College in Dublin, and Magdalen College, Oxford. From his earliest days as a student at Oxford, Wilde shocked the establishment by treating the superficial as important and the important as trivial. Many years later, the artist Andy Warhol would adopt the same approach. But Wilde did it first; he may fairly be described as the twentieth century's first pop celebrity.

At Oxford he won the Newdigate Prize for poetry in 1878 and graduated with first-class honors in classics and the humanities. He also originated an aesthetic cult whose symbols were peacock feathers and blue china, and propounded the philosophy of art for art's sake.

Oscar Wilde's first publication was a volume entitled *Poems*, in 1881, which precipitated something of a scandal when it was condemned as being plagiaristic. Undaunted, Wilde set out on a tour of the United States and Canada in 1882, lecturing on aesthetic philosophy—and whatever else came into his head. Flamboyant, ebullient, and shocking, he made his way across the nation leaving a trail of outrage and laughter behind him. The Americans were baffled by him—and loved him. He is reputed to have told a customs official, "I have nothing to declare except my genius," which became one of his most widely quoted epithets.

Ellmann calls one of the chapters describing this trip *Indoctrinating America*. Wilde was something of a surprise to the American reporters who met him on his arrival. Instead of the small, delicate individual they expected, they found themselves confronted by a man "who was taller than they were, with broad shoulders and long arms and hands that looked capable of being doubled into fists. [Wilde] might be lionized, but not buffaloed."

Meeting Walt Whitman was a highlight of the trip. To Whitman, Wilde was "a fine handsome youngster," and the American poet later remarked, "Wilde had the *good sense* to take a great fancy to *me*."

Wilde spent the next six years in London working as a book reviewer. In 1884 he married Constance Lloyd, who bore him two sons. His literary career truly began in 1888 when he published *The Happy Prince and Other Tales*, a charming collection of fairy stories, but his only novel, *The Picture of Dorian Gray*, was denounced as immoral when first published in 1891. When he turned his hand to plays he produced hit after hit, however, writing comedies such as *Lady Windermere's Fan, An Ideal Husband*, and *The Importance of Being Earnest*. His satirical comedies were both astringent and perceptive; audiences could not get enough of them. Wilde's star shone brightly indeed and he reveled in fame.

In 1891 Wilde met with Lord Alfred Douglas, known as Bosie; a physically beautiful, emotionally shallow young man who eventually stimulated in Wilde what may have been a latent natural proclivity toward homosexuality. Lord Alfred's father, the Marquess of Queensberry, violently objected to the relationship and accused Wilde of being a sodomite. Wilde responded by taking an action against Queensberry for criminal libel. Wilde lost, and was himself then arrested and charged with homosexual offenses. He was tried and sentenced to two years at hard labor, much of it spent in Reading Gaol.

His wife, Constance, undertook to divorce him, but though she eventually withdrew the divorce proceedings, she changed her name to

Holland in an effort to distance herself and the children from Oscar's disgrace. He would never see his sons again.

At the height of his career Wilde had been celebrated on two continents, as famous for his witticisms as for his writing. Upon his release from prison he was a broken man, bankrupt, his health ruined, an exile who would spend the rest of his life in Italy and France, living on handouts from the few friends who remained to him.

But he was still Oscar Wilde. Although he claimed that in prison he had learned humility, he wrote, in a memoir in the form of a long letter entitled *De Profundis*, "The gods had given me almost everything . . . I treated Art as the supreme reality, and life as a mere mode of fiction; I awoke the imagination of my century so that it created myth and legend around me."

He tried to continue with his writing in hopes of reclaiming his reputation. But the only creative work he was able to complete was a poem drawing upon his prison experiences, entitled *The Ballad of Reading Gaol*.

Constance died in 1898. In the autumn of 1900, while in Paris, Oscar fell ill with encephalic meningitis. He died a pitiful death on the 30th of November. In a cheap coffin and a shabby hearse, his remains were taken to the cemetery at Bagneux and buried there on December 3rd.

Lord Alfred had arrived in Paris on December 2nd, and was the chief mourner at the funeral.

Wilde's life was so exotic that if it were a novel, it would be considered too outrageous to find a publisher. One would simply not believe the story as fiction. As a biography it is irresistible. The scandal that ultimately destroyed Wilde is not the *cause célèbre* it once was, but the pain it brought him still touches the human heart.

I suggest you read Ellmann's biography and then go and read *The Ballad of Reading Gaol*. It is not the greatest poem ever written, but the agony contained in its lines is the cry of every man who ever killed the thing he loved.

FALLON, IVAN

The Luck of O'Reilly

Warner Books, New York, 1994

The biography of Anthony J. O'Reilly, reputedly Ireland's richest man and a self-made multimillionaire, features a unique blend of Irish and American elements. Everyone knows about the Kennedys. Their saga, with one generation building upon another in the climb to riches and prestige, is an American success story. But Tony O'Reilly's meteoric rise is due only to his own talents.

Henry Kissinger calls Tony O'Reilly "Renaissance Man." For almost two decades O'Reilly has been one of the top executives in America; in 1992 he was the highest paid man in the country, earning over $75 million. He had taken over as CEO of the H. J. Heinz Company of Pittsburgh in 1979, at a time when the century-old firm was valued at something less than $800 million. By 1994, its value was over $9 billion. This astounding increase was credited largely to one man, the first chairman outside of the Heinz family—a man born in a middle-class suburb of Dublin in 1936, with several skeletons in the family closet.

The Luck of O'Reilly is not an authorized biography, the author tells us. The book was written with the subject's cooperation but not always his approval. O'Reilly is a man who has literally invented himself, and as such there are elements of his life he might wish overlooked. But Ivan Fallon has been a diligent researcher, uncovering facts even his subject did not know.

Tony O'Reilly's father Jack, who was born in 1906 in Drogheda, led a double life. When he was old enough to seek employment, he arbitrarily changed his name from John Patrick Reilly to Patrick John (the name of his older brother) O'Reilly, and stated his age as twenty-one rather than eighteen. Thus he was able to land one of the scarce and highly desirable civil service jobs in the newly formed Irish Free State. Over the next forty years he rose to the top of the Customs and Excise Service.

In the meantime he fell in love with a Wicklow girl, Judith Clarke, whose family did not approve of him. In 1928, when she was heavily pregnant, they were married in a hasty ceremony. In a short space of time Judith bore Jack O'Reilly two more children, all living together in a cramped flat. Ever more frequently Judith and the children returned to Wicklow, leaving young Jack O'Reilly alone in Dublin—where he fell in love again. And again. The first was a girl called Petite O'Hagen; the second a tall beauty named Aileen O'Connor. Meanwhile, Judith had borne him his fourth child in five years, seriously damaging her health. The marriage was disintegrating when Jack moved in with Aileen O'Connor.

They pretended they were man and wife—a lie that did not come true until thirty-eight years later. Such an arrangement would have been shocking in the Catholic Ireland of the thirties. Their son Anthony was born the year before Eamon de Valera introduced the first Irish Constitution. Jack O'Reilly was good to his second family. In 1942 he sent young Tony, aged six years and four months, to the Jesuit-run Belvedere College to begin his formal schooling. The boy grew up living and breathing Ireland's tumultuous and painful recent history. Then, when he was only sixteen, he learned some of the truth about his own background. In a move that would become characteristic of Tony O'Reilly, he used this emotional setback to fuel his ambitions.

From the age of eighteen, when he first played rugby for Ireland, O'Reilly was a star. Determined to excel at everything he undertook, he set athletic records that still stand today. He also scored the highest marks in Ireland on his law exams. By his mid-twenties, he was the youngest-ever head of an Irish state enterprise. A dairy industry of five hundred thousand people was dependent on his judgment. His launch of the Kerrygold butter brand was one of the most successful in the world. Then he was spotted by Heinz and soon soared to the top of the corporate ladder. The "Heinz years" provide a behind-the-scenes look at how business really works in America, and how an Irish boy can fit into the American scene.

Although channeled, O'Reilly's sheer raw energy could not be totally contained. Over the years his interests have spread far beyond the Heinz Corporation, leading him to invest in one firm after another. His newspaper interests are rapidly developing into a worldwide network. He saved Waterford Wedgwood from bankruptcy and nursed it back to health; built up the biggest supermarket chain in Northern Ireland; and he has somehow found the time to be a major force in the American Ireland Fund and to devote himself to various other international causes. Having homes both in America and Ireland, he exemplifies the modern jet-set executive.

This impressive list of achievements has come with a price, however. Fallon also details the business mistakes, the near failures, and the outright disasters. He examines O'Reilly's personal life and draws interesting interpretations from the influences of childhood. O'Reilly's marriage to Susan Cameron, the pain of divorce, and his subsequent marriage to the Greek heiress and horse breeder Chryss Goulandris tell much about the man.

Tony O'Reilly is a complex individual: a renowned wit and raconteur, he is driven, caring, and courageous. These qualities have won him powerful friends. The book is filled with famous names—Nelson Mandela, George Bush, Margaret Thatcher, Paul Newman. But O'Reilly has also made enemies, and more than once the reader senses a house of cards on the verge of toppling. Yet in the business world of inspired risk-taking and high-stakes success, O'Reilly has managed a remarkable high-wire act that leaves one breathless at times.

The Luck of O'Reilly is a multidimensional examination of big business as played by the heavy hitters. It is also very much the story of modern Ireland taking a new place in the world.

FINGALL, ELIZABETH

Seventy Years Young: Memories of Elizabeth, Countess of Fingall

Collins, London, 1937; Lilliput Press, Dublin, 1995

This biographical memoir provides a perfect counterpoint to *Peig* (see p. 66). Here is the "big house" life of the Anglo-Irish ascendancy in all its opulence; the pampered existence of the Irish ruling class, who were much more English than Irish. I have chosen the book for this collection because it is an accurate firsthand depiction of one aspect of Irish life, almost up to the present time.

In 1883, seventeen-year-old Elizabeth Burke, nicknamed Daisy, married the eleventh earl of Fingall of Killeen Castle, County Meath. She was a Burke from Moycullen, County Galway, a landed family of Norman/Irish antecedents; her husband was a member of the British peerage. Most of her very long life revolved around foxhunting and hunt balls, house parties that lasted for weeks, glittering jewels and glamorous clothes, and even more glamorous yachting parties. She met an endless parade of prominent personalities, from politicians to royalty. Hers is the genuine voice of a woman at the center of a world of privilege.

Daisy tells us in the very first chapter, "My memory is like one of those toy kaleidoscopes." When she looked into one as a child, myriad colors shifted constantly before her wondering eyes. How could one catch them and force them into a pattern? She goes on to add that "I have the same difficulty as I sit looking at this kaleidoscope of life."

Yet she very successfully traces out the pattern for us, beginning with the secure and happy childhood she knew in Galway, between the shimmering waters of Lough Corrib and the jagged peaks of the Twelve Pins. She and her brother and sisters had a genteel governess imported all the way from Dublin, who was miserable in "the wilds of Connemara." But Daisy cherished every detail of her home and recreates it for the reader in glowing detail.

Her friends must have been surprised when lovely, lively Daisy married a man known as "the somnolent Earl" because of his propensity for dozing off after dinner—in spite of the fact that he was only twenty-four at the time of the wedding. They made an unorthodox couple. Daisy longed for travel and the social whirl; Fingall limited his interests to foxhunting and country pursuits. The marriage might have failed had not Daisy discovered a more sympathetic companion in the neighboring castle of Dunsany.

Lady Fingall's friendship with Horace Plunkett, the third son of Lord Dunsany, appears to have been the thread that held her life together. It was probably never consummated sexually; he was a highly moral man and the earl of Fingall was his cousin. But he remained a bachelor for her sake and no one doubted he was in love with her.

Plunkett was a leading political moderate in the era between Parnell and the Easter Rising, but he is better known as the father of the co-operative movement in Irish farming. He succeeded in uniting farmers and industrialists, north and south, Catholic and Protestant, in a successful attempt to extract from the British administration what would become Ireland's first independent government ministry—the Department of Agriculture and Technical Instruction.

Daisy Fingall became involved in many aspects of his life, serving as hostess for his dinner parties and decorating his house in Dublin's fashionable Foxrock. A member of the British Parliament since 1892, when Horace Plunkett challenged the status quo he was attacked from all sides of the political spectrum. Daisy describes these attacks on him in terms that reveal a considerable amount of political acumen on her part. Her fondness for Plunkett is obvious. In later life she made a fascinating throwaway remark to a much younger acquaintance: "My dear man, I never slept with King Edward or Sir Horace Plunkett!"

Cushioned by her husband's money, Daisy made numerous visits to England and the Continent. Queen Victoria's Diamond Jubilee in London, for example, was just the first step on a journey of indulgence that took Daisy to a German spa for the sulphur water, then on to a tiny village in the mountains frequented by the great Paris beauties who came to rejuvenate their complexions in baths made glutinous with rose petals.

But Daisy was no mere pampered beauty. Beneath a seemingly frivolous veneer was a woman with a poetic soul and a philosophic turn of mind. Although her memoirs read like research material for a romance novel, they also contain a sharply-honed picture of a society in flux. Upon the death of Edward VII in 1910, she writes: "There was a feeling of foreboding in the air those days after his death, although there was no talk of war then; a feeling too of the ending of a chapter—a chapter that had held peace."

The earl of Fingall was a member of the ruling class about to be swept away by the tide of change. But unlike many of their aristocratic contemporaries, the earl and his countess would not pull up stakes and depart after Ireland won its independence from Britain. Instead, they chose to live on in a land much less congenial to their sort than formerly.

Daisy sold some of her jewels and her satin and brocade ball gowns to raise money for charitable causes during World War I; she was an eyewitness to the events of the Easter Rising; she lived long enough to see her world of Dublin drawing rooms and Meath hunting fields become as remote as prerevolutionary Russia. Yet she never lost her spirit. In time she would sum up the vanished past and her own credo: "Live. Laugh. Love. Well, we lived, laughed, loved. It was a friendly world."

GOGARTY, OLIVER ST. JOHN

As I Was Going Down Sackville Street

Rich Publishers, London, 1937; O'Brien Press, Dublin, 1994

G ogarty was a close friend of James Joyce and one of the leading figures of the Irish literary renaissance. In *Ulysses,* Joyce used Gogarty as a model for "stately, plump Buck Milligan." For a short time in 1904 the two men shared uncomfortable lodgings in a Martello tower overlooking Dublin Bay. The tower has now become a museum to Joyce. There was a great rivalry between the two men, culminating in Joyce's abrupt departure from the tower. But although the friendship was over, Gogarty remained enthralled by Joyce's style, as is apparent in his autobiographical memoir, *As I Was Going Down Sackville Street* (1937).

Oliver St. John Gogarty—his middle name pronounced "Sinjin" in the British fashion—was born in Dublin in 1878, the son of a well-to-do family. His birthplace was in what is now Parnell Square, where the Irish Writers' Centre and the Irish Writers' Museum stand today. Educated at Stoneyhurst in England, Gogarty twice won the Vice-Chancellor's Prize for English verse and went to Oxford for two terms in a vain attempt to emulate Oscar Wilde by winning the Newdigate Prize.

He graduated from Trinity College with a degree in medicine and became a nose and throat surgeon. But although he rapidly built up a large practice, his first interest was always writing. Soon he was holding court for the Dublin literati. In places like the Bailey Restaurant in Duke Street, Gogarty became famous both for his free spending and his Rab-

elaisian wit. He made it his business to know everyone worth knowing—
and in time he would tell all he knew about them.

During the Irish Civil War in 1922, Gogarty sided with the Free
Staters, those who supported the Anglo-Irish Treaty. When Michael
Collins's body was returned to Dublin after his assassination in Cork,
Gogarty was the doctor who examined it. The war affected him in other
ways as well. Gogarty's country house in Connemara was burned down;
he was taken prisoner in Dublin by the republicans, but escaped by
swimming the Liffey River. Afterward he ceremoniously presented the
river with two swans in gratitude.

After the war Gogarty rebuilt the house in Connemara as a hotel,
which he ran on idiosyncratic lines, entertaining friends such as W. B.
Yeats and Augustus John, the painter. He also won a gold medal for his
book of verse, *An Offering of Swans* (1923). Gogarty was nominated to
the first Irish Senate, where he worked to improve the deplorable conditions in Dublin slums. He was a self-admitted snob—but a snob with
a social conscience. As time passed he developed an obsessive dislike of
Eamon de Valera and the increasing Irish conservatism that de Valera
fostered. It was ill-suited to Gogarty's flamboyant personality.

Witty, eccentric, and vastly entertaining, *As I Was Going Down
Sackville Street* was originally written for the U.S. market. Gogarty had
been encouraged to produce "a book of memoirs for an American publishing firm." The result was assembled without conventional construction, beginning in the late 1930s and working backward over a period
of twenty years. It provided Gogarty with an ideal opportunity to air
both his political views and his personal prejudices.

Sackville Street would prove to be the most profound of Gogarty's
several autobiographical memoirs, giving a true insight into the man's
character. It veers from passages of poetic beauty to others of the most
spiteful and malicious gossip. Everything is recounted; no one is spared.
But there is more here than titillation. W. B. Yeats once wrote to a
friend, "Everybody is reading it. . . . You can open it anywhere, like the
Imitation of Christ." It's easy to understand what he meant. Choosing a
page at random, I read: "To-day I will be a millionaire. I will do just as
I please. It is a fine day in Dublin, and my tastes are more than money
can buy. I have never confused money with wealth, that is why I am a
millionaire." And on another page, "Any new idea, no matter whence
it comes or how rotten it may be, will stampede the Irish into enthu-

siasm. . . . Politics is the chloroform of the Irish people, or, rather, the hashish."

After the publication of *As I Was Going Down Sackville Street*, Gogarty fought and lost a notorious libel action as a result of his mischievous reminiscences. It seemed there was no one in Dublin he had not vilified—or infuriated. Turning his back on Ireland, Gogarty moved to America in 1939 and died in New York in 1957, controversial to the end. His celebrity as a colorful personality tended to obscure his considerable accomplishments as a writer until in 1964 Ulick O'Connor published the first of what would be several biographies about him, and people "rediscovered" the work of Gogarty.

Sackville Street is a fascinating read, full of innuendo, as wicked and much wittier than modern tabloids. Although he wrote many other things, in this particular book I find a voice I recognize: the educated raconteur who holds court in a corner of all the best pubs in Dublin. You don't have to be Irish to enjoy Gogarty.

HOLROYD, MICHAEL

Bernard Shaw

Chatto & Windus, London, 1988–90; Random House, New York, 1988–91.
Vol. One: The Search for Love; *Vol. Two:* The Pursuit of Power;
Vol. Three: The Lure of Fantasy.

To his own generation, Shaw's greatest creation was himself. Playwright, wit, socialist, and polemicist, as a young man he possessed irresistible charm. In old age he deliberately exemplified the curmudgeon, making a virtue of irascibility.

George Bernard Shaw was the scourge of all that was most oppressive in English society. In his writings and public speeches he used the unfamiliar weapons of reason and commonsense, sprinkled with unanswerable humor. Yet, as Michael Holroyd's monumental biography makes clear, this multifaceted facade was a paradoxical method of personal concealment. Shaw spent his long lifetime trying to come to terms with a world that had abandoned him in his childhood.

He was born in 1856 in Dublin, the only son of an unsuccessful Anglo-Irish merchant. He would later write, "I am pure Dublin. . . . We are a family of Pooh Bahs—snobs to the backbone. Drink and lunacy are minor specialities." But it was only outside Ireland that he was recognized as being Irish. Although Shaw never forgot his Irish roots, it appears he often wished to do so. Holroyd tells us, "He claimed to be at least as indigenous as the half-American Winston Churchill or a half-Spaniard such as Eamon de Valera, both excellent examples of advantageous cross-breeding." Shaw once assured G. K. Chesterton, "I am a typical Irishman; my family come from Yorkshire."

The family was colorful. Shaw's father, George Carr Shaw, was second cousin to a baronet, a man of landed pretensions with no land to fall back on. The Shavian circle included eccentric aunts and inebriate uncles who would later appear as characters in Shaw's writings. According to Shaw himself, his mother, Bessie Gurly, was possibly the descendant of noble Huguenot stock driven to Ireland to escape religious persecution. But that might have been one of Shaw's flights of fancy.

George Carr Shaw was twice Bessie's age when they married, an advanced alcoholic with chronic diarrhea, a weak mouth, a squinting eye, and a number of unpleasant mannerisms. When they drove off after their wedding, Shaw attempted to kiss his bride. She found his embrace so disgusting that she was still protesting about it thirty years later. But as Bessie's son would one day say of her, "Misfortunes that would have crushed ten women broke on her like waves on granite."

Holroyd follows Shaw through his early days in Dublin, "rich only in dreams," when his family consisted of two older sisters and a curious *ménage-à-trois*. George and Bessie Shaw shared their life with a Svengali-like figure named George John Vandeleur Lee. (Fearing that he may have been Lee's illegitimate son, Bernard Shaw later dropped the George from his own name.)

In 1872, Lee suddenly decided to move to London, and Mrs. Shaw, tired of genteel poverty, followed him with her two daughters, leaving husband and son to fend for themselves. Four years later young Bernard joined her, having made up his mind to be a writer. From 1876 to 1885 Shaw labored to write five novels, none of which had any success. He joined the Fabian Society in 1884 and through sheer, dogged willpower overcame his shyness to become one of the most effective speakers in the country. The tide of fortune began to turn in his favor.

Shaw's first play, *Widowers' Houses*, its theme the evils of slum landlordism, was produced in London in 1892. It was followed by *The Philanderer, Mrs. Warren's Profession, Arms and the Man* (upon which the operetta *The Chocolate Soldier* was based), *Candida*, and *The Devil's Disciple*.

A series of tantalizing and poignant love affairs led to Shaw's marriage in 1898. Of marriage he wrote, "There is no gratification which a woman can afford you, that will not be sweeter when the woman is not your wife, except the possession of boys and girls to continue the record when you are in your coffin. Therefore marry the woman who will bring you the finest children." Shaw chose Charlotte Payne-Townshend to be the mother of his children, and thus started on the "terrible adventure" that was to turn him into "a respectable married man."

From 1898 on, almost every year saw a new Shaw play. *Man and Superman* (1903) and *John Bull's Other Island* (1904) were both well received in London. By the outbreak of World War I, Shaw was established as the leading dramatist and wit of his day. His courageous stand on behalf of his native country after the rising of Easter Week, 1916, resulted in British resentment against him, however. His idea of justice and his clear thinking on the real nature of war were anathema to a people caught up in the fever of the times.

Shaw himself considered *Heartbreak House* (1919) his best play, though most critics assign that honor to *Saint Joan* (1923). In 1925 he was awarded the Nobel Prize for Literature.

Shaw had become a dedicated vegetarian after reading the poet Shelley's little known work, *A Vindication of Natural Diet*. He attributed his health and energy to the fact that he neither smoked nor drank alcohol, although he did fall ill with pernicious anemia in 1938. His wife died in 1943 after a long illness. In spite of his theories, they had no children, and the remaining seven years of his life were reclusive and solitary. In September 1950 he fell and fractured his thigh; he died on November 2.

His will benefited the National Gallery of Ireland, where as a poor boy Shaw had first found the intellectual stimulus he craved. The enormous royalties from *My Fair Lady*, the film version of his play *Pygmalion* (1912), have multiplied the value of this bequest many times over.

MacMahon, Bryan, translator

Peig

Talbot Press, Dublin, 1974; Educational Company of Ireland, Dublin, 1990

The autobiography of Peig Sayers speaks to us in what is perhaps the purest Irish voice available to readers today. Born at the remote western edge of County Kerry, Peig Sayers tells us, "My people had very little property: all the land they possessed was the grass of two cows." Her father was a poor farmer called Tomás Sayers; her mother's maiden name was Brosnan.

Peig never specifies the year of her birth, but she was an old woman in 1935 when she dictated these memoirs. Indeed, she never dates anything by years; the life she lived was governed by the seasons. Peig was what is called in Ireland "a native speaker." She came from an Irish-speaking family and grew up with Irish as her first language. Both the Anglo-Saxon culture and the modern world passed her by. Her story, originally available only in the Irish language, is told in the simple words but incredibly rich imagery of a bygone era.

Her memories are of a poverty then common to the west of Ireland. Yet Peig in her own eyes was wealthy, for she had a keen awareness for detail and almost total recall. She relates that her parents had two sons and a daughter in the first six years of their marriage, and "that was the sum total of the family that lived!" Afterwards, nine Sayers children had died, one after the other. Then at last Peig was born. Understandably, she was everyone's pet, but her brother Seán doted on her most of all.

"If even a puff of wind blew about my ears Seán would think that I'd lose the life!"

Because hardship had stripped Peig's mother of her strength, the little girl's older sister Máire carried the burden of the household. It is the small things that make this book so valuable: the perceptive character studies, the daily routines, the vignettes of a way of life unchanged for centuries. Through Peig, the reader enters into a strangely enchanted world. The life she is describing represents, in miniature, rural life as it was lived throughout much of Ireland until the 1950s. And for all its harshness and difficulty this remains the quintessential image of Ireland for many, the source of an enduring nostalgia.

Peig's father often spoke of the Great Famine, which was still having a major influence on Irish life. Writing of friends who were emigrating to America, she says, "The parting from friends was a sorrowful sight, for parted they were from that day forward as surely as if they were buried in a grave."

When Peig was not yet fourteen years old, her father arranged for her to "go into service" in Dingle. Although it was a tiny town then, Dingle seemed a daunting metropolis to the young girl after the quiet of country life. "Grand tall buildings stood on all sides of me and people were passing each other backwards and forwards. The two eyes were popping out of my head with fright."

Peig describes her new life as a maid-of-all-work in considerable detail. The chapter she calls "Exciting Stories in Dingle" gives us a fresh look at the west of Ireland, through numerous vignettes amusingly related. Obviously she was enjoying herself, and her employers were kind to her. But the work was hard and Peig was often homesick, particularly for her mother. Eventually her health gave way and she had to return home. Once she regained her strength, she went back into service in a different, less salubrious household. She comments, "Hardship was my comrade early enough in life and it still kept a firm grip on me." When her health threatened to break down a second time, Peig Sayers left service for good.

An unexpected happiness awaited her. In keeping with traditional custom, a marriage was to be arranged for Peig. Three men were under consideration; when they came to call on her father, she modestly says, "Each one of them was too good a man for me even if I were seven times a better woman than I was." Ultimately, Peats Flint was chosen to be her husband. With unconcealed delight, Peig describes him as "a fine handsome man, and as I can gather from the whispering going on around me I'm not the first woman who cocked her cap at him!"

She writes admiringly of the cottage belonging to her new in-laws, "very nicely and tastefully done up, the walls bright with whitewash, new furniture too, and gleaming sand spread on the hearth. A neat lamp hung by the side of the wall and the dresser was laden with lovely delph. A great grey cat with a gloss on its fur lay in the corner."

The newlyweds went to live in the even more remote Blasket Islands, where Peig tried to recreate such a home for herself. Island life was vibrant with close-knit relationships, colorful traditions, marriage feasts and christenings, the laughter of the young and the wisdom of the old. And when tragedy came, Peig's simple but touching account of the death of children and husband tells us all there is to say about sorrow and loss.

The faith and mysticism of the islanders is richly contrasted with their earthy practicality. Electricity, the telephone, even indoor plumbing were unknown to Peig and her neighbors—but they did not miss them. Their survival skills had been honed through a hundred generations of wresting a living from demanding soil and unforgiving sea. To counter the inherent tragedy of existence they had a great sense of fun that surfaces again and again in Peig's story.

Though she lived well into the twentieth century, the world we know today would be more alien to Peig than hers is to us. The life of this remarkable woman was much more exciting than one might expect, given its narrow boundaries. One of her greatest gifts was the ability to recognize the drama inherent in daily life. When Peig was an old woman she dictated her memoirs to her "poet-son," and we are forever indebted to him for faithfully transcribing them. Because it provides the most authentic evocation we have of a uniquely Irish way of life, *Peig* is an Irish classic and is taught in the school curriculum. I reread the book again and again, savoring a lingering trace of my own ancestors.

MCCOURT, FRANK

Angela's Ashes

Scribners, New York, 1996; Simon & Schuster, New York, paperback, 1998

Winner of the 1997 Pulitzer Prize for Autobiography, *Angela's Ashes* is a sometimes funny, sometimes heartbreaking memoir of growing up in two worlds—New York and Ireland.

The era is 1930–50, the narrator a man intimately acquainted with poverty. McCourt spent his early childhood in the tenements of New York and then in the slums of Limerick. This early life is depicted as one of unrelenting privation, as harrowing in its own way as the Ireland of the famine. He begins by telling us, "My father and mother should have stayed in New York where they met and married." Instead, when McCourt was four, the family returned to Ireland with Frank, his three-year-old brother Malachy, and twins Oliver and Eugene, a year younger. Margaret, the baby, was already dead.

The decision to return was an unhappy one. "When I look back on my childhood," McCourt writes, "I wonder how I survived it at all. It was, of course, a miserable childhood: the happy childhood is hardly worth your while." This is certainly true if one is setting out to capture the reader's sympathy from the first page, as McCourt does. He plunges straight into a catalogue of woes: a feckless drunkard father, a pious complaining mother, a succession of bullying schoolmasters—and an Irish climate he describes as unrelentingly wet, turning "noses into fountains, lungs into bacterial sponges."

We are told that the senior McCourt, also named Malachy, had fought with the old IRA and fled Ireland with a price on his head . . . and that he had been dropped on that same head as a baby. But a similar fate had befallen the author's uncle Pat, his mother's brother. As for the mother herself, the eponymous Angela, she was born only a few weeks after this event—by which time her father had run off to Australia in an effort to escape his guilt for dropping and crippling his son.

With such a common bond, Angela Sheehan and Malachy McCourt seem cruelly fated to meet. Both immigrants, they come together in New York during the time of the Great Depression, which serves as yet another indicator of what they can expect of life. The author describes his careless conception as "a knee trembler . . . the act itself done up against a wall, man and woman up on their toes, straining so hard their knees tremble." The result was Frank McCourt, whose imminent birth resulted in his parents' shotgun marriage.

From there on, things went steadily downhill. Frank's early childhood memories of New York tenement life are strikingly clear for a boy who left when he was four. He recalls an occasion when there was nothing to eat but cabbage leaves floating in the melted ice in the icebox. Between bouts of drinking, the father, who cannot seem to hold a job, exhorts his sons to someday "die for Ireland." The mother mourns her dead baby; Frank dreams of the mythic Irish hero Cuchulain. But the family's actual return to Ireland is anything but heroic. As their ship leaves New York Harbor, affording one last glimpse of the Statue of Liberty, Angela McCourt leans over the rail and vomits.

In Ireland, McCourt presents us with a harrowing picture of a dysfunctional family held together by a mother's determination. Told from the viewpoint of a child, the story has a child's simple and credible voice. The book follows a thread of unraveling relationships as the McCourts arrive first in rural County Antrim, home of Grandpa McCourt. Country life is a revelation to young Frank, who has to ask his father to identify animals he has never seen before: cows and sheep. But the boy does not have long to acquaint himself with livestock, for soon they are on their way to Limerick and the other grandparents.

In the western Ireland city of Limerick the family endures the grimmest poverty, sustained only by Angela's will to survive. She is the undoubted heroine of the story, an agonized figure in the vortex of a tragicomic life. Frank McCourt seems to have total recall, entertaining the reader with page after page of brilliantly realized, often hilariously funny vignettes—such as the time the only piece of corned beef in the house is given to the newest baby while his hungry siblings watch enviously. The baby promptly throws the scrap of meat to the dog. McCourt's memoir concludes when he is nineteen and at last on his way back to America. The final scene depicts the boy's first real sexual experience in all its mindless ecstasy—and a priest knocking at the door.

Although set in two countries, *Angela's Ashes* is pervasively Irish. Speech patterns, customs, and relationships are shaped by Ireland, and McCourt exemplifies the Irish talent for storytelling. In person, the author is a genuine and unassuming man in spite of the overwhelming success of his best-selling book; his wife has been quoted as saying she married a schoolteacher, then unexpectedly found herself married to a millionaire. McCourt's years as a teacher of English in the American school system have stood him in good stead. From a synthesis of genes, environment, and circumstance he has created a fully fleshed memoir of a unique life, as every life is unique. But not every writer is as well able to tell his story as Frank McCourt.

Any literary work in Ireland has its critics. Some complain that McCourt presents an inaccurate picture of the poverty of Limerick during that era; others assert it was every bit as bad as he says. These, however, are the facts of life as Frank McCourt saw them. All personal memoirs may be suspected of having a certain fictional element, if only because human memory is imperfect and tends to recreate the past according to the present need. But in *Angela's Ashes*, McCourt presents a focused view of one aspect of the Irish-American experience, and his book is a valuable contribution to the social history of both countries.

NORMAN, DIANA

Terrible Beauty: A Life of Constance Markievicz

Hodder & Stoughton, London 1987; Poolbeg Press, Dublin, 1988

In counterpoint to the life of Countess Fingal is that of Con Markievicz, the famous "rebel countess." Born Constance Gore-Booth, she was originally a pampered product of the ascendancy. This class consisted of the Protestant English and Anglo-Irish lords and landlords who were in the "ascendant" over the native Irish until the present century. Although events would make them as outdated as the dinosaur, they were "no petty people," in the words of W. B. Yeats. Some of them were highly intelligent and exceptionally decent. Their sons fought and died, bravely, in two world wars; their daughters struggled no less bravely in the face of declining family fortunes.

But when Constance Gore-Booth was born in London in 1868, the daughter of Sir Henry Gore-Booth and Georgina Hill Gore-Booth, herself a granddaughter of the earl of Scarborough, a glittering future might safely have been expected for her. From the beginning it was apparent that she and her younger sister Eva were going to be beauties, and their parents and two brothers doted on the little girls. Constance was educated by a governess at Lissadell, County Sligo, where the Gore-Booth family had extensive country estates. In 1887, she was presented at the court of Queen Victoria and hailed as "the new Irish beauty." But others admired her looks as well.

In County Sligo, Constance and her sister Eva had met W. B. Yeats, who was a friend of the family. Inspired by the girls, he wrote,

The light of evening, Lissadell,
Great windows open to the south,
Two girls in silk kimonos, both
Beautiful; one a gazelle.

And Yeats told the girls stories—stories of Ireland's romantic Gaelic past.

From the beginning, Con, as she was known, was an individualist. Not content with the life planned for her—a traditional marriage to another member of the ascendancy, big houses, travel, society balls—in 1893 she enrolled in the Slade School in London to study art. She shocked both friends and family by smoking cigarettes and wearing trousers, and then shocked them again when she set off for Paris in 1898 to continue her studies.

In Paris, she met Casimir Dunin-Markievicz, a Polish count six years her junior. He was already married and had two sons, but was estranged from his wife, who died in 1899. "Casi" was a gifted portrait painter; his large oil painting of Con, *Constance in White*, was exhibited in Paris during the Great Exhibition of 1900. Casi was undeniably handsome and possessed considerable charm, but he was also somewhat impoverished, Catholic, and his Polish title was a minor one. He was not what Con's parents had wanted for their daughter. Nevertheless, the couple were married in London in 1900. Their only child, a daughter they called Maeve Alys, was born at Lissadell the following year.

After spending some time in Paris and the Ukraine, the count and his wife settled in Dublin in 1903. Soon Con had joined the Gaelic League and was taking a lively interest in the burgeoning Irish theater. She also helped found the United Arts Club in Dublin in 1907, which is still a popular gathering place for members of the creative arts.

Con's marriage was as idiosyncratic as her character; she and Casi began to spend increasing amounts of time apart. She rented a cottage at Ballally in the Dublin Mountains as a hideaway and there came across some back issues of nationalistic magazines left by a previous tenant—the writer Pádraic Colum. Reading them, she began to take an interest in the cause of Irish freedom.

In 1908 Con joined the political party, Sinn Féin; in 1909, she founded Na Fianna Éireann, an organization for Irish boys somewhat on the model of Baden-Powell's Boy Scouts. There seemed no limit to

Con's energy. She became first a suffragette, then an active supporter of the labor movement. A crack shot with rifle and pistol, she was called by her bemused husband "my loose cannon."

Most of her contemporaries loved her, with the exception of the playwright Seán O'Casey, who positively hated her. But even he admitted she was clothed with physical courage "as with garment." The celebrated beauty became a lean, tireless woman who cared nothing for appearance, but burned with a white-hot flame fueled by injustice. During the lockout of workers in Dublin in 1913, she ran a soup kitchen in Liberty Hall. About this time, Casi left for the Ukraine; he would never live in Dublin again.

During the Easter Rising in 1916, Con Markievicz was an officer in James Connolly's Citizen Army. As she did everything else, Con threw her whole heart into the rebellion meant to set Ireland free. She fought in the front lines with the men and was arrested when the rising finally collapsed. Sentenced to execution by the British, her life was spared because she was a woman—an excuse that infuriated her.

Con was released in the amnesty of 1917, and received into the Catholic Church two weeks later. In the general election of 1918 she became the first woman ever elected to the British Parliament, but in the Sinn Féin tradition refused to take her seat. When Dáil Éireann, the first Irish parliament, was formed in 1918, Con served as minister for labor. She vigorously opposed the Anglo-Irish Treaty that partitioned Ireland; in 1922, she toured America to enlist support for the republican cause.

By 1927 her health was failing, and Casi came from Warsaw to be at her bedside. Upon her death, Ireland accorded the rebel countess a hero's funeral. Thousands lined the streets to mourn her.

Constance Markievicz was the most remarkable Irishwoman of her generation. One need not have a drop of Irish blood to be enthralled by her character and her life.

SEÁN O'CASEY

Autobiographies, Vols. One and Two

Macmillan, London, 1939; Carroll & Graf, New York, 1984

S eán O'Casey, one of the best known of all Irish playwrights, devoted the last years of his life to writing a lengthy autobiography. Each of these two volumes is divided into three books, which serve as "acts." The first volume contains *I Knock at the Door, Pictures in the Hallway,* and *Drums Under the Windows*. Any of these titles could grace a play.

In telling the story of his life from his own point of view, O'Casey adopts the idiosyncratic style of writing in the third person. This device does serve to distance him somewhat from his subject, but also allows him to shape the material according to his sense of theater. From the first page, O'Casey's unique style is evident in the writing. He tells us, "In Dublin, sometime in the early 'eighties, a mother in child-pain clenched her teeth, dug her knees home into the bed, sweated and panted and grunted, became a tense living mass of agony and effort . . . and pressed a little boy out of her womb into a world where white horses and brown horses trotted tap-tap-tap over cobble stones. . . ."

I Knock at the Door follows "Johnny," as Casey refers to himself, through his early years and the adventure of going to school. The author sets the stage in exhaustive detail, describing Dublin at the end of the nineteenth century with a sharp, not altogether loving eye. In his case, eyes themselves were an unexpected problem. He tells of the time when small pearly specks appeared on his eyeballs, and relates, harrowingly, the primitive medical treatment he endured. His fury shimmers off the page as he says, "It was a time when only a few brave men separated themselves from this dung-heap of ignorance."

Eventually, O'Casey's eyes were saved, although they would continue to trouble him all his life. But at least he was able to observe what was going on around him, commenting on such events as the Castle Ball in all its preposterous, overdressed splendor. By comparison his own existence was bitterly hard, an existence of struggle and poverty that showed no sign of improving. O'Casey's chapter titles almost tell his story: "His Father's Wake"; "Hail, Smiling Morn"; "The Tired Cow"; "The Street Sings"; "Pain Parades Again"; "Life Is More Than Meat."

Pictures in the Hallway opens with a chapter intriguingly entitled "A Coffin Comes to Ireland." In this book we are able to watch the boy becoming a young man, still enmeshed in the complex, often stifling family relationships that were so much a part of Irish life. He took work as a manual laborer, which he continued to do until 1926, and was largely self-educated, reading omnivorously. His mother disapproved of his growing interest in the theater; theatrical people were highly suspect, both as to their motives and their morals. But inevitably sex and even love came to young John Casside.

Drums Under the Windows covers the period of O'Casey's life that was profoundly affected by the rising tide of Irish nationalism, the years leading up the Easter Rising of 1916. By now he had joined the Gaelic League, which had been organized for the purposes of furthering an interest in Irish culture and the Irish language, and was styling himself Seán O'Casey. But he found much of the struggle for Irish independence bewildering. Issues did not seem clear-cut; he could see right and wrong on both sides. O'Casey's black humor sometimes surfaces, as when he writes, "Ireland's no worse now than she was before she was as bad as she is now." Chapters bear such titles as "House of the Dead," "Home of the Living," "Lost Leader," "Prepare, Everyone with Weapons," and "The Bold Fenian Men."

Vol. Two consists of *Inishfallen, Fare Thee Well; Rose and Crown;* and *Sunset and Evening Star*. At last, Seán O'Casey tells us in the chapter entitled "Mrs. Casside Takes a Holiday," he had written something for money. He had penned a little booklet called *The Story of the Irish Citizen Army*, and a Dublin publisher had promised to print it—provided they could get it past the British censor.

O'Casey writes with something approaching awe and reverence of that first check earned through his writing—the princely sum of £15. He describes the bank where he tries—unsuccessfully—to cash his check as one would describe a cathedral barring the gates of heaven.

Inishfallen covers the Irish Civil War, the infamous British Black and Tans, and Michael Collins— "Collins wasn't a great man, but he was the makings of one." When Collins met a cruel death on a lonely road in County Cork, O'Casey depicts himself as increasingly embittered by a cycle of violence that seems endless.

Rose and Crown focuses more on the theater and O'Casey's expanding career as playwright. At last he was able to give up the hard manual labor by which he had supported himself all these years and concentrate on his writing. His most successful plays are from this period: *Shadow of a Gunman (1923); Juno and the Paycock (1924); and The Plough and the Stars (1926)*. All were drawn from his background of Dublin working-class poverty, and combine the ring of truth with a sharp wit and an ingrained pessimism. Characters he created, such as Joxer Daly and Fluther Good, have since passed into the mythology of the Irish stage.

Sadly, O'Casey's subsequent seven full-length plays never received either the critical or financial success of those early works. The final book in his autobiography, *Sunset and Evening Star*, is filled with memories and nostalgia, the attempt of a talented man to sum up a life. But a writer's work is never done. O'Casey concludes by saying, "Even here, even now, when the sun had set and the evening star was chastely touching the bosom of night, there were things to say, things to do. . . ."

He died in 1964, still attempting "to make gold embroidery of out dancin' words."

As an autobiography, this sprawling work is sometimes tedious and overblown. But it never falls to engage the attention, and the view it offers of Irish life in this century is as engrossing as good theater should be. For many Americans, the plays of Seán O'Casey are the closest they have come to hearing an authentic Irish voice.

SYNGE, JOHN MILLINGTON

The Aran Islands

First published 1907; Blackstaff Press, St. Paul, Minnesota, 1988

John Millington Synge was born in the village of Rathfarnham, in the foothills of the Dublin Mountains, in 1871. He came from ultra-conservative Protestant landowning stock. His father, John Hatch Synge, was a barrister who specialized in the buying and selling of property; his mother, Kathleen, was the daughter of a staunchly Protestant County Antrim family. When young John was only a year old, his father died of smallpox. His mother then moved into Orwell Park, a fashionable area in the city of Dublin.

John was the youngest child and fourth son of the family, and was provided with the education deemed suitable for his status. His early schooling was in Mr. Herrick's Classical and English School on Leeson Street; later he went to Trinity College and attended lectures at the Royal Academy of Music. Meanwhile, his mother rented a succession of handsome houses for her family. In addition they were entertained during the summer at Glanmore Castle, which belonged to relatives.

It was a strange irony that led J. M. Synge to turn his back on all this and find the inspiration for his life's work in the most primitive part of peasant, Catholic Ireland. Synge originally planned to be a musician. In 1893, he went to Germany to study music, but soon turned his interest to literature instead and he settled in Paris. There he became acquainted with William Butler Yeats, who advised him to go home and explore his roots if he wished to become a writer.

Acting on Yeats's advice, Synge spent the summers of 1899 to 1902 in the Aran Islands off the west coast of Ireland. He immersed himself in the culture he found there, discovering that he relished both the geographic isolation and the warmth and simplicity of the islanders. Their life could not have contrasted more strongly with his own, yet they seemed content in a way no city person could know. Synge spent his days and nights talking with the natives and listening to the story-tellers who entertained around the cottage firesides. From these sources came the inspiration for an outpouring of work that would make him one of the leading writers of the Celtic Revival.

The Aran Islands (1907) is Synge's very personal memoir. He writes of the islanders in a beautiful simple prose that exactly suits the topic: "I am in Aranmor, sitting over a turf fire, listening to a murmur of Gaelic that is rising from a little public-house under my room." Describing a funeral, he says, "The keen of grief is no personal complaint . . . but seems to contain the whole passionate rage that lurks somewhere in every native of the island."

With obvious love, Synge introduces an assortment of unique people. His gift is not limited to characterization, however. Synge has an excellent ear for language, and the Irish dialogue he reproduces loses nothing in his English translation. On one occasion when he shows a fifteen-year-old boy how to use newspaper to make a draft and stir up a fire, the boy reports, "I'm after trying the paper over the fire and it burned grand. Did I not think, when I seen you doing it, there was no good in it at all; but I put a paper over the schoolmaster's fire and it flamed up. Then I pulled back the corner of the paper and I ran my head in, and there was a big cold wind blowing up the chimney that would sweep the head from you."

As Synge observes the life of these people, we are able to watch their influence seeping into his soul. Their courage, their steadiness, their melding of themselves with the natural world, all change him forever. *The Aran Islands* is ostensibly their story, but on a deeper level it is as fine a portrait of self-discovery as any man has ever written.

Synge was also in the process of acquiring a naturalist's eye. He writes of being in a boat "on an evening of superb light, with a golden haze behind the sharp edges of the rocks, and a long wake from the setting sun making jewels of the bubbling left by the oars." He tells us that he lay "half in a dream, looking at the pale oily sea about us, and the low cliffs of the island sloping up past the village with its wreath of smoke." With such visual images to draw upon, it is no wonder that the Irish artist Jack Yeats, brother of W. B. Yeats, illustrated the first edition of Synge's book.

Drawing on his island experience, Synge subsequently wrote such remarkable plays as *Riders to the Sea* (produced in 1904) and *The Playboy of the Western World*. The latter caused a riot in the Abbey Theatre in Dublin the first time it was produced in 1907. The opening-night audience was shocked by his depiction of peasant life in the west, and denied that Irish men and women ever behaved in what they considered such a coarse, earthy way. People shouted abuse at the author and stormed out of the theater.

But in addition to being a talented writer, Synge was an honest one. His characters were more true to life than the good people of Dublin wanted to admit. He had shown his audience a reality not known in the theater of the early 1900s, one that Seán O'Casey would subsequently develop with an equally acute observation of city life.

Besides his plays and this book, Synge wrote a number of essays and sketches depicting the wilder parts of Ireland which he had explored. Even the least of these writings brims with charm compounded of the man's own personality, his devotion to his subject, and the remote beauty of the land he observed.

J. M. Synge was never robust, and in 1909 his health broke down completely. He died and was buried in the family tomb at Mount Jerome in Dublin. No widow mourned him, for he had never married, but his last, unfinished play, *Deirder of the Sorrows*, (produced by the Abbey in 1910) reputedly was inspired by his love for Molly Allgood, an actress in the Dublin theater.

WALLACE, MARTIN

100 Irish Lives

Barnes & Noble, Rockleigh, New Jersey, 1983

Any American with an interest in Ireland must sooner or later encounter a number of names with which he or she is unfamiliar. Irish history abounds in saints, kings, bards, patriots, and politicians. Many of these have full-scale biographies in print, but others, though important to Ireland, are relatively unknown elsewhere. The author says of his work, "They are a disparate lot." As if to prove his point he includes several rogues in their number, for, as he tells us, "No impression of Ireland would be complete without them."

100 Irish Lives is a book I have used as a basic reference tool again and again. Within its pages one finds names, dates, thumbnail biographies, and illustrations that present basic facts about the chosen subjects in a lucid and informative style. Maps, a list of important dates in Irish history, and an index of names add to the usefulness of this concise volume. Martin Wallace has arranged his subjects chronologically, beginning with the dawn of literacy and Sts. Patrick, Colmumcille, and Columbanus, whose names are most connected with that literacy. They are followed by Brian Bóru, arguably the first nationalist and Ireland's greatest high king, who died in 1014 after winning the Battle of Clontarf, the greatest military victory in Irish history.

The Middle Ages also offer two saints, Malachy and Oliver Plunket. But it was not an era characterized by sainthood. Other figures whom Wallace examines include Garret More Fitzgerald, eighth earl of Kildare, who although accused of treason at one stage in his career was subsequently restored to power by King Henry VII, who said of him, "Since all Ireland cannot rule this man, this man must rule Ireland."

Fitzgerald's entry is followed by that of Grace O'Malley, the pirate queen from Mayo, a contemporary of Elizabeth I, who lived and died an unrepentant Gael. Richard Bingham described her as "nurse of all rebellions in the province for forty years." Mícheál O Cléirigh, who in the seventeenth century was responsible for compiling the *Annals of the Four Masters*—Ireland's massive, year-by-year history beginning with folkloric accounts of the Great Flood—provides a fascinating look at Irish scholarship. Jonathan Swift, less than a hundred years later, introduces us to a very different form of scholarship and moves the collection into the international arena.

Subsequent entries include Arthur Guinness, founder of the famous brewery that still bears his name; Oliver Goldsmith, the poet; Edmund Burke, the political philosopher; Henry Grattan, who won the granting of a short-lived, independent Irish Parliament in 1782; Robert Emmet, the romantic hero of 1778; Thomas Davis of the Young Irelanders; John Mitchel, whose career as nationalist and journalist involved both Tasmania and America; Charles Stewart Parnell, the "uncrowned king" of Ireland; Lady Gregory, moving spirit behind the Celtic Revival; and Edward Carson, whose relentless opposition to Home Rule for Ireland would ultimately lead to the Easter Rising.

Other prominent figures of the nineteenth and early twentieth centuries include Douglas Hyde, Eoin MacNeill, Roger Casement, Maude Gonne MacBride, Patrick Pearse, Erskine Childers, and James Larkin. Less familiar, but often equally influential, are people such as P. W. Joyce, Sir Horace Plunkett, and Sir Hugh Lane. Each fits into the unique patchwork that comprises Irish history. The book as a whole is invaluable.

WILLIAMS, NIALL, AND CHRISTINE BREEN

The Luck of the Irish: Our Life in County Clare

SoHo Press, New York, 1995

In 1987 these two authors abandoned "the New York rat race" to live out a dream by emigrating to Ireland. They settled in Kilmihil in County Clare, adopted two children, and set about adjusting to the mammoth differences between Ireland and America. The charming chronicle of their first year's adventures, entitled *O Come Ye Back to Ireland*, sold out almost immediately.

The Luck of the Irish, their fourth and most ambitious book on the subject, continues to expound on the earlier memoirs that described the nuts-and-bolts of life in the west of Ireland: how things work (or don't) and how different the rural Irish lifestyle is from American perceptions. In a matter-of-fact style laced with healthy dollops of humor, the couple tell us about their daily routine, their friends and neighbors, their disappointments and successes.

Mostly written by Williams, with some journal entries and sketches by Breen, the story is no longer about adjustment, however. The couple consider their survival in the bleakly agrarian west to have been a major achievement. At the time of their immigration, Ireland had not yet become the "Celtic tiger economy" of the late 1990s. Committing oneself and one's future to a poor country was an act of considerable courage. But "After ten years we are still here," the authors report with pride.

For Dublin-born Niall Williams, the village of Kilmihil provides a sense of belonging and community. His days are filled with his family, as well as with part-time teaching, gathering turf for winter fuel, taking part in the Tidy Towns Committee, and directing a play. His wife describes herself as "a mother first," and spends most of her spare time gardening and painting.

Unlike many expatriates, the authors wisely have chosen to embrace Ireland's traditional ways rather than continuing to try to maintain an American lifestyle. Their book is filled with useful clues for anyone who would like to emulate them. The daydream of moving to Ireland, of retiring to a cottage (or a castle) and immersing oneself in Celtic bliss, has fueled many an Irish-American imagination. Williams and Breen will tell you how it really is.

HISTORY

BERLETH, RICHARD

The Twilight Lords

Alfred A. Knopf, New York, 1978

American schools such as the ones I attended while growing up do not teach much about Irish history. In *The Twilight Lords*, I discovered many of the missing puzzle pieces.

The author, a popular historian of considerable ability, tells the story of the destruction of the old Gaelic aristocracy during the reign of Elizabeth I. He begins with an assessment of the English political situation in 1579: "As the second decade of her reign drew to a close, Elizabeth's Ireland was a possession still largely outside the Tudor order, a land always to be reformed tomorrow, never today." Then in the autumn of 1579 there was an Irish uprising, a not uncommon occurrence. The native Gaelic chieftains who ruled the numerous Irish tribes resented any attempt by the English to interfere in their affairs. The queen's opponents seized upon the rebellion as an opportunity to discredit her policies. They warned that Catholic Spain and the papacy would use the island, to the west—an island, incidentally, rich in valuable natural resources—as a back door to England in order to overthrow the Protestant Elizabeth.

As always, Elizabeth could be persuaded to act by any perceived threat to her sovereignty. In lucid prose, Richard Berleth clarifies the complex political maneuvers by which she undertook to complete the conquest of Ireland, a conquest that had begun with the Norman invasion of that island in 1170.

The Irish had ultimately triumphed after a fashion over the Normans. They had assimilated their would-be conquerors into their own culture, making them "more Irish than the Irish." Many descendants of the Normans now spoke Irish, wore Gaelic dress, and resisted any English attempt to force them to pay taxes to the crown. Elizabeth Tudor, having determined to bring the "wild Irish" to heel once and for all, set about the task.

Step by step, Berleth outlines the campaign both from the Elizabethan point of view and from the Irish side. A huge cast of characters, many with familiar names, such as Essex and Drake, Hugh O'Donnell and Hugh O'Neill, is introduced together with details of their lives. But sixteenth-century Ireland as Berleth depicts it is far from familiar. In contrast to the rigid, bureaucratic society of England, its men and women inhabit a Celtic twilight of heroes, myths, and legends.

Further confusing the picture are men like Gerald Fitzgerald, earl of Desmond—one of those Norman descendants. He ruled in Munster like the feudal lord he was, but as Berleth tells us, "One moment he is England's grateful client, the next, its implacable foe." Elizabeth could not be sure which side he would take. Reared to enjoy princely wealth and power, and an aristocrat first and last, Gerald disdained administration. He would always put his own interests first. He harbored no national vision and cherished no dream of Irish independence. But he had not the slightest intention of giving up one jot of his power to the English queen.

Once the "final conquest" was undertaken, a bloody twenty-year struggle ensued. On one side it is the story of the Gaelic chieftains and their clansmen—grouping and regrouping, quarreling and forming new alliances in defense of their way of life as well as their tribal lands. They were warriors from an age long gone, charging to the attack in shirts of chain mail, riding stirrupless with lances held high, fielding battle lines of gallowglasses (the mercenaries of the clans) whose weapons were six-foot battle-axes and whose name was a byword throughout Europe for savagery and valor.

On the other side is a dark, almost forgotten aspect of Elizabeth's reign. The English initially lost not only army after army of seasoned troops in battle against the Irish, but something more precious—the flower of their civilization. Statesmen, soldier-heroes, idealists, poets, scholars, and adventurers were dragged into the quagmire. Some went to Ireland to fight, some to win the queen's favor, some to make fortunes, and some to govern, convinced they would bring enlightenment to a pagan race. All—Sir Walter Raleigh, Edmund Spenser, the Sidneys, Burghley, even the queen's last love, the earl of Essex—were in their different ways harmed by the undertaking.

Two islands—two cultures diametrically opposed in almost every respect—were pitted against each other. The Irish sought survival of an ancient way of life; a tribal, pastoral culture, where Christianity existed cheek by jowl with a strongly surviving pagan tradition. Gaelic Ireland was controlled by no bureaucracy, but by the two-thousand-year-old Brehon Law, which has been described as the most humane ever promulgated.

England, on the other hand, sought supremacy in what it considered "the modern world." One would do well to remember, however, that in *A Distant Mirror* the historian Barbara Tuchman depicts medieval Europe only two hundred years earlier as so savage and brutal its inhabitants hardly seem human.

But the Elizabethans were convinced of their superiority and equally convinced it gave them the right to build an empire. Ireland was to be the first jewel in that crown, no matter what the cost. With an easy-to-follow tactical analysis of the Irish campaign, Berleth brings events to life. He quotes at length from Sir William Stanley, who writes of the Battle of Glenmalure in what is now County Wicklow: "It was the hottest piece of service for the time that ever I saw in any place . . . I lost divers of my friends. They [the Irish] were laid all along the woods as we should pass, behind trees, rocks, crags, bogs, and in covert." The vanguard of the English army realized that to continue to advance would mean annihilation and soon began to claw their way out of the glen. They had encountered what was in effect guerrilla warfare, the natives making the most of their knowledge of the land and striking from concealment, without warning. Against the English line it was chillingly effective.

But in the end, the tide began to turn. Numerical supremacy and the powerful Elizabethan war machine of arms and armorers inevitably spelled doom for the Gaelic way of life. As the cannon boomed and the arquebus barked, the smell of gunpowder stained the sweet Irish air.

Meanwhile, the greedy scramble for land had well and truly begun. Sir Walter Raleigh received Lismore Castle and several thousand acres along the upper Blackwater River. The poet Edmund Spenser was granted the lease of sizable properties at Enniscorthy—a leasehold he sold only three days later, for cash. He then acquired more property further south. Everyone was doing it. One man after another swore fealty to Elizabeth and rushed off to "fight for her in Ireland"—and claim a substantial reward.

Matters came to a head at the Battle of Kinsale late in 1601. Elizabeth had finally found the commander she needed in Charles Blount, Lord Mountjoy. At Kinsale, he was pitted against a confederacy of Irish chieftains led by the redoubtable Hugh O'Neill, earl of Tyrone, who had spent years in the English court and acquired a keen understanding of the English mind. But others among the Irish were less willing than he to adapt new strategies.

Kinsale is one of the towering tragedies of Irish history, and like so many battles, had its elements of farce. As Elizabeth had feared, the Spanish had allied themselves with the Irish. Don Juan de Aguila landed below the town with a Spanish force of four thousand men. Mountjoy promptly bottled up the Spanish on the Kinsale promontory, where they fumed impotently and sent messages to the Irish that were never received. Meanwhile, Hugh O'Neill frantically dashed south to take advantage of the arrival of his allies, but due to a confusion of orders among the Irish leaders he was unable to break through the English siege lines.

During three long, bloody months, the battle degenerated into a war of attrition. Berleth describes it as a contest of the trenches in which the Irish lost their principal advantages—mobility and the element of surprise. Don Juan surrendered in December without ever having got into the battle. When the fighting was finally over, the English counted one thousand two hundred Irish dead; undoubtedly, many more had been killed or wounded. Of the nearly nine hundred Irish prisoners taken, all but a few of the highest rank were hanged. The Spanish survivors were generally spared.

Kinsale was the Irish equivalent of the Battle of Hastings, a turning point from which there was no going back. When it was over, Hugh O'Neill withdrew into the wilderness of Ulster, waiting for Elizabeth to die or weary of the expense of pursuing him. From there, he sent Red Hugh O'Donnell to Spain to raise a new army. Then in Madrid, in 1602, O'Donnell was poisoned by English agents. There would be no second Spanish attempt to help Ireland.

In the year following Kinsale, Ireland floundered. There was still fighting, but the famine that Mountjoy had wreaked upon the South by destroying its cattle and crops soon spread across the land. Fynes Morrison, who served as secretary to the English commander George Carew, is quoted: "It was a common practice among [the Irish] to thrust long needles into the horses of our troops . . . and be ready to tear out one another's throats for a share of them. No spectacle was more frequent than to see multitudes of these poor people dead with their mouths all colored green by eating nettles, docks, and all things they could rend up above ground." These same horrors were to be repeated two hundred and fifty years later, with the Great Famine. Ireland, once so rich in cattle and timber and gold, was despoiled.

Three months into 1603, O'Neill was persuaded to surrender. With promises of favorable terms he met Mountjoy at Mellifont Abbey, just north of the Boyne River. Disarmed and heartbroken, he had at last been worn down. The scene was recorded by an eyewitness, Thomas Gainsborough: "It was one of the deplorablest sights that ever I saw: and to look upon such a person, the author of so much trouble, and so formerly glorious, so dejected, would have wrought many changes in the stoutest heart."

O'Neill was kept kneeling before Mountjoy for one hour. Subsequently, he was made to perform a number of acts of submission, then eventually taken to Dublin Castle. After the formal ceremony of surrender on April 3, he was at last told: Queen Elizabeth had died on March 24. He had outlived his enemy after all. The irony was one an Irishman could appreciate.

Although the Battle of Kinsale was one of the great turning points in Irish history and laid the foundation for the next five centuries, it is little known outside Ireland. But of the many books written about the Elizabethan era, none has moved me more deeply than *The Twilight Lords*. Through Berleth's words I can glimpse them still, out of the corner of my eye—those vivid Gaelic chieftains.

I miss them.

CAHILL, THOMAS

How the Irish Saved Civilization

Doubleday, New York, 1995

The book begins, intriguingly, with a chapter entitled "The End of the World," subtitled "How Rome Fell—and Why." "On the last, cold day of December in the dying year we count as 406, the river Rhine froze solid, providing the natural bridge that hundreds of thousands of hungry men, women, and children had been waiting for. They were the *barbari*." When the hordes of barbarians entered the Roman ambit, the lamp of literacy began to sputter and go out. Almost.

In a writing style as compelling as that of any novelist, Thomas Cahill paints picture after picture of the ancient world. On a sociological level, he describes what people wore, what they ate, even their haircuts, so we are able to picture them clearly. As a scholar, he describes the classical philosophies endangered by the fall of Rome, the priceless written words of Plato and Aristotle and Augustine. Then in a soaring sweep to what he calls Unholy Ireland, Cahill examines paganism in a chapter entitled "A Shifting World of Darkness." The epic bardic tales from that time serve as a springboard to introduce Christ's own bard, St. Patrick, and lead on to a discourse on Holy Ireland, which became Literate Ireland.

Cahill shows us how, far from the despoilation of the European Continent, monks and scholars laboriously preserved the intellectual treasures of Western civilization. They kept the lamp of literacy alight as the Dark Ages closed in elsewhere. From such lofty heights, he switches easily to a discussion of the contents of an ancient human stomach that was unearthed in a bog. It is this constant sense of movement, of surprise, that makes Cahill's book such a delight. Anything that serves to establish connections between Celtic legend and Irish history, Celtic lore and Irish politics, is grist to his mill. Quoting from an ancient poem, *The Voyage of Bran*, he gives us a clear vision of the Celtic mind in very few words:

A hawk today, a boar yesterday,
Wonderful instability!

Cahill goes on to point out that the magical state of flux that so stimulated Celtic imagination also had its dark side, an uncertainty as to personal identity. Many centuries later, this quality would make the Irish susceptible to intimidation by imperial England. But that was still far in the future when the early Irish monks sat on their high stools, crouching over sheets of vellum and pots of ink as they transcribed texts that otherwise would have been lost forever. They are Cahill's heroes. He describes them as happy men; men with a sense of purpose. They engaged with the text they worked on and endeavored, from time to time, to improve it. Thus they not only became conservators of Western literacy but would also have a powerful influence on the medieval mind.

When Cahill's book was first offered to Irish publishers, it was rejected. Its subsequent publication and huge success in America provides a wonderful example of how blind people can be to the jewel on their own doorstep. Thomas Keneally, author of *Schindler's List*, describes *How the Irish Saved Civilization* as "shamelessly engaging, effortlessly scholarly, utterly refreshing." It is all of this and more.

Perhaps Cahill's unabashed love and admiration for the Irish is what denied him a publisher in Ireland. The Irish are suspicious of praise. For the last eight hundred years they have been told by the English that they are inferior, which has led them to discredit anyone who has a good thing to say about them. This lamentable tendency is disappearing as we approach the twenty-first century. Soon the day may come when Ireland is as self-confident as any other nation and blows its own horn with a vengeance. Until then, fortunately, there are writers like Thomas Cahill.

COOGAN, TIM PAT

The Troubles

Hutchinson, London, 1995; Roberts, Rinehart, New York, 1996, paperback, 1997

Here is "what went wrong" in Northern Ireland, minutely detailed by a highly experienced and respected Irish journalist.

In his introduction, Tim Pat Coogan sets out the historic background for what he calls "Islands at War." Then he moves on to examine the six counties that comprise Northern Ireland today: Antrim, Armagh, Derry, Down, Fermanagh, and Tyrone. "There were a number of sparks blowing about the Six Counties in the 1960's," he tells us, "any one of which might have ignited a conflagration." By explaining the socioeconomic background of the area, Coogan shows us the heart of the trouble. Northern Ireland was almost an apartheid society. Protestant and Catholic lived side by side but there was very little contact between them. The Protestants had the power; the Catholics had their church and their poverty. The two cultures were locked together in an artificially created statelet, the result of the Anglo-Irish Treaty of 1921 and the Act of Partition which was a concomitant of that treaty.

Coogan says the conditions endured by Catholics were not due to inherent cruelty on the part of the British government, but were rather the result of misjudgments and bureaucratic inefficiency. In an effort to maintain control over "the rebellious native Irish," the authorities had severely distorted the democratic concept of one man, one vote. The result was a skewed society. A near-feudal system of superior/inferior was the norm, with the Protestant unionists in the ascendancy.

As civil rights issues were coming to the fore in America, it was only to be expected that their influence would eventually touch Northern Ireland as well. The first organized civil rights march, a peaceful protest by Catholics against intolerable conditions, took place on August 24, 1968. Four thousand people carried banners and placards and sang "We Shall Overcome." But the followers of Ian Paisley organized a counter-demonstration and the police turned the civil rights marchers back.

In the city of Derry, a second civil rights march was planned for October 5. Like its predecessor, it was intended to be nonviolent in the best Martin Luther King, Jr., tradition. However, hard-line unionists viewed the protest as an effort "to remove Derry from the Queen's Dominions." They insisted the Catholics meant to bring down the government.

The peaceful civil rights marchers were met with calculated violence. Men and women were knocked to the ground with batons wielded by the police, while others fled in panic from the bruising force of a water cannon. Spectators shouted taunts and insults from the sidelines as frightened children screamed for their mothers.

In the following weeks and months the pattern of protest and retaliation intensified. Confrontations escalated between members of the "Provisional" Irish Republican Army and loyalist paramilitaries. The roar of bombs began to haunt the streets not only of Derry but of other northern cities. The IRA planted a bomb in a bar on Belfast's Protestant Shankill Road; the loyalist Ulster Volunteer Force set off a bomb in a Catholic bar which claimed sixteen lives.

The year 1971 saw the institution by the British of the policy of internment. This meant the authorities could arrest anyone, man or woman, whom they even suspected of being involved in republican activities. No proof was required. The person could then be held in prison indefinitely—without trial. Democratic principles were simply ignored. Understandably, the resentment over internment was intense.

The resultant long-expected conflagration was touched off on January 30, 1972—Bloody Sunday.

A peaceful civil rights march through Derry's Catholic Bogside area went seriously wrong when British paratroopers fired indiscriminately on the crowd. Thirteen Catholics were killed outright; another man died later. None of those killed were carrying any weapons. Witnesses claimed some of the shots came from the walls of the city, with the "paras" firing down on Catholics as if shooting ducks in a pond. According to Brian Cashinella, quoted in *The London Times*, the paratroopers "seemed to relish their work, and their eagerness manifested itself, to me, mainly in their shouting, cursing, and ribald language. Most of them seemed to regard the Bogsiders and people who took part in the parade as legitimate targets." Newspaper photographs around the world carried the grim pictures: Northern Ireland was at war.

Bloody Sunday was to prove a watershed. After that, the issue was no longer civil rights but a question of nationalist identity. Coogan describes the complex political processes by which the unionists "played the Orange card" in the British Parliament, and what he calls "the greening of the IRA" that resulted. He names names, gives dates, and backs up his statements with copious footnotes. An extensive bibliography is also included.

As a trained journalist, Coogan attempts to maintain an objective viewpoint, and succeeds in demonstrating that there has been considerable wrong on both sides. He points out that the toll of the dead and maimed is almost equal on both sides. However, only IRA violence has received much international coverage. By focusing on the period 1966–95, Coogan presents a horrifying picture of the levels of hatred and deliberate misunderstanding still possible in what we would like to call an enlightened age. It is hard enough for those of us who live in Ireland to grasp the situation, which changes almost daily. For people abroad, it remains baffling. Yet there are beginning points, root causes, even a kind of logic involved here.

Tim Pat Coogan argues that the unfinished business in the North is in fact a much broader and deeper conflict, involving politics in Britain, Ireland, and America, intractable constitutional issues, and two disparate cultures dating back to the sixteenth century and earlier. It is the story of two conflicts, one secret, the other overt. There is no book on the subject that I can recommend more highly than *The Troubles*, both in terms of its lucid writing and its understanding of the situation. Irish Americans need to know.

FOSTER, R. E.

Modern Ireland 1600–1972

Allen Lane, London, 1988

Modern Ireland contains much material never published before. R. E. Foster writes with clarity and precision. He dates modern Ireland somewhat arbitrarily from 1600, citing the incomplete Elizabethan conquest as the beginning of the land's "modernity." In his prologue, "Varieties of Irishness," he explains that the dates of reigns (English, not Irish), administrations, and battles provide convenient markers for the beginning of modern Irish history.

Spreading out from this focus like concentric ripples in a pool, Foster traces the development of today's Ireland from the Battle of Kinsale in the winter of 1601—an English victory. His first chapter, entitled "Wild Shamrock Manners: Ireland in 1600," depicts the Irish before that time as primitive and savage, people much in need of the civilizing influence English conquest would provide. This, in my opinion, is a highly biased and Anglicized view, but it will give the reader a clear idea of the prejudices with which the Irish have been confronted for so many years. That reason alone would give *Modern Ireland* a certain value; a way of presenting another viewpoint. However, the book's overriding value lies in its depth of historical information and research.

In Chapter 2, " 'Nationalism' and Recusancy," the author says that "Gaelic society was measured against a 'standard of outlandish reference,' " providing an index of comparison for observation of American Indians and Africans on the Gambia River." He goes on to explain that the

English saw both Irish laws and Irish bards as "arrogantly archaic and mystifying; a world at once bogus and perverse, which could only be civilized by means of plantation." Thus he neatly sums up the English justification for the following four hundred years.

In subsequent chapters Foster traces step by step the various procedures undertaken to bring "enlightenment" to Ireland, while relieving it of its natural resources. He also explains quite cogently the difference between the Old English, the descendants of the original Norman invaders who had become thoroughly Gaelicized, and the Old Irish. Both worked together to form an alliance to resist English domination.

"Cromwellian Ireland" tells the story of Oliver Cromwell's arrival in Ireland in 1649 as commander in chief and lord lieutenant, and his subsequent campaign to subdue the rebellious Irish once and for all. The massacres and expropriations that he undertook have made his name a horror in Ireland down the centuries, and Foster does not pretend otherwise. He does, however, attempt to balance the scale of public opinion by setting out the reasons behind Cromwell's actions and the subsequent results in terms of beneficial effects.

From there the author moves on to Restoration Ireland, and then to a detailed recounting of the foundations of the "ascendancy," the Protestant society whose ascendancy over the native Catholics made English law and custom the model for Irish behavior. Foster also views Irish patriotic rhetoric in its political context. He quotes John Fitzgibbon, the ascendancy earl of Clare, as reminding "the gentlemen of Ireland that the only security by which they hold their property . . . is the connexion with . . . and dependence upon, the Crown of England." Subsequent chapters deal with the Famine, Ireland Abroad, the Politics of Parnellism, the "New" Nationalism, and on to "War and Revolution." This chapter addresses the effect of World War I on Anglo-Irish relations, and the separatist struggle that began with the Easter Rising of 1916 and continued through the War of Independence in 1919, the Anglo-Irish Treaty of 1921, and the subsequent civil war of 1922–23. The Irish Free State and the career and influence of Eamon de Valera are examined in chapters that follow. Chapter 23, entitled " 'Modern' Ireland?" continues the patronizing tone Foster has used throughout this book, but fortunately combines this with a detailed and useful look at the development of the society that would become the economic tiger of the late 1990s—an outcome that Foster certainly does not foresee.

A huge volume, as befits a huge topic, *Modern Ireland* includes a copy of the Proclamation of the Republic, an extensive historical chronology, a section of detailed references, and a bibliographical essay. Foster is a thorough researcher who provides his readers with a wealth of material.

This book has a definite pro-British bias. One example is the denigration of the words "patriot" or "patriotism," when applied to the Irish, by always enclosing them in quotation marks. But that in no way diminishes the value of a seminal work. Indeed, it unconsciously illustrates part of the problem of modern Ireland. Only by exploring the last four hundred years of Irish history through British eyes can Americans achieve an understanding of the tangled relationship between the two countries.

HERM, GERHARD

The Celts

First published in Berlin, 1975; St. Martin's Press, New York, 1977

The Celts was Germany's number one best-seller when first published in that country. The Germans have always been aware of their Celtic forebears and the importance of their role in the development of Europe—an awareness very few Americans share.

Gerhard Herm's book was the first major nonfiction work in the modern era to popularize the Celts. It tells the epic story of a race who were also ancestors of the modern Irish. In fact, the Celts can be found in the family histories of most Western European peoples. From their homeland in the Bavarian Alps, they spread their culture and influence throughout what is now southern Germany, northern Italy, the Balkan peninsula, Galatia in Turkey, France (Gaul), Galicia in Spain, Switzerland, Belgium—and the British Isles. At one time Ankara, Cologne, Belgrade, and Milan all spoke variants of the Celtic language. Budapest on the Danube was known as *Ak-Ink,* the Celtic name for "sweet water."

At their zenith in the first millennium before the Christian era, the Celts had a civilization rivaling Greece and Rome for complexity, diversity, and richness. Originally fierce naked warriors who collected enemy heads as trophies of war—Herm tells us they put them atop poles to guard their houses, or cleaned and lined the skulls with gold to use as drinking vessels—the Celts developed highly stylized art forms of mesmerizing beauty. They also invented soap, wore trousers, and were the first to introduce forged iron to the Romans. From Continental

Celtic tribal law would evolve the ancient Irish Brehon Law, which is the second oldest codified law after that of Hammurabi. It was furthermore a law under which women in many ways held equal rank with men. Herm describes the opening of a Celtic tomb at Vix, in present-day France. The tomb belonged to a young noblewoman. She had been buried wearing a half-moon-shaped diadem of twenty-four-carat solid gold, beside "a bronze receptacle five feet high and weighing four hundred and fifty pounds; the largest known vessel of Antiquity."

Far-roaming, adventurous, and loving their independence, the Celtic tribes never had enough cohesiveness to form a nation, never mind an empire. Theirs was a warrior aristocracy that defined itself through combat. The Greeks classified the Celts, together with the Scythians and the Iberians, as one of the three great barbarian races. The Romans called them *furor celticus*. Herm writes of the development of the Celtic world through trade and its eventual clash in Gaul with its nemesis, Julius Caesar. The brave and doomed defense conducted by the Celtic chieftain Vercingetorix makes for moving reading.

The author also details the religious beliefs of the Celts in a chapter entitled "The Mastery of Death: Deities and Druids." Here he makes plain that Druids were no fantasy-fiction creation, but the intellectual class of their race. Druid practices predated Christianity but also acknowledged the immortality of the human soul, as well as endeavoring to manipulate the environment through rituals and symbols. Herm describes the process by which these brilliant, artistic people were eventually crowded farther and farther westward. He examines the Celtic inspiration behind the Arthurian legends, and demonstrates how the Celtic influence found its final refuge on the Atlantic rim. Today, six regions still comprise what is known as "the Celtic fringe,'" with an ever-increasing interest in their Celtic heritage: Ireland, Scotland, Wales, Brittany, Cornwall, and the Isle of Man.

Gerhard Herm was born in 1931 and educated in Munich and the United States. He has produced a number of documentary films for German television and his books on early European and Mediterranean civilizations have been translated into almost thirty languages. He writes in an easy, fluid style, utilizing the tension and drama of the novelist to capture and hold the reader's interest. There are many books on the Celts, but in my opinion this one remains a seminal work. If you read only one volume on the ancestors of the Irish, it should be Herm's *The Celts*.

JOYCE, PATRICK WESTON

Social History of Ancient Ireland

Educational Company of Ireland, Dublin, 1913; reprinted in facsimile edition in two volumes by Arno Press, New York, 1980

The early Irish culture is here explored in incredible detail. In his introduction, P. W. Joyce explains, "My survey generally goes back only so far as there is light from living record—history or tradition. I am content to stand near the outer margin of the fog, and observe and delineate the people as they emerge from darkness and twilight."

Beginning with the pre-Christian era, Joyce opens Vol. One with a chapter entitled "Laying the Foundation." His sources of information include surviving artifacts, folkloric history, and oral tradition, and he combines these elements skillfully to present a portrait of human habitation in Ireland since the Ice Age. But it is the Gaelic tribes, descendants of the Celts of Continental Europe who settled Ireland over two and a half thousand years ago, with whom he is most concerned. Joyce gives us access to these fascinating people as no one else has.

The author explains that the primary focus of succeeding chapters will be on the sixth through twelfth centuries A.D. This period includes the coming of Christianity to Ireland, and the resultant advent of literacy.

The first Christian missionaries to Ireland found a country of "vast forests, and great and dangerous marshes, quagmires, and bogs." But outside those expanses of wilderness were open plains, sweeping grasslands, fertile fields under cultivation, and pastures well stocked with cattle and sheep. Gold glittered in rivers and streams. The island was abundantly wealthy in fish, game, and natural resources.

Joyce describes the complex sovereignty of the times. Four provinces—Leinster, Munster, Connaught, and Ulster—were each ruled by provincial kings. From Tara, in Meath, the so-called royal province, an *Ard Rí*, or high king, had dominion over the provincial kings—though not over Ireland as a nation. The concept of nationhood had not yet entered the Irish psyche.

After descriptions of government and the military system, Joyce moves on to warfare—an in-depth examination not only of battle customs but also of the warrior mind-set of the early Irish. From museums and other sources he has acquired numerous illustrations of all forms of early weaponry, including types whose name and purpose are drawn direct from Irish mythology. The terrifying *Gae Bulga* of Cuchulain, a multiheaded spear with supernatural abilities, is an outstanding example.

In a chapter entitled "The Structure of Society," Joyce dissects the complicated interweaving of an entire social system. And the chapter on "The Brehon Law" alone is worth the book. Brehon Law is perhaps the most humane system of law ever devised, formulated according to a realistic understanding of human nature—not as it aspires to be but as it truly is. One of the primary considerations of the law was "the restoration of amity between the offender and the offended." For this purpose a highly elaborate system of compensations was devised, allowing for everything from murder to the smallest offenses. The people themselves were charged with enforcing this law. But they were in no sense vigilantes; family and tribal pride was the control mechanism—and used most successfully.

Paganism is discussed next, and no author has made a more thorough examination of the belief system of ancient Ireland. Once more Joyce draws upon the oral tradition, demonstrating that Irish mythology is not "fantasy" but the retelling of what was once the central religion of the people. He gives equal time to Christianity, allowing us to see the blurring of lines that occurred as the newer religion was grafted upon, rather than supplanting, the older. This single fact explains how the Irish were bloodlessly converted. Subsequent chapters in Vol. One include: "Learning and Education"; "Irish Language and Literature"; "Annals, Histories and Genealogies"; "Music"; and "Medicine and Medical Doctors."

Vol. Two concentrates on social and domestic life, including "The Family," "The House," "Food and Fuel," "Personal Adornment," "Agriculture," "Metal and Stoneworking," "The Skilled Trades," "Locomotion and Commerce," "Public Assemblies," "Sports and Pastimes," "Social Customs," and "Death and Burial Rites."

Every conceivable detail that might interest us is discussed at length. For example, in "The House" we are told that ordinary dwelling houses were nearly always built on a timber framework, the most common types being deal (pine), oak, and yew. The walls were made of wickerwork composed of hazel rods, firmly interwoven. The rods, Joyce tells us, were "peeled and polished smooth. The whole surface was plastered on the outside and made brilliantly white with lime, or occasionally striped in various colours."

Royal residences, more elaborate, were sometimes of stone, and were encircled by protective banks and palisades. Their interiors were opulent, with carved cedar panels and inlays of precious metals such as bronze, copper, and silver. Ingenious arrangements for cooking, heating, bathing, and sanitation show the Irish to have been far from primitive. The furniture and other appurtenances of home life are described and illustrated with the same loving detail that pertains throughout the book. The chapter dealing with food, for example, contains a meticulous sketch of an ancient butter-printer made of willow wood; and the chapter on personal adornment contains such fascinations as a pair of Irish shoes now in the National Museum. Ingeniously made, the soles and straps are cut from one piece of fine leather.

"Death and Burial Rites" describes the Brehon laws pertaining to the end of life, together with the religious observations that surrounded it—right down to foods considered appropriate for the funeral feast. Joyce remarks that the Irish always kept a *fé* (pronounced "fay"), or aspen rod, for measuring bodies and their graves. He quotes a very ancient verse lamenting a dead king:

> Sorrowful to me to be in life,
> After the king of the Gaels and Galls;
> Sad is my eye, withered my clay,
> Since the *fé* was measured on Flann.

These two volumes supply a wealth of information, enough to reconstruct an entire society. P. W. Joyce's work, together with that of Professor Eugene O'Curry (*Manners and Customs of the Ancient Irish*), constitutes a large part of the intellectual treasure of Ireland.

KENEALY, CHRISTINE

This Great Calamity

Roberts, Rinehart, Boulder, Colorado, 1995

This recent best-seller looks at the Great Famine in the light of new material. As scholars continue to study the famine and its ongoing effects on the Irish psyche, each study brings fresh insights. For that reason I have included two books on the famine in this library.

Christine Kenealy opens with the statement: "The major tragedy of the Irish Famine of 1845–52 marked a watershed in modern Irish history. Its occurrence, however, was neither inevitable nor unavoidable." And therein lies the real tragedy.

In Chapter 1, "The Rags and Wretched Cabins of Ireland," Kenealy explains that the received wisdom of the British establishment in relation to Ireland had always been determined by the fashionable philosophy of political economy rather than by hard facts. In fact, it is Kenealy's detailed examination and analysis of British political policy that gives her work its importance.

Ireland in the first half of the nineteenth century was still an agriculturally rich country. The peasants produced vast quantities of livestock and grain on rented land, but the bulk of this produce was shipped to England by the landlords, most of whom were members of the ascendancy. Irish tenant farmers were left with a subsistence diet consisting of little more than potatoes and buttermilk. This was deemed by the authorities to contain everything that was needed to support life. They pointed out, as proof, the "sturdiness" of the peasant class.

But the poverty of this very large class was wretched, as Kenealy demonstrates: "The increasing realisation amongst members of the [British] government that a system of poor relief needed to be introduced in Ireland was due largely to a belief that Britain needed to be protected, rather than to any concern for the problems of the native poor." Britons were horrified at the idea that starving Irish men and women might come swarming to their shores.

Various schemes to ameliorate the situation were undertaken. Mostly they just made matters worse. That was the situation in 1845, when a potato blight of unknown origin attacked crops throughout Europe. In Ireland, tenant farmers went to bed secure in the knowledge that the little patch of "praties" they were raising for themselves was producing enough food to see them through the winter. They awoke the next morning to find their crop already in a state of decomposition, "the potatoes withering, turning black and rotting, during which process a putrid smell emitted from them."

After a critical examination of the blight and its causes, Kenealy turns to a stark topic: "We Cannot Feed the People." The Poor Laws Commission, which the administration had created to keep the destitute marginally fed and under control, broke down. Workhouses were crowded past capacity. Yet the British administration steadfastly continued to refuse to make supplies from its own stores available to the starving. Charles Trevelyan, secretary of the treasury, instructed his agents: "You must . . . draw out the resources of the country before we make our own issues." While whole families died in the most appalling circumstances in the west, three thousand cattle a day were shipped out of Queensland port in County Cork to London. A huge profit continued to be made from Ireland even as its people starved.

But not everyone was so callous. A number of organizations and private individuals tried to help. From October 1847 until October 1848, the British Relief Association advanced almost £250,000 to the Poor Law Union for the aid of Irish paupers. This must be compared with a mere £156,060 spent for that purpose by the British government during the same period.

Eviction was another horror visited upon a nation already on its knees. Tenants who could not pay the rent on their land were thrown out of their pitiful cabins and had to watch as their former homes were torn down or burned. Kenealy treats both the landlords responsible and the administration that supported them with contempt as she describes the various regulations introduced to justify this behavior.

The book ends with the conclusion that the response of the British government was inadequate in terms of humanitarian criteria—and, increasingly after 1847, deliberately so. Kenealy follows with appendices analyzing the potato crop failures, the effects of the Public Works Scheme, and the Poor Law Union.

Although the Great Famine devastated much of Ireland, it had results far beyond those shores. America was the beneficiary of the largest wave of famine emigration. The starving, frightened, desperate Irish who fled to the New World would have an influence far beyond their numbers. But the memories they brought with them would continue to haunt them, and their children, for generations.

Modern Americans have never endured famine; the television image of starving thousands in some desolate corner of the Third World has little reality for them. But for the Irish it is still very real. Because we had our famine—or famines, for there was more than one—we are the first to offer aid when famine strikes anywhere else. Annually the Irish people give the largest proportion of food aid in relation to their population size of any nation in the world. We have been hungry. We do not forget.

MACARDLE, DOROTHY

The Irish Republic: A Documented Chronicle of the Anglo-Irish Conflict and the Partitioning of Ireland, with a Detailed Account of the Period 1916–1923

Victor Gollancz, London, 1937; Irish Press, Dublin, 1951, reprinted 1965

T*he Irish Republic* has long been out of print, but it is essential to any Irish major collection in American colleges and universities and is therefore readily available. As a result of ongoing demand, another reprint is anticipated soon. The book is considered by many historians to be the definitive work on the foundation of the Irish state.

Dorothy Macardle has in effect chronicled the birth of a nation. Her style is simple without being simplistic; she is wonderfully easy to follow. The book is divided into chronological sections, organized so that each step along the path to independence is clearly demonstrated and seen in the larger historical context. Part One, *A Broken Nation*, sets out the history of the Irish relationship with Britain from the Elizabethan era to 1911. Macardle writes that "There is a sort of magnificence in the barbarities of Elizabeth I's agents in Ireland," a point she promptly illustrates with the deliberate devastation of the province of Munster. In six months of 1582, more than thirty thousand native Irish starved to death as a result of Elizabeth I's scorched-earth policy. The queen's officers gleefully reported "a populous and plentiful country suddenly made void of man and beast." From this grim beginning, Macardle moves forward to discuss the Act of Union with England in 1800, the patriot Robert Emmet, the politician Daniel O'Connell, the Land League, the growing power of the Irish Republican Brotherhood, and other elements that set the stage for the second part of the book, The Irish Volunteers (1912–1915).

In this second section, the author tells the story month by month, an approach that gives a strong sense of immediacy to the gathering voices demanding Irish independence. A meticulous historian, Macardle views the situation from all sides, including those of the British administration in Dublin Castle.

Part Three, The Republic Proclaimed (1916), continues the month-by-month chronicle. World War I is the background, and the British considered any attempt by Ireland to win its freedom as an act of treason against them in time of war. Macardle sets out the predicament of the British authorities with a certain sympathy, but her heart is with the rebels—right through their terrible executions.

Part Four, Resurgence (1917 and 1918), demonstrates that the sacrifices of Easter Week were not in vain, for they awakened the Irish people to an almost extinguished sense of pride and nationhood. Individual chapters describe the jockeying for position as various forces competed to shape the future. Michael Collins, Eamon de Valera, and the revivified republican movement feature prominently.

Part Five tells of The Government of the Republic (1919). At the time, "republic" was still an aspirational term only; Ireland did not yet have its independence from Britain. But we follow the determined efforts of its leaders to make that dream a reality, including attempts to gain support from President Woodrow Wilson. Forming their own government, the Irish made it plain they had no intention of returning to the passive past. Part Six, Suppressing a Nation (January to July 1920), sets out the methods used by Britain to discourage the Irish urge toward freedom. Coercion and partition became part of the British political language, while the Irish referred to flying columns, guerrilla warfare, and hunger strikes.

Part Seven, The Extreme Penalty (August to December 1920), marks the onset of serious reprisals. The Irish town of Balbriggan was burned by the Black and Tans, a British military unit gone out of control. Cork City was subsequently burned as well. Spies were used by both sides. The British authorities seemed unable to stop the escalation of conflict. Part Eight is A State of War (January to June 1921), giving a clear picture month by month and sometimes almost day by day of the

Irish War for Independence. Macardle demonstrates the desperate efforts of politicians on both sides to arrive at an acceptable truce. Part
Nine, Negotiations (June to October 1921), focuses on the relationship
between Eamon de Valera and Lloyd George and the political chess
game they were playing. A veritable catalogue of duplicity, this segment
of the book, perhaps more than any other, explains Ireland's lasting
mistrust of Britain.

Part Ten, Articles of Agreement (October to December 1921),
covers in detail the machinations behind the scenes that resulted in the
infamous treaty that would allow Ireland Free State status—at the cost
of six northern counties. The next three parts describe the subsequent
national convulsion as Irish public opinion divided on the subject of the
treaty. Republicans led by Eamon de Valera took up arms against their
former comrades, now known as Free Staters, led by Michael Collins.
Part Fourteen, entitled bitterly, The Republic Defeated (January to May
1923), refers to the fact that the Free State, consisting of only twenty-
six counties, won out over the republican desire for a unified island. Part
Fifteen describes Ireland Partitioned (May 1923 and After).

Extensive biographical notes follow, together with statements and
documents, election returns, a list of the executed republicans, and other
information hard to obtain anywhere else. As with every aspect of Irish
history, the period covered by *The Irish Republic* is one of considerable
complexity. Today's political situation is the direct result of actions taken
and decisions made then. While retaining her own political bias,
Macardle manages to give a well-balanced overview that explains the
events surrounding Ireland's fight for independence—a fight that in so
many ways parallels America's own struggle.

MacManus, Séamus

The Story of the Irish Race

First published in Ireland, 1921; latest reprint Devin-Adair, New York, 1986

M any years ago, my father gave me this book as a Christmas present with the admonition, "Learn something more about your Irish roots." I did. From *The Story of the Irish Race* sprang my lifelong fascination with the history of my people. Since then I have discovered that many other readers have had the same experience. This book is almost ubiquitous in the collections of Irish Americans. There are some mistakes in Séamus MacManus's research, but there is no mistaking the passion with which he writes. MacManus loved Ireland, and the history he presents in these pages is the one many of us learned at our father's knee.

Beginning with a foreword in which the author tells us, "This is a rough and ready picture of the more prominent peaks that rise out of Ireland's past," the book opens with the coming of the Milesians (the early Gael) to Ireland. Other vivid legends of prehistoric conquest include Ireland's own version of the aftermath of the Great Flood, with the arrival of fifty women and three men on an ark! The men died of exhaustion soon after, we are informed.

MacManus relates highlights from the epic saga of Cuchulain, the Hound of Ulster, who was Ireland's Hercules. The legends continue with Fionn MacCumhaill, leader of the first army of Ireland, and the establishment of the great royal site at Tara of the Kings. As is appropriate for the folkloric history of a Celtic people, myth and reality are interwoven throughout this period. Even when MacManus reaches St. Patrick and the golden age of saints and scholars, well within the ambit of written history, he cannot resist adding touches of Irish magic.

This is all material that other books have covered; but the author's style, reminiscent of the Irish *seanchai* (storyteller) of the past, brings fresh life to his subjects. He frequently intersperses dramatic incidents with humor and uses the Irish idiom to full advantage. Describing the brutal burning of a poet's home by a tenth-century chieftain, MacManus informs us that the damages assessed against the chieftain afterward included "the breadth of the poet's face in gold."

The Vikings, Strongbow, Oliver Cromwell, Wolfe Tone, the Rising of 1798, the Act of Union, Robert Emmet, Daniel O'Connell, the Great Famine, Charles Parnell, the Land League, the Easter Rising—names and events that appear again and again in Irish history—all are presented in an eminently readable style with numerous embellishments. The book follows Ireland and the Irish to the foundation of the state and the enactment of the Irish Constitution in 1937.

Séamus MacManus, who was born in 1869 in County Donegal, went to the United States in 1899. There he found a ready market for his writing, soon making a name for himself with fairy tales, poetry, novels, and humorous plays. *The Story of the Irish Race* was his most ambitious work, however, and the one for which he is best remembered today.

Although MacManus returned to Donegal each year, America remained his base for the rest of his life. He died in New York in 1960. For Irish Americans who want to learn more about Ireland without having to wade through hundreds of pages of dry and scholarly text, *The Story of the Irish Race* is the answer.

The New Gill History of Ireland, 6 Vols.

Gill & Macmillan, London and Dublin, 1993–96

Among the numerous histories of Ireland produced in the last twenty-five years, the Gill Series has been outstanding for its detailed scholarship. Originally consisting of eleven volumes, it has recently been republished in a totally revised and updated six-volume edition called *The New Gill History*. The series consists of:

MEDIEVAL IRELAND *The Enduring Tradition*, by Michael Richter

SIXTEENTH-CENTURY IRELAND *The Incomplete Conquest*, by Colm Lennon

SEVENTEENTH-CENTURY IRELAND *The War of Religions*, by Brendan Fitzpatrick

EIGHTEENTH-CENTURY IRELAND *The Long Peace*, by Eamon O'Flaherty

NINETEENTH-CENTURY IRELAND *The Search for Stability*, by George Boyce

TWENTIETH-CENTURY IRELAND *Nation and State*, by Dermot Keogh

Each of these volumes—which in their totality comprise a complete history of Ireland—is written by an expert in the particular era.

. . .

Medieval Ireland opens with a dissertation on the Celts and a survey of the island in prehistoric times. The Gill histories avoid relying on folkloric history, drawing instead upon such tangibles as archeology and accepted documentary evidence. However, *Medieval Ireland* does refer to the *Táin Bó Cúailnge*, the epic saga of the Cattle Raid of Cooley, as "the best information on the upper strata of society in pre-Christian Ireland." The *Táin* is considered world literature—see entries under Mythology and Folklore.

In its second part, *Medieval Ireland* delineates the beginnings of Christianity in Ireland and the formation of the early Irish Church, which is undergoing a resurgence of popularity today as "Celtic Christianity." Christian Ireland in the seventh and eight centuries is thoroughly examined, giving an accurate story of the island's famous saints and scholars. The arrival of the Vikings is set in its geographical context with considerable background on the Scandinavian cultures. The inexorable rise to power of Ireland's greatest high king, Brian Bóru, is explored, as is his victory over the Vikings at Clontarf in 1014.

The arrival of the Normans in the twelfth century is one of the definitive events in Irish history, setting the stage for the final third of the book. Here the author examines Ireland under foreign influence, devotes considerable time to exploring the political situation in the thirteenth, fourteenth, and fifteenth centuries, and concludes with the end of the Middle Ages. He finishes by summing up the enduring tradition left to us from this period, and provides both a bibliography and a most helpful list of Irish words.

Sixteenth-Century Ireland focuses on the Elizabethan era, beginning with the "natural environment" of the island in 1500. The ancient and highly stratified Gaelic society is explained in order to demonstrate how irreconcilable its tenets were with those of England. Religious and court politics play a central role in this volume, as they did in Ireland during that period.

Each of the four provinces is examined separately, as different situations existed. Munster, the southwest part of Ireland, was to suffer worst under the Elizabethans. The author describes the campaigns conducted there with the journalistic coldness needed to maintain a distance from such disturbing events. Ulster and the so-called Nine Years' War are also given close scrutiny, as the hatred engendered then would leave reverberations to the present day. The book concludes with a chapter entitled "Reformation to Counter-Reformation," making clear the divergent religious forces that were to have such a long-lasting effect on Ireland. This prepares the way for the third volume in the Gill Series.

Seventeenth-Century Ireland first examines the identities and allegiances in place at the start of the century. English policy toward the Catholics was increasingly important. Ireland eventually became the battleground where two kings, one Protestant and one Catholic, fought each other for the English throne. The Jacobite Wars between James Stuart and William of Orange were to have a profound effect on Ireland when the Catholic James was defeated at the Battle of the Boyne (1690).

Individual chapters in this volume are devoted to risings, revolutions, crises, plots, and insurrections, giving a picture of an island in turmoil. The century began with the defeat of the old Gaelic order and would end with Ireland supposedly "secure for the Crown." But the English crown could never be certain of the troublesome island to the west. The chapter entitled "Theology and the Politics of Sovereignty" examines the ways in which the religious question continued to be used as a tool for the gaining and holding of power.

Eighteenth-Century Ireland was strongly influenced by the Restoration in England, which ushered in a new era of elegance. The Protestants who had been "planted" in Ireland by Oliver Cromwell had uneasy possession of their lands, but the recurring waves of revolution and rebellion that had marked the seventeenth century had eroded the political and economic position of the Catholic majority. The Catholic Irish aristocracy had fled abroad after the Jacobite Wars, drawn by dual loyalty to the pope and the exiled house of Stuart. In the vacuum of leadership left behind a number of new political figures emerged, ushering in an Irish parliament—although under English control.

The latter part of the century was an age of uncommon brilliance in the Irish House of Commons, with men like Henry Grattan holding audiences mesmerized by their oratory. But insecurity always lay at the foundations of Irish politics. By 1800, it was obvious that England meant to take back the small measure of power it had ceded to Ireland. The Act of Union would be the first important Irish event of the new century.

Nineteenth-Century Ireland tells the story of two disasters: first, the Act of Union that welded Ireland to what would be known as "Great Britain," making this island part of an empire in which it had little say. The second, and more overtly dramatic disaster, was the Great Famine. But the author does not focus on the famine so much as upon the Union and its consequences. The seething unrest over the question of land and landownership was very much a part of this century, as explored in a chapter entitled "The Land and Its Nemesis." So too were the contradictory philosophies of Irish nationalism and Irish unionism, both of which can date their birth in modern guise from this period.

The subtitle of this volume is "The Search for Stability," but there was no stability to be found in nineteenth-century Ireland. The old verities of the eighteenth century were swept away. The author tells us, "It was in the British interest to promote stability and order through reform. The problem was, however, that the British government was not always in a position to pursue such a policy wholeheartedly or even sympathetically. There was, after all, a difference between Great Britain and Ireland." That one simple statement sums up a seemingly insoluble problem. In this volume it becomes clear that Britain will always pursue its self-interest while finding it unforgivable that Ireland should want to pursue its own in turn. Under a cloud of misunderstanding, the twentieth century began.

Twentieth-Century Ireland is the largest book in the series, and covers a century not yet ended as of this writing. The period from 1900 to the beginning of the 1990s was one of unprecedented change. As so frequently in this series, the author looks at these years from a perspective somewhat different from that of the other writers. Instead of focusing on the Easter Rising, he turns his attention to the Irish Civil War as the more important event, in light of the Irish political parties which it spawned. The entire book is a detailed history of Irish politics, in fact, from the tentative early struggles to create a nation in the shambles of a land divided to the triumphant accession of Ireland's first woman president, Mary Robinson.

Two world wars had a profound effect on the nation, though by the second Ireland had a declared policy of neutrality. That policy was central to the so-called Valera Constitution. The author looks at the pragmatic necessities for such a policy, one chosen for the sake of survival as a result of all the history that had gone before. Ireland, geographically cheek by jowl with Britain, could hardly afford to alienate the kingdom that had been its antagonist for so many centuries. But neither could it afford to set itself against possible allies on the European Continent, nations that had never been other than friendly to Ireland and the Irish.

This millennium has been a long, uphill struggle for the people of this island, but by its close we find ourselves in a totally new position. As a full partner in the European Community, Ireland at last has status on the world stage. Through a careful reading of the entire Gill Series one can appreciate just how hard the struggle has been—and how much the Irish have achieved.

RAFTERY, BARRY

Pagan Celtic Ireland

Thames & Hudson, New York, 1994, paperback, 1998

Our impressions of pre-Christian Celtic Ireland—1000 B.C. to 600 A.D.—have come down to us primarily through the great Irish sagas, which recount heroic struggles between kings or mystical encounters with pagan deities. In the modern era these images are being increasingly challenged, and sometimes unexpectedly supported, by the discoveries of archeology.

The millennium preceding the coming of Christianity to Ireland was one of great transition. The Bronze Age was giving way to the Iron Age. A proliferation of imposing hill forts appeared on the Irish skyline, protected by stone and earthwork banks so solidly built that many remain today to tease the imagination. Within these, sometimes on artificially raised mounds, were various buildings. Today, little remains of the buildings themselves except postholes and an enigma. Were the hill forts the homes of chieftains, defensive structures for a clan, commercial trading centers—or sites of some archaic ritual? Scholars have argued about the subject for years.

In this book, Barry Raftery approaches head-on the question of just who built the forts and why. Step by step he takes the reader through the reconstruction of a near-mythic time, based on the tangible artifacts remaining. He reveals the rise of an aristocratic elite, the Celtic warrior class, that expressed its power by building highly visible monuments such as the hill forts. Located on high ground, these were like huge signs advertising the power and prestige of their occupants.

Raftery begins by examining the transition from bronzesmith to blacksmith, citing numerous examples of the spectacular personal ornamentation which was a fixture of the Bronze Age. Using illustrations from the National Museum of Ireland and other sources, he makes visible a culture with a highly developed artistic sense and astonishing craftsmanship. The Bronze Age culture gave way to the Iron Age in Ireland around the fourth century B.C. The transition was not clear-cut, however, but took place over a period of time as a new wave of settlers arrived from the European Continent. With them they brought knowledge of smelting and forging iron, effecting a change more remarkable than that of the development of the combustion engine in our own era.

Using a variety of artifacts, the author builds up a picture of a people who were far from primitive. Exquisitely engraved horse bits and harness ornaments show us what importance they attached to incorporating beauty into the most mundane objects. Raftery investigates the wooden roads they built to allow them to travel safely across Ireland's bogs. He describes the construction of one of these, the largest roadway in prehistoric Europe, as "a gigantic undertaking comparable to the effort involved in the building of the great royal centers." Using the latest archeological discoveries, Raftery places a skin of reality over the shadowy everyday lives of the common people. Their art and technology, their cults and rituals, reveal themselves in these pages. He offers many surprises. Speaking of the great Neolithic tumulus at Newgrange, in County Meath, which was erected almost six thousand years ago, he points out that thousands of years after its building the huge mound was still the recipient of sacrificial gifts. "No fewer than twenty-five Roman coins have come to light over the years, ranging from the period of Domitian (A.D. 81–96) to Arcadius (A.D. 385–408)."

The author also employs aerial photography to illustrate a variety of strongholds dating from this period, including hill and promontory forts, as well as Tara, the ultimate royal site, in County Meath. Here the High kings of early Ireland created a veritable city unrivaled in prestige.

At the end of his book Raftery challenges many of the hypotheses that have been taken as gospel about the inhabitants of early Ireland, commenting: "Archaeology presents us with a perplexing picture which is largely at variance with that presented by philology, early Irish history, folklore, and tradition." Some of Raftery's conclusions have been widely questioned and will continue to be argued among archeologists and historians for decades. But his book is invaluable both for its scholarship and for the intellectual stimulation it provides. The romance of ancient Ireland casts a powerful spell upon Irish Americans; this is worth examining in the cold light of scientific reason to see just how well it stands up.

Professor Barry Raftery is a recognized authority on Iron Age Ireland. No man is better equipped to examine the subject in detail; but in addition to his professional expertise and field experience, he brings to this scholarly book a lucid writing style that makes it a pleasure to read.

STEPHENS, JAMES

The Insurrection in Dublin

Maunsel & Co., Dublin, 1916; Dufour Editions, Chester Springs, Pennsylvania, 1993

James Stephens gives one of the best eyewitness accounts of the Easter Rising of 1916. Dublin-born, he was employed as registrar at the National Gallery from 1915 to 1924. But his passion was writing and he had already published several books (see *The Crock of Gold*, under Mythology and Folklore, p 182).

He awoke as usual on Easter Monday, 1916, and went to his office, unaware that he was in a city soon to be at war. On his way home for lunch, Stephens tells us, "I noticed that many silent people were standing in their doorways—an unusual thing in Dublin outside of the back streets." Because there had been the sound of rifle fire throughout the morning, he felt faintly uneasy but concluded that military recruits were probably practicing at one of the urban army barracks.

Then, a "sleepy, rough-looking man about 40 years of age, with a blunt red moustache and the distant eyes one sees in sailors," told Stephens, " 'The Sinn Féiners seized the city at eleven o'clock this morning. The Green is full of them. They have captured Dublin Castle and taken the Post Office.' " It was the beginning of the most dramatic week in Dublin's history. James Stephens was right in the middle of it, recording with a writer's eye.

As a member of the Gaelic League, Stephens knew many of the leaders of the rising. He was also well aware that several hundred thousand Irishmen were fighting with England, instead of against it, in the

Great War. He had to ask himself: Was the rising an act of treason or of patriotism?

When the Easter Rising broke out in Dublin, the population also had to deal with events on a practical level. The inconvenience of suddenly finding oneself without fresh vegetables or newspapers, or being denied access to certain areas because they are being shelled, is clearly portrayed in Stephens's writing. This was not his rebellion; it just happened. He was caught up in it as a witness, not a participant, and he describes it from the point of view of a baffled and irritated civilian.

Nonetheless, Stephens's hour-by-hour account of the events of Easter Week has a sense of immediacy. Reading it, we are there as he tells us: "This night [Thursday] was the most sinister and woeful of those that have passed. The sound of artillery, of rifles, machine guns, grenades, did not cease for a moment. From my window I saw a red flare that crept to the sky, and stole over it and remained there glaring; the smoke reached from the ground to the clouds, and I could see great red sparks go soaring to enormous heights." Gossip and rumor ran riot. No one seemed to know anything definite, but Stephens faithfully reported whatever he was told. This element of confusion only adds to the reality.

When the momentous week was ended and the leaders of the rising had been executed, Stephens took stock of his thoughts. He concludes by allowing the reader to observe his mental processes. Stephens was a gentle man appalled by the violence he saw, but he gradually was able to make sense of it. In what is perhaps the most telling statement in the book, he says, "There is no religious intolerance in Ireland except that which is political." This is as true today as it was in 1916.

Stephens strikes an objective philosophical balance. He sees the right and wrong on both sides, which is no small accomplishment for someone who has just been through a major trauma. But though the city he loved was in places reduced to rubble, he found reason to hope for a better future as a result. Nowhere in this book is the author's talent for words more obvious than at the very end, when he says: "From this day the great adventure opens for Ireland."

WOODHAM-SMITH, CECIL

The Great Hunger

Hamish Hamilton, London, 1964; Penguin USA, paperback, 1995

This is the best known study of the potato famine, the work against which all others are judged. When I first read *The Great Hunger* many years ago, I was left with a sense of shock and outrage that lingers still.

In 1841, the population of Ireland was given as 8,175,124, a figure many believe was underestimated. By 1851, it had dropped to six million and was still dropping. Those who could, emigrated. Those who could not, died of starvation and the diseases that result from extreme malnutrition. No one will ever know for sure just how many the Great Famine killed, but it is accepted as being in excess of one million.

In dispassionate prose Cecil Woodham-Smith piles horror upon horror, setting the famine in both its historical context and its grim reality. Her dissertation on the potato, with an elaborate description of the advance of the disease, is unforgettable: "If a man could imagine his own plight, with growths of some weird and colourless seaweed issuing from his mouth and nostrils, from roots which were destroying and choking both his digestive system and his lungs, he would have a crude idea of the condition of the potato plant."

The small details are the most painful. There is a nightmare on almost every page. A British Army officer wrote, of a visit to County Clare: "I confess myself unmanned by the intensity and extent of the suffering among the women and little children, crowds of whom were to be seen scattered over the turnip fields like a flock of famishing crows, devouring the raw turnips, mothers half naked, shivering in the snow and sleet, uttering exclamations of despair while their children were screaming with hunger."

Compare these scenes with the arrival of Queen Victoria on a state visit to Ireland in 1849. Her "beautiful pink silk dress" is much admired, and she basks in what she perceives to be the love and devotion of her loyal Irish subjects. The famine is not mentioned. Dublin is a "city in jubilee." Whatever horrors lurk beyond the carefully scrubbed and polished face of Ireland presented to the queen are well hidden, lest they offend.

From such material it is easy to create sensationalist writing, but Woodham-Smith mostly resists the temptation. Her narrative is balanced and objective as she attempts to apportion blame between the blight that destroyed the potato on which many Irish peasants relied for subsistence; their landlords, who in some cases were nearly as poverty-stricken as themselves; and the lack of comprehension on the part of the British government.

Close to the end of her book, Woodham-Smith says, "It is not characteristic of the English to behave as they behaved in Ireland; as a nation, the English have proved themselves to be capable of generosity, tolerance and magnanimity, but not where Ireland is concerned."

America was different. The author relates that "donation parties" for Ireland were held across the country. The Catholic churches in New England sent $19,000; the Catholic diocese of Boston subscribed a total of $150,000. But many of the contributions were nondenominational. The city of Cincinnati sent $30,000 and New York contributed more than $200,000. Perhaps the most touching of all donations came from the Choctaw Indians, "our red brethren," who raised $170.

Kind as the intentions of the donors were, they did not address a basic reality: people in Ireland were starving not for the lack of money, but for the lack of available food. Those who broke down and attacked governmental stores in an effort to feed their children were executed or deported. In an attempt to flee the famine, at least eight hundred thousand Irish men, women, and children sailed for the United States and Canada. Many did not survive, packed into "coffin ships" that sealed their doom. Others fled to England, especially Liverpool, hoping to build new lives and forget the bleakest chapter in all of Ireland's long and turbulent history.

But once the Irish reached other shores, their difficulties were not over. Woodham-Smith follows them through "a bitter struggle, as bitter, as painful, though not as long-drawn-out, as the struggle by which the Irish at last won the right to be a nation." She describes New York in 1847 as a city bursting at the seams as tens of thousands of emigrants poured in. There was a danger of sanitation breaking down in some parts of the city; those who had escaped the rotting horror of the potato in Ireland would have to confront "the most offensive and poisonous exhalations" in a city threatened with cholera and overpopulated grave-yards. As the number of famine immigrants mounted, the original American impulse of generosity toward them dried up.

This focus upon the immigrant experience makes *The Great Hunger* a must-read for Irish Americans.

HUMOR

CULLEN, LEO

Clocking Ninety on the Road to Cloughjordan and Other Stories

Blackstaff Press, Belfast, 1995

This critically acclaimed debut collection of seventeen intercon-nected short stories is the work of a compassionate yet unsenti-mental Irish writer. Leo Cullen's gift is the ability to transform the mundane events of day-to-day existence into magical or amusing situ-ations. The subtly motivated tales offer a rich impression of family life in rural Ireland during the 1950s. They focus on Connaughton—an undertaker, hotelier, victualler, and racehorse owner—and his sensitive, wide-eyed, idolizing son, Lally.

The stories' intriguing titles give an idea of the diversity of the con-tents: "Why Did the Hen Cross the Road?"; "The Day of the Long Knives"; "Clouds Over Suez"; "The Finger Stump"; "All Eternity." Taken separately, each story reveals a different and slightly skewed view of the rural Irish scene. Together, they also form a chronological history of the author's personal road through life.

The title piece is a typically Irish play on words. The town of Cloughjordan is pronounced "Clock Jordan," inspiring "Clocking Ninety on the Road to Cloughjordan." The story concerns a family drive in a new Fiat that becomes a death-defying test of nerves. It will remind everyone who has ever gone for a family drive under similar circum-stances of their own experience.

In keeping to the title theme, many of the stories revolve around forms of transportation. "The Funeral of Canon Cross" tells of a funeral cortège led by the author that disintegrates into a farcical motor race. "The View from College Hill" has Connaughton and his father taking a terrifying air ride with a former war ace.

The tales are doubly enriched by the author's careful observation of even secondary characters and their lives. Fanning, the butcher, smells of "hard, lardy carcass exteriors." When out for a drive, Barry, the local coffinmaker, wishes he were in his hearse instead of a private motorcar. We are told that he prefers "the glassed-off silence, the faint residue of pine, of life itself within the hearse."

When Lally discovers the pleasures of illicit drinking in the fourteenth story, "Whiskey When You're Sick Makes You Well," the author switches to a first-person narration. The remaining tales shift in tone toward a knowing cynicism, indicating Lally's growing maturity. Yet they are no less keenly observed. There is something very Irish about the collection; it is typical of Irish humor to focus on the dark side of life and find something hilarious about it. But the stories are universal too, as in the one about the married man who discovers he enjoys the company of a wandering Jack Russell terrier more than that of either his wife or his mistress.

Each interconnected story is a beacon of memories, expanding and deepening the integrity of the author's comical vision of life. I recommend them to American readers not only for the entertainment and amusement they afford but also because they illumine the Irish character.

DONLEAVY, J. P.

The Ginger Man

*First published in Paris, 1955; Corgi Books, London, paperback, 1963;
Abacus, New York, 1997*

Gaudy, bawdy, and picaresque, *The Ginger Man* first burst on the
public consciousness during the 1950s like a roar of rowdy laughter. International critics were soon to be acclaiming it a work of comic
genius. Conservative Ireland was shocked.

Donleavy tells the then-contemporary story of Sebastian Balfe Dangerfield, an Irish American with an English accent who is a Trinity
College law student. Feckless, unwashed, charming, and penurious,
from the first page Dangerfield goes careening through life at a heedless
pace, carrying all before him.

Marooned in "the ould country," he dreams of ready money and
ready women while stumbling from the public house to the pawnbroker.
Any girl who will stand still long enough will be subjected to his blandishments. The copious dialogue is authentic, related in the staccato,
often incomplete sentences of the time. The point of view moves back
and forth from third person omniscient to the inside of Sebastian's
skull—a place of lustful chaos as revealing as an unmade bed.

The hero is in perpetual search for freedom, wealth, and the recognition he feels is his due simply for the wonder of being himself. His
ego is overwhelming, reminding the reader just what it was like to be
young and think the world revolved around one.

Donleavy, like James Joyce before him, takes the reader on a tour
of Dublin and environs. But this is a newer Dublin, a middle-of-the-

century Dublin with social revolution just glinting on the distant horizon, painfully out of reach. Lyrical and ribald by turns, *The Ginger Man* captures a specific moment in time.

Time and fashion have moved on. The book no longer has the capacity to shock. It is now possible to appreciate its quality from a literary point of view, enjoying the development of character as well as the joyous, exploding humor. Donleavy's Ireland was very alive at the time he wrote *The Ginger Man*. In these pages it still is.

NA GCOPALEEN, MYLES [BRIAN O'NOLAN]

The Best of Myles

Penguin Books, New York, 1983

Brian O'Nolan was born in 1911 in County Tyrone. He was a brilliant student at University College in Dublin, and after graduation did linguistic research in Germany before joining the Irish Civil Service. His lifelong passion was writing, however. Inspired by James Joyce, he wrote several novels under the pseudonym of Flann O'Brien. His acknowledged masterpiece is *At Swim-Two-Birds*. This witty novel, which explores endless permutations of fantasy, satire, and farce, was first published in 1939. Hailed by critics and much admired by Joyce himself, at first it sold poorly. Only with reissue in 1960 did the book receive the popular acclaim it deserved.

But it was under the name of Myles na gCopaleen (na Gopaleen) that O'Nolan gained undying fame in Ireland by writing a satirical column—"Cruiskeen Lawn"—for the *Dublin Irish Times* from 1939 until his death in 1966. In the Irish language, Myles na gCopaleen is normally translated as "Myles of the Little Horses," but the author always claimed it should be "Myles of the Ponies." He insisted that the "autonomy of the pony must not be subjugated by the imperialism of the horse"—a witticism that reveals a great deal about the condition of being Irish. Irish humor frequently revolves around the situation with England; another way of laughing at the dark side of things.

The Best of Myles contains some of the most hilarious excerpts from Myles's columns. Everything was grist to his mill and no irreverence was beyond him. He fearlessly poked fun at anyone, reminding us that in ancient times the professional satirist was the most feared man in Ireland and could bring down a king. His style depended upon an adroit use of language and a seemingly endless ability to play upon words. For example, from one of his columns:

> What's this I have in me pocket? Dirty scrap of paper. Some newspaper heading I cut out. "LANGUAGE IN DANGER." Of course if I was a cultured European I would take this to mean that some dumb barbarous tonguetide threatens to drown the elaborate delicate historical machinery for human intercourse, the subtle articulative devices of communication, the miracle of human speech that has developed a thousand light-years over the ordnance datum, orphic telepathy three sheets to the wind and so on. But I know better.
>
> Being an insulated western savage with thick hair on the soles of my feet, I immediately suspect that it is that fabulous submythical erseperantique patter, the Irish [language], that is under this cushion—beg pardon—under discussion.
>
> As far as I remember, I founded the Rathmines branch of the Gaelic League. Having nothing to say, I thought at the time that it was important to revive a distant language in which absolutely nothing could be said.

Myles na gCopaleen could address the other end of the linguistic spectrum as well. His articles about "the brother" are classics, not only for the way in which he describes his truly appalling and lunatic kinsman, but also for the steady stream of Dublin slang he injects into every sentence. "The brother" became a byword, as did na gCopaleen's Plain People of Ireland, a breed distinguished for their love of a well-turned cliché. Some of the most successful columns consisted of a dialogue Himself held with Himself, the party of the second part being disguised as the Plain People of Ireland.

He also created the Research Bureau, given to such zany inventions as a copper snow-gauge to put inside your fireplace on the theory that a certain amount of snow would filter down the chimney. American readers who recall Rube Goldberg will recognize a kindred spirit. The bureau proffered a scheme to lay railroad lines across bogs, using a device fitted beneath the engine to scoop up turf and thus provide a constant supply of fuel for steam. Proving he was ahead of his time, na gCopaleen anticipated the dummy cellular phone by inventing a mock telephone, which would give people the status of being "on the phone line" without the inconvenience of phone bills or having to talk to people they wished to avoid.

To read Myles na gCopaleen is to acquire some insight into the milieu that bred James Joyce, for the same witty, fantastical turn of mind informs the writing of both men. It is uniquely Irish, giving the lie to the pseudo-brogue that is so often mistaken for the real thing.

My favorite essay is the one in which a man standing on the curb is inadvertently submerged beneath a load of dumped sludge. When he flounders free, he remarks, "Where else could that happen but in Ireland!" Myles na gCopaleen comments that this is the man's universal apothegm. To him, it defines and explains the whole of Ireland and everything Irish. More particularly, it covers the late arrival and departure of trains and buses; nonrepair of watches and shoes by date promised; the election of illiterate, venal, criminal, or otherwise inadequate persons to public office; the discovery that a beggar speaks excellent Greek; the discovery that a university professor cannot speak good English; the participation by ecclesiastical authorities in real estate, financial, and speculative enterprise . . .

Like Myles na gCopaleen, I have heard that man. We all have. Perhaps that's what makes it so funny.

IRELAND AND AMERICA

Real Lace: America's Irish Rich

Harper & Row, New York, 1973; Syracuse University Press, 1997

America's wealthy Irish-American Catholics comprise a class apart. While proud of their Irish heritage, they have embraced America and the American way of life wholeheartedly and would list themselves as American rather than Irish on any résumé. They may go back to visit "the ould sod" of their ancestors, but when they do, they travel on American passports and their accents identify them as foreigners.

Yet they are still of Ireland. As Stephen Birmingham points out, in nearly every case their origins were desperately humble. Fleeing from the Great Famine in the 1840s, they found themselves virtually penniless in the slums of New York and Boston. There they were regarded as an invasion and a curse. Seeking work, they encountered the humiliation of signs that sternly announced, "No Irish Need Apply." When they could find employment, it was usually doing tasks that even the emerging blacks considered too menial.

But these immigrants possessed a singular advantage over the hordes of others descending upon America's shores: they spoke the language, albeit with a variety of rich accents. They were also survivors, as they had proved simply by making it to America against long odds.

In *Real Lace*, Birmingham illustrates how the Irish—or at least some of the Irish—emerged, frequently in less than a generation's time, and climbed out of poverty into positions of social and business prominence. Families like the Bradys, Buckleys, Butlers, Cuddihys, Fords, Mackays,

McDonnells, Murrays, and above all the Kennedys became the new "Irishtocracy."

Birmingham's probing eye seeks out not only the individual stories but also their meaning in the larger social context. Thus he begins *Part One—The F.I.F.s* (First Irish Families) with the collapse of McDonnell & Company, one of New York's oldest and most respected brokerage houses, in the 1970s. Its downfall came about as a result of the 1969–70 stock market decline. But an inspection of the family saga reveals a far-reaching network of marriages connecting McDonnells with the top of the American social register and a number of international fortunes. Fords, Cuddihys, Murrays . . . the F.I.F.s formed a complex organization. If one family in this structure caught cold, they might all sneeze. America's economic substructure, as the author demonstrates, had become surprisingly vulnerable to its newly rich Irish Americans.

To find out just why, Birmingham goes back in time to discuss the potato famine and its implications. This is familiar ground, but he looks at it from a fresh point of view: that of subsequent American influence. In chapter after chapter he follows the fortunes of those who fled Ireland, revealing the means by which they gained access to power and how they used that power. Along the way he relates some delicious tidbits. He describes a New York lady of ancient Sephardic Jewish heritage visiting a Gentile friend in Newport—whose old guard occupied the pinnacle of WASP society. At one point the Newporter said to her guest, "I do think our two peoples are getting closer together, don't you?" The Jewish lady replied that she hoped so. To which the non-Jewish Newport lady remarked flatly, "Of course we'll never accept the Catholics."

Part Two, The Wheeler Dealers, introduces the long-term effect of the great wave of Irish immigration on this century. Birmingham extends his examination from the McDonnells to their extensive connections. This allows him to observe and comment on almost every famous family of Irish origin in America.

Although a number of biographies have dealt specifically with the Kennedy family, none has ever set them in the context of the "Irishtocracy" before. It is this which provides the background that explains their achievements—and failings. Birmingham begins with the man whom the older-established families considered the founder of the clan. Not the legendary "Honey Fitz" Fitzgerald, but the quintessential Kennedy: Joseph Patrick, banker, ambassador, film tycoon, lover of Gloria

Swanson, and eventually father of the president of the United States: "Born in East Boston in 1887, the son of a saloon keeper who had elevated himself—though just barely—from the 'shanty' Irish status of his immigrant father to where he might be considered, by Boston's Protestant elite, 'lace curtain,' young Joe Kennedy early showed himself to be a man of restless drive, energy, and ambition, for whom business scruples came second."

The author goes on to trace the Kennedy career in relation to other members of Irish-American society, such as Mike Meehan and Bernard E. Smith. Both of these men could be described as diamonds in the rough. With his brash ways, Meehan wangled entrée to a seat on the Stock Exchange. Smith, an even tougher character, also made enormous profits through the exchange. Birmingham writes, "He had been in the stock game to make money for Ben Smith, and no one else. As for America, to hell with that too. What had America ever done for him?"

But it was Joseph P. Kennedy who would turn out to have the most lasting influence on America. He wanted to make money too, yet for him, money was only an incidental tool. The saga of his rise to fortune as one of Wall Street's ablest and most agile wheeler-dealers is breathtaking. Kennedy left a trail characterized by the double cross—and along the way, managed to alienate many of the F.I.F.s. His ruthless social pretensions were bitterly resented by longer-standing members of the Irishtocracy.

As others have done, Birmingham writes of Joseph P. Kennedy's personal morality—or lack of it. But again he shows it in the larger social context, setting the stage for the most famous Kennedy of them all, his son John Fitzgerald. For its searching and explanatory study of the Kennedy clan alone, this book belongs in every Irish-American library.

COFFEY, MICHAEL, EDITOR, AND TERRY GOLWAY

The Irish in America

Hyperion, New York, 1997

This broad-spectrum look at the Irish in America, past and present, was produced to commemorate the 150th anniversary of the Great Famine. The famine set in motion one of the largest migrations in history. The novelist Peter Quinn describes it as "the amazingly rapid transformation of a substantial portion of the most thoroughly rural people in the British Isles into stereotypical denizens of American cities."

The book centers on six themes prominent in the Irish-American experience: The Famine, The Parish, The Precinct, Work, The Players (sports, entertainment, and the arts), and the New Irish. It contains hundreds of illustrations and photographs addressing these themes, and more than two dozen original essays written especially for this project. Included among the essayists is the historian Ellen Skerret, who writes on the role churches played as real and symbolical focal points of Irish neighborhoods in American cities. The political strategist Robert Shrum discusses "The Greening of the Presidency," examining the importance of the Irish vote in American politics. Pulitzer Prize-winning author Frank McCourt reflects on his impoverished Irish childhood and the worldwide problem of hunger. Jason Robards contributes an essay on performing the plays of the Irish-American playwright Eugene O'Neill, while the comic Denis Leary writes "On Being Born Irish-American: A Glossary." Leary is also responsible for the quote: "We're cops, firemen, athletes, doctors, lawyers, bagmen, senators, presidents, and heads of state. Okay, so we still haven't had our own pope. But look at the bright side: neither have the French."

In addition to the guest essayists, the book features an ongoing narrative of Irish-American history written by Terry Golway, journalist and columnist. He chronicles the lives of the ordinary people, telling how they dealt with immigration to America, how they adapted to American society, how they changed their adoptive nation, and their contributions and legacies.

Retired firefighter-turned-author Dennis Smith describes being Irish in America as having the chance to plan a future, acquire an education, get married, raise a family, and provide for them. Joe Kennedy, grandfather of President John F. Kennedy and the first of his family born in America, had a different viewpoint. In response to being identified as Irish, he replied, "I was born in this country! My children were born in this country! What the hell does someone have to do to become an American!"

The experience of women is not overlooked:

Though a highly masculine world, like the parish and the precinct, Irish-American journalism was not completely closed to women. One of the most fabled journalists of the late nineteenth and early twentieth centuries was Elizabeth Cochrane, better known to her successors as Nellie Bly. The daughter of an Irish-American judge, she won stardom as a feature reporter for Joseph Pulitzer's *New York World*. Though she gained her greatest notice by carrying out the sort of circulation-building gimmicks the newspaper loved—she traveled around the world in seventy-two days—she was a crusader and a muckraker, filing first-person reports about the conditions of factories and slums. In today's journalism she'd be a tabloid star, with her combination of reporting skills and heart-on-her-sleeve outrage. Some might argue that there was nothing particularly Irish about Nellie Bly. But they very likely are unfamiliar with her work.

That is true of all the people described in this book. Their Irishness comes through, sometimes in spite of themselves.

CONYNHAM, CAPT. D. P.

The Irish Brigade

William McSorley & Co., New York, 1867; facsimile reprinted by Old Soldiers Books, Gaithersburg, Maryland, 1994

The Irish have made a tremendous contribution to American military history, beginning with the many brave Irishmen who accompanied George Washington that horrendous winter at Valley Forge. The story of the Irish Brigade during the Civil War is an outstanding example of their efforts and achievement.

Knowledge of the Irish Brigade is essential for anyone seriously interested in the military history of the United States. In the spring of 1861, in response to the call of President Abraham Lincoln for troops to quell an incipient rebellion in the South, the New York militia volunteered their services. Among them was the 69th Regiment, also known as the Irish Regiment for its large percentage of first- and second-generation Irish men. The 69th was under a cloud, however. Col. Michael Corcoran was about to face a court-martial for disobeying orders. Born in County Sligo, Ireland, Corcoran had refused orders to parade his men in honor of the Prince of Wales.

Impending civil war and the need to field men was an overriding concern, so the court-martial against Corcoran was dissolved and he was returned to the 69th on April 20. By the 22nd, he had received orders to embark his men for active duty. Corcoran was an Irishman, but he was now an American, too. He proudly led his men off to war behind a wagon carrying the slogan: "No North, No South, No East, No West, but the whole Union."

The Irish Brigade would be catapulted into some of the most savage fighting of the Civil War. Their baptism of fire was the first Battle of Bull Run, which the author describes as "a series of minor engagements culminating in a general action at Manassas." His eyewitness account of that battle is extremely clear, relating every step of the way and thrilling to read in spite of ultimate military disaster for the Federal forces.

At Bull Run, the Irish Brigade was under the command of Brig. Gen. Thomas F. Meagher, whose name would ever after be synonymous with that of the 69th. A special correspondent for the *New York World* is quoted as writing, "It was a brave fight—that rush of the Sixty-ninth to the death-struggle! . . . . No Southerner but feels that the Sixty-ninth maintained the old reputation of Irish valor—on the wrong side." Both Meagher and the Irish Brigade were on their way to immortality.

Meagher had been born in Waterford in 1826. His father was a friend of Irish politicians such as Daniel O'Connell and patriots like William Smith O'Brien, and had been one of an Irish deputation that went to Paris in 1799 to congratulate the French on their new republic. Not surprisingly, Meagher's son Thomas became involved in Ireland's own endless struggle for freedom. He was eventually arrested in 1848 and deported to Tasmania. He escaped and fled to America in 1852, where he was enthusiastically welcomed by other expatriate Irish.

Thomas Meagher became one of the heroes of the Civil War and his career is well documented in this book; but so are the careers of a number of other Irish Americans. Readers will find numerous names familiar to them, and perhaps some of their own ancestors as well. Conyngham felt that the many Irish regiments who had fought for America down through the years deserved special recognition. His focus upon the Irish Brigade, with which he himself served, reads almost like a novel, with memorable descriptions, painstaking detail, and dialogue that rings true. His accounts of the many battles in which the brigade took part are often harrowing, but he also tells us of camp life.

He describes the celebration of St. Patrick's Day among the Irish Brigade: "For days previous vast preparations had been made, a race-course marked out, and on every side was the following announcement—*Grand Irish Brigade Steeple-Chase.*" Conyngham tells of the banquet Meagher had prepared for his men, which included thirty-five hams, a roast ox, an entire pig stuffed with boiled turkeys, countless small game, eight baskets of champagne, ten gallons of rum, and twenty-two gallons of whiskey. Nothing went to waste; a general invitation was issued to all the officers of the Army of the Potomac. Afterward they returned to war; to the cold, bleak details of a winter campaign, movingly described.

A wealth of data is to be found within the pages of this book, enriched by fascinating anecdotal evidence. Originally written in 1866, Conyngham's history of the Irish Brigade was penned by an actual participant while memories were still fresh. In an appendix, he gives names and thumbnail biographies of brigade officers and a detailed list of engagements fought, together with the dates. He also includes A Concise History of the Twenty-Eight Regiment Massachusetts and a Sketch of the Officers and Services of the One Hundred and Sixteenth Pennsylvania Volunteers, Irish Brigade.

In recent years several books have been written about the Irish Brigade, but this one is my choice. Even someone with no interest in war stories will find Conyngham's account riveting. The small details of everyday life are as richly described as the panorama of battle; the sociological structure revealed in *The Irish Brigade* is as authentic as that in the work of Dickens or Austen. And the eyewitness account of American history is invaluable.

Doyle, David Noel, and Owen Dudley Edwards,
editors

America and Ireland, 1776–1976: The American Identity and the Irish Connection

Greenwood Press, Greenwich, Connecticut, 1980

This book consists of a collection of essays representing the proceedings of the United States Bicentennial Conference of Cumann Merriman, held in Ennis, County Clare, in August 1976. The conference, sponsored by the organizers of the Merriman School, is a major seminar which is held annually in the west of Ireland to study various aspects of Irish culture. This particular event celebrated America's two hundredth birthday and focused on the relationship between Ireland and America.

The book opens with a foreword by Michael O'Kennedy, former minister of foreign affairs for Ireland, in which he says: "At a time when opportunities were denied to them at home, America provided a road to material progress to millions of Irish men and women." The introduction is by William Shannon, former American ambassador to Ireland. After further addressing the "export of talent" that saw many of Ireland's brightest and best emigrate to America, Shannon moves on to look at the present and the future, saying, "The Irish commitment to internationalism makes the United States and Ireland amicable comrades in the search for world order."

The book is divided into three parts: The American Identity, The Irish Presence, and Interpreting the Tradition. Essays address such diverse topics as The Writers of the American Revolution, A Profile of Irish America, The Influence of America on Irish Nationalism, The

Political Irish, The Irish Way Out West, The Irish in the Labor Movement, The Irish Neighborhood, and Irish Traditional Music in the United States.

In the first essay, "Edmund Burke and the American Revolution," Conor Cruise O'Brien discusses the writings of the eighteenth-century British statesman and political thinker as they relate to the misuse of power and its implication for the British colonies. Although Burke's concern, Cruise O'Brien tells us, was not primarily with America but with the interests of Great Britain, the man took into account not only the resources of the colonies but the feelings of the colonists.

Burke had Irish Catholic connections and had attended Trinity College in Dublin, both of which helped influence his thought and writings. A dedicated conservative, he served as agent for New York from 1770 to 1775. He initially espoused the policies of George III's administration, but slowly began to champion the viewpoint of the colonists instead. He is quoted as saying of British policy in America, "God forbid that our conduct should demonstrate to the world that Great Britain can in no instance whatever be brought to a sense of rational and equitable policy, but by coercion and force of arms." These became prophetic words indeed in light of subsequent Irish history.

Every essay in this book illumines a different aspect of the American-Irish relationship. For example, León Ó Broin's work on "The Fenian Brotherhood" will be a revelation to many who are unaware of the intense involvement of Americans in the Irish struggle for independence that culminated in the Easter Rising. Early in the twentieth century, John Devoy and the Irish Republican Brotherhood supplied both money and weapons to republicans in Ireland to aid them in mounting a rebellion against British rule. The Irish Republican Union, the Emigrant Aid Society, and the Phoenix Society all had been founded in America with the purpose of providing a support system for immigrants, and they also became a powerful political force working on behalf of Irish freedom.

Andrew M. Greeley calls his essay "The American Achievement: A Report from Great Ireland." The title merely hints at what proves to be a perceptive, often humorous, but always informed dissection of the largest of the "Irish colonies."

In her essay on "The Irish-American Literary Connection," Peggy O'Brien uses Jonathan Swift as a springboard for examining and interpreting writers as diverse as Nathaniel Hawthorne, Walt Whitman, and Sylvia Plath, proving that Ireland has a long reach indeed.

"The Irish in American Business and Professions," by E. R. R. Green, begins with the author recalling a childhood in Northern Ireland. The corner shop that the family passed on their way to town was described to them as the result of a legacy left by an American millionaire to his kin back in Ireland. That early identification of America with money and success is explored on many levels in Green's essay. John Maxwell Nesbitt, first president of the Insurance Company of North America, serves as an exemplar. Born in County Down, Nesbitt had come to Philadelphia at the age of seventeen, taken a job as a lowly clerk with a shipping merchant, and eventually worked his way up to become one of the most prominent businessmen of his time.

Each essayist in *America and Ireland* is a specialist in his or her field. Taken as a whole, their work amounts to an exceptionally informative and multidimensional portrait of the Irish in America. This is a book to be read one essay at a time; slowly, thoughtfully, but with great pleasure and considerable pride.

LAXTON, EDWARD

The Famine Ships: The Irish Exodus to America, 1846–51

Bloomsbury Press, London, 1996; Henry Holt & Co., New York, 1997

On one level, this is a chilling, indeed a horrifying, book. I found some of its passages more painful to read than eyewitness accounts of the sinking of the *Titanic*. Ireland today is a booming economy known throughout Europe as the "Celtic Tiger." One hundred and fifty years ago, things were very different. In a nation with a population of eight million at that time, Catholic Irish peasants led an existence of bare subsistence. Then the potato crop failed. In the years that followed, according to the passenger lists from the files of the Port of New York, 651,931 Irish people arrived in that city as a result of 2,743 desperate voyages. It is interesting to note that only 325 ships made more than one voyage apiece, however. Reading Edward Laxton's book, the reasons are obvious.

For as little as ten dollars, refugees fleeing the Great Famine were sold tickets to America and a better life. Or so they thought. The reality was that the ships they boarded were little more than rotting hulks. Laxton tells us that hundreds of poor men, women, and children of all ages huddled together in the holds, without light, without air, half-submerged in their own excrement. Desperately seasick and forced to breathe this fetid atmosphere, they soon became sick in body and dispirited in heart. Thousands would perish at sea in the most appalling circumstances, dying of typhus and dysentery in the stinking holds of ships unfit for human occupancy. The filthy vessels became known as "coffin ships."

No one in a position of responsibility cared. Once they had paid their money, the Irish emigrants were expendable, mere cargo to be delivered or dumped overboard depending upon the circumstances. Winter sailings were particularly difficult. Many a ship was beaten back into port by strong winds off the Atlantic. A vessel might be one, two, even three weeks into its voyage, with supplies greatly depleted, and still have the coast of Ireland dishearteningly in sight, reminding the unfortunate passengers of all they were leaving behind.

In one of the letters quoted in the book, a passenger named Henry Johnson describes a six-day storm at sea. The man in the next berth had been ill for some time of a bowel complaint, and died the first night of the storm. As the waves grew wilder, the ship began to roll and pitch violently. Johnson was thrown against the corpse in a great tangle of women, children, barrels, and boxes. His was a nightmarish experience, but by no means unique.

One heartrending quote is taken from a journal kept by a schoolteacher who, together with his wife, succumbed to fever and was buried at sea: "In reverent memory of all who have perished in this holocaust and of all who have suffered in any way . . . I dedicate the message in this little book. Farewell, Gerald Keegan."

Part of the horror of the story lies in the fact that many of the leaky, overcrowded sailing ships that carried Keegan and those like him were Irish-owned and sailed by Irish crews. Many vessels never completed their voyages at all, but took their unfortunate passengers and their crews to the bottom of the ocean. Laxton recounts their stories in stark, brutal detail.

Those who survived the Atlantic crossing set out to make new lives for themselves in the New World. Among them was the Ford family, former tenants on a farm at Ballinascarty. The party included seventy-one-year-old grandmother Rebecca, her son and his wife Thomasina, and their seven children, of whom a boy named William was the eldest. In the New World, William Ford would marry and have a son whom he named Henry. The rest is automobile history.

Another immigrant came from a farm in County Wexford. Although his parents' rented holding of twenty-five acres was large by the

standard of the day, the vegetables and grain they grew were not suffi-
cient to support the entire family. So in 1849 young Patrick set off for
America aboard the *Washington Irving*. The trip to Boston took thirty-
one days and nights—long enough for a romance to develop between
Patrick Kennedy and a girl called Bridget Murphy. In America they
married and raised a family; their great-grandson was John Fitzgerald
Kennedy.

Not everyone who sailed aboard the famine ships had such a future
awaiting them, of course. Many would ultimately fight and die in the
American Civil War; others would find they had traded one sort of
poverty for another as they took up hard menial labor in the cities or
working on the railroads. But in spite of the strength and skills they
brought, they were not always welcome. The author tells us that the
governments of both the United States and Canada began to feel that
the massive Irish emigration fleeing the famine was unbalancing the
population.

The Famine Ships is thoroughly researched, drawing upon passenger
lists from U.S. immigration files, crews' papers for the specific voyages
from the marine archives, and a wealth of firsthand reports from the
survivors themselves. The story the book tells is one of greed and the
most callous exploitation, but also a celebration of the Irish spirit and
the will to survive. Any history of the Great Famine is incomplete without this chapter, which is of such particular relevance to America.

MILLER, KERBY, AND PAUL WAGNER

Out of Ireland

Elliott & Clark, Washington, D.C., 1994

There is the story of Irish immigration to America told through numerous photographs and the letters of actual immigrants. The authors state that more than seven million men and women came out of Ireland to settle in America. Their story speaks to their forty million Irish-American descendants through these images.

The authors remind us that "every Irish immigrant's story is unique and intensely personal." The opening chapters are entitled "This Unfortunate Country" and "The Hunger"; they examine the conditions in Ireland in the eighteenth, nineteenth, and early twentieth centuries. Hunger, poverty, and social injustice were the principal factors behind wholesale emigration from Ireland. But some people left home and family and set off across the Atlantic simply because they were lured by the American dream.

The very first illustration in the book is a group portrait of eighteen Irish immigrants arriving in America on a steamship. They appear well nourished and nicely dressed, members of the Irish middle class. These are people at the beginning of a great adventure. As the authors tell us, by the twentieth century many Irish people had friends and relatives already well established in America and could be sure of a support system waiting for them.

Earlier immigrants were rarely so fortunate. Chapter 4, "No Irish Need Apply," points out that American streets were not paved with gold as many had believed; instead, the immigrants themselves were expected to pave the streets, and for very low wages. Discrimination against them was rampant. Photographs of railroad crews, loggers, and divers working on bridge construction show how hard and dangerous life could be for the newly arrived Irish.

The many black-and-white photographs on these pages have the fascination of allowing us to look upon faces long dead, in circumstances that no longer exist. Both Ireland and America are well represented. A thatched cottage in nineteenth-century Gweedore has Bridget O'Donnel and her huge brood gathered for the camera. A little farther on is an interior scene showing a family in Galway reduced to skeletons by illness and starvation during the famine.

Across the Atlantic, an Irish housemaid in New York City stares past the camera with a wistful gaze, dreaming of home. A prospering farm couple in the Midwest sit for formal studio portraits, looking stiff but triumphant. Irish-American politicians in top hats are photographed at the St. Patrick's Day Parade. An Irish Catholic nun poses with her young charges in Louisville, Kentucky.

For some, the New World was a terrible disappointment; for others, a challenge. Step by step, Irish men and women began pulling them-selves up by their bootstraps. The authors describe their entry into pol-itics, commerce, and the hierarchy of the Catholic Church. Romance and freedom awaited many as well, narrated in the chapter entitled "Love and Liberty."

One immigrant's story, in "Miraculous Energy," tells of a young man named Tim O'Brien. The letters he wrote to his mother back in Ireland brimmed with excitement and the certainty of imminent success. When he arrived in Canada from Belfast as a brash eighteen-year-old determined to conquer the world, O'Brien was too impatient to go through the red tape of U.S. immigration. In 1921, he hijacked a train crossing the U.S.-Canadian border at gunpoint and entered the United States illegally. New York amazed and astonished him; he wrote to his mother in Ireland, "Here no-one shines his own shoes." Soon he set off again, this time for South America. After wandering alone and on foot through the Amazon jungle, he next wrote his mother from Brazil, then was on his way by ship to New Orleans. Lionized by the press as a great adventurer, the young man headed for Hollywood to cash in on his fame and become a movie star.

He didn't succeed, although the letters he wrote home to his mother boasted of being friends with Charlie Chaplin and Douglas Fairbanks. One letter comments, "God, I never knew I was alive 'til I got out here and woke up." For a time O'Brien made a good living selling religious statues to Catholic migrants from Mexico; but when that career failed, he began exhibiting a collection of shrunken heads on the boardwalk at Long Beach and charging twenty-five cents to regale customers with his experiences in the jungle. It was an unfortunate career choice. The heads had been stolen from a Los Angeles anthropologist, not acquired in the Amazon as he claimed, and he was soon arrested. When a judge naively released him on bail, Tim O'Brien set off for Venezuela to make a new fortune. No one ever heard from him again.

The final, and for me the most moving photograph in the book, is of a young Irishwoman on the Aran Islands. Her hair is windblown, her face full of hope. She appears to be gazing west—toward America.

MILLER, ROBERT RYAL

Shamrock and Sword

University of Oklahoma Press, Norman, Oklahoma, 1989

During the U.S.-Mexican War of 1847, many Irish-born immigrant soldiers left the U.S. Army and formed the "San Patricios," or St. Patrick's Brigade, to fight for Mexico against what they perceived as American imperialism.

Since arriving in America, the Irish immigrants had found life difficult. Although most of them were farmboys with little education and no knowledge of military skills, the U.S. Army had seemed to offer a golden opportunity to better themselves. However, once they joined the army, they found life even harder. Racism and persecution were rife in the ranks. The Irishmen were treated very badly, their origins ridiculed, their Catholicism condemned. They found themselves still at the bottom of the pecking order, abused by Americans in the New World as they had been oppressed by the English at home.

In the plight of impoverished Catholic Mexico, struggling against the powerful United States, they saw a cause with which they could identify. The Irishmen enlisted with the Mexicans with one proviso: that they be allowed to fight under their own flag, the banner of St. Patrick. Led by Clifden-born John Riley, the San Patricios would become national heroes to the Mexicans. They were awarded full military honors; an impressive memorial was erected to them, and their memory is kept alive to the present day with festivals and celebrations. But they were condemned as traitors by the American government.

Many of St. Patrick's Brigade died in battle. Those who were captured during the conflict were court-martialed by the U.S. Army. Fifty were executed; others were whipped and branded. John Riley was branded with the letter "D" on both cheeks and wore the disfigurement the rest of his life. On the last day of the war, as the Americans awaited the outcome of the final battle, they stood the condemned San Patricios on wagons with ropes around their necks. There they remained throughout the long day until the American flag was raised at last, heralding victory. Then the horses were whipped up and the Irishmen were hanged.

This true account of war, intrigue, defection, and brutal military justice makes riveting reading. Military buffs will treasure the book, but for all Irish Americans it helps to demonstrate how the history of the New World shaped—and was shaped by—our people. It also gives a fascinating insight into the vastly differing interpretations of one event from two national perspectives. Again, the analogy is very strong. The history of Ireland as perceived by the Irish is very different from the British version. A book like *Shamrock and Sword* demands that one stop and think. Histories are almost always written by the victors; but where does the *truth* lie?

The story of St. Patrick's Brigade is being filmed on location in Mexico as a major motion picture entitled *One Man's Hero*. The film has been twenty years in the making. The late John Wayne originally wanted to play the leading role, but his friends and advisers talked him out of it. They insisted the American public would never accept the Duke in the role of "a traitor to America."

Times have changed, however. People no longer blindly accept that their country is always in the right. Whether the conflict is America versus Mexico, or England versus Ireland, there are always two sides to every story. The title of the movie tells it all: One man's traitor is, indeed, another man's hero.

O'CARROLL, IDE

Models for Movers: Irish Women's Emigration to America

Attic Press, Dublin, 1990

This book examines an element of Irish emigration that has been neglected. Historians have far too often ignored women altogether, or at the most included them in a very general way. Yet there can be no doubt that the women played a crucial role in the establishing of Irish America. Ide O'Carroll, an emigrant herself who moved to Boston in 1986, began by wondering what became of all these women over the years. Were they successful in their search for freedom and happiness? What particular forces drove them to emigrate—and will they ever return?

In her foreword, the author points out that we must also consider the lives these women had led in Ireland, their position in society, and the homes from which they came. O'Carroll gives a thumbnail history of each of the great waves of Irish emigration, beginning with the nineteenth century. But because she wanted to interview living women, she ultimately focuses on those who left Ireland for America in the twentieth century.

The 1920s in Ireland, following the civil war, were a time of tremendous conservatism. The nation was brand-new and still suffering from the trauma of its birth. The place of women, as later stressed in the Constitution of 1937, was in the home—period. With the exception of Dublin, Ireland was a rural society, and women made a substantial contribution to the small-farm economy with their unpaid labor.

The 1950s would see a new wave of emigration from Ireland. There were still few opportunities for paid employment in agriculture and industry, and Irishwomen wanted to take part in the higher standard of living the postwar period was bringing elsewhere.

Emigration in the sixties, seventies and eighties saw women leaving Ireland who were more highly educated than their predecessors. They were well aware of the feminist movement gaining strength in America. Fueled by expectations of more societal freedom and equal employment opportunities, they headed across the Atlantic in droves. Many of them arrived in America as undocumented aliens.

O'Carroll has conducted extensive personal interviews with a number of women, whose stories are often accompanied by photographs. The book is divided into chapters determined by chronology, beginning in the nineteenth century. One of the stories from early in the present century is that of Sadie Patterson, who was born into a working-class Protestant family in Belfast in 1906. Her role in working outside the home was accepted by Protestant society, but even so, life was hard. She tells us, "We who produced the finest linen in the world had to be content with newspapers on our tables, too poor to buy what we produced. We slept on sheets made from flour sacks." Sadie Patterson helped organize female workers in the linen mills and later became the first female official of the Transport and General Workers' Union.

The situation for Catholic women was different. During the revolutionary period, 1916–22, they had proudly taken their place beside their men, even on the battle lines. But as the new state took its first fledgling steps toward autonomy, the author tells us that the patriarchal Catholic Church began relentlessly pushing women back to kitchen and kettle. Just one example is the fact that married women were banned from working in the civil service. Given this situation for women who had recently not only helped win freedom but tasted it for themselves, it is not surprising that they began to look beyond Ireland for their futures.

The story of Bridie Halpin is subtitled "Up Us! Profile of an Immigrant in New York." Bridie was an active revolutionary and member of Cumann na mBan, the women's arm of the Irish Volunteers. In 1921, she was deeply disappointed by the treaty that brought the Free State into being by partitioning Ireland. For her ongoing republican activities she was subsequently imprisoned for a time by the new Free State government. It is not surprising that she decided to emigrate to America and work from there to bring about a "proper" settlement of Irish affairs. It took Halpin seventeen years after her first formal application to receive permission to settle in America—a full twenty years after her release from prison. She spent the rest of her life in New York working for Irish causes, and died in 1988.

Of course, the majority of women did not leave Ireland for political reasons. Terry Ryan Ryder was born in a tenement in Dublin in 1936. As a young child she contracted tuberculosis, which meant spending her young girlhood in and out of hospitals, expecting to die. But Terry was hard to kill. She grew up, went to secretarial school, and worked continually to better herself. The ultimate step in her plan was to go to America. She finally got work as a housekeeper and baby-sitter for a family on Cape Cod. The tuberculosis lingered, seemingly a lasting reminder of the hard years in Dublin, but she went on to become a business executive and enjoy a happy marriage.

Rena Cody was born in County Tipperary in 1952. She speaks frankly of how hard it was for her to get established as an immigrant in America: "I was very tired and quite burnt out ... I traveled on the Greyhounds for about three months ... a lot of isolation, loneliness. ..." She stuck with it, eventually becoming an Immigrant and Refugee Outreach worker at Neponset Health Center in Boston. Rena represents a younger generation of emigrants, one that is successfully carving its own niche in the New World.

O'Connor speaks proudly of these women as role models, demonstrating the growth that has occurred in individual lives inspired by an American dream.

WILSON, ANDREW J.

Irish America and the Ulster Conflict

Catholic University Press of America, Washington, D.C., 1995

In this thoughtful work, Andrew J. Wilson explores both the political and the socioeconomic story of Irish America's longtime role in the Ulster crisis. Northern Ireland has endured almost thirty years of protests and violence between loyalists and nationalists. One side is determined to remain part of the United Kingdom while the other side ardently desires a united Ireland. The antagonism is intense; the problem has seemed intractable.

To set the stage for his examination of this situation, the author begins with a summary of Irish-American involvement in Irish politics since 1800. He describes the founding and development of various militant and constitutional nationalist groups in the United States, such as the Irish Republican Brotherhood, the Ancient Order of Hibernians, and so on. Then he moves on to examine the impact such organizations have had on events in Northern Ireland.

Wilson gives a comprehensive account of Irish-American support of the IRA, and also analyzes tactics used by various militant groups to win publicity and public sympathy for their cause. In his examination of Irish-American support for constitutional nationalism, he focuses on the influence of the Friends of Ireland group in Congress and its attempts to shape British policy in Ulster.

The lobbying of such prominent American politicians as former Speaker of the House Thomas P. O'Neill, former governor of New York

Hugh Carey, Senator Edward M. Kennedy, and Senator Daniel Patrick Moynihan is detailed. Wilson shows how these men influenced U.S. government policies and in turn provided the Dublin government with leverage to use in diplomatic relations with the British. This leverage has been crucial in reaching the current level of cooperation between the British and Irish over the fate of Northern Ireland.

The result of extensive research and interviews with leading activists on both sides of the Atlantic, this book is a serious, scholarly examination of a complex situation. Although not easy reading, it will prove worthwhile for all those with an interest in modern history and American diplomacy as applied to Ireland.

MYTHOLOGY AND FOLKLORE

COLUM, PÁDRAIC

A Treasury of Irish Folklore

Crown Publishers, New York, 1967

Some titles can be misleading, but this book is a genuine treasury. Here you will find Fionn MacCumhaill and St. Patrick cheek by jowl with Turlough O'Carolan the blind harper and heroic Michael Collins. Fairy stories to read aloud to children are interspersed with intriguing historical episodes and thumbnail biographical sketches of Ireland's heroes.

Pádraic Colum begins with a section he calls The Irish Edge: essays on the wit and wisdom of the Irish. Many of the writings are his; others are from well-known authors. In the very first sketch, "A Man's Life," Colum tells us: "You see, my boy, a man's life naturally divides itself into three distinct periods. The first is that when he is planning and contriving all sorts of villainy. The second is when he is putting into practice the villainy he contrived before. The third is when he is preparing for another world."

In the next section Heroes of Old, Colum writes of the Tuatha de Danaan, the "magical people" who were the antecedents of the latter-day "fairies" of Ireland. From here he moves on to tell of Cuchulain, of Deirdre of the Sorrows, of Fionn, and of the romance of Dermot and Grania—the foremost ancient tales of Ireland.

The section entitled Great Chiefs and Uncrowned Kings covers a wide range of historical figures, from triumphant Brian Bóru to the Two Hughs—Red Hugh O'Donnell and Hugh O'Neill—who were tragically defeated in Ireland's struggle against conquest by Elizabeth I. Here also is the Irish pirate queen, Grace O'Malley, whose tale is all the more extraordinary for being true. Colum gives us brief but entertaining essays that will stimulate the reader's interest and urge wider exploration of the subjects.

Ireland Without Leaders tells of the eighteenth century and the failed Rising of '98. This section is followed by New Leaders At Home and Abroad, which concludes with Charles Parnell and Michael Collins. Colum never forgets the power of language. From a speech by Daniel O'Connell, the Irish statesman who was responsible for Catholic emancipation in Ireland, he quotes: "Among the means to raise money in Ireland for James the First [of England] was invented a scheme to inquire of every man what right he had to his own property, and to have it solemnly and legally determined that he had none."

Ways and Traditions, Fireside Tales, and The Face of the Land follow, drawing upon the extensive collection of stories and folklore Colum had gathered over the years. He concludes with Ballads and Songs, reminding the reader that music is central to the Irish experience.

Pádraic Colum (1881–1972) was a member of the Irish literary renaissance early in this century. His father had been master of the workhouse in County Longford, but young Pádraic's first job was in the Railway Clearing House in Dublin. He soon turned to writing, however, producing plays and song lyrics. His best known song, the haunting "She Moved Through the Fair," tells the story of a maiden who died before her wedding day; it is a part of every Irish traditional singer's repertoire.

Together with the writer James Stephens, and Thomas MacDonagh, who would be one of the leaders of the Easter Rising, Colum founded the *Irish Review*, an important nationalist periodical. Colum and his wife moved to the United States in 1914, where both became teachers of comparative literature at Columbia University. Colum wrote a series of folk tales for the *New York Tribune*, including legends of Hawaii. His *Collected Poems* were published in 1953; the following year, he was awarded the Gregory Medal by the Irish Academy of Letters.

Pádraic Colum's extensive writings covered a wide range from poetry to biography. With *A Treasury of Irish Folklore* he formed a bridge between Ireland and America, between his birthplace and his chosen home, making the best of the former easily accessible to the latter.

DAMES, MICHAEL

Mythic Ireland

Thames & Hudson, New York, 1996

Irish Americans love to visit Ireland. They come seeking the magic they are certain is there, but they also bring a lot of the romance with them. And they come equipped with a list of names; special places which represent Ireland to them. Tara, the seat of the ancient high kings; Uisneach (pronounced "Oosh-nah"), the mysterious druidic ritual site at the heart of the island; Anna Livia, better known as the River Liffey, a pagan goddess whose story predates that of human settlement.

The Americans come to Ireland for two weeks or for a whole summer, only to discover that one cannot know all of this small island in a lifetime. But this book will suggest new methods of discovery.

Michael Dames begins *Mythic Ireland* by telling us that the Age of Myth is supposedly over. The gods of humanity's childhood were supplanted first by the Christian God, and then by a god-free concept of scientific reason. But, he argues most persuasively, Irish mythology is far from dead, springing as it does from the living land. He proceeds to explore two Irelands: one the tangible and physical; the other the Ireland of the imagination. Perhaps more than any other country in Europe, Ireland has retained its mythological heritage almost intact, surviving in folk tales, literature, place names, and topography. Mountains and lakes are the homes of gods and goddesses, saints and monsters. Pattern, beauty, and the logic of the seasons are revealed in their stories.

Dames guides the reader through each of the four provinces of Ireland—Ulster, Munster, Leinster, and Connacht—as well as the so-called fifth province, the central region of Meath. After a general discussion of the importance of local myth, rite, and symbol comes Part One, Ulster: Saint Patrick and the Hag. The author focuses his Ulster explorations on St. Patrick's Purgatory on Lough Derg, described by the geographer Giraldus Cambrensis as early as 1186: ". . . a lake in Ulster containing an island divided into two equal parts. On one stands a church of special sanctity, glorious for the visitations of angels and the multitude of saints who visibly frequent it. The other, being covered with rugged crags, is the resort of devils only and the theatre on which crowds of evil spirits perform their rites."

This evocative quote leads Dames to discuss similar sites elsewhere in Europe, related classical mythological references, the dichotomous relations of heaven and hell on earth, and the concept of purgatory and purification. Thus he gives the reader a broad view not only of St. Patrick's Purgatory itself, but also of its place in the cosmos.

From a central site in each of the four provinces, the tale spirals out to examine related myth—and reality. Dames tells of the enchanted island of Tir Na n'Og, the Country of the Young, which might be described as the Irish Brigadoon. By cleverly placing Tir Na n'Og in juxtaposition with what he calls "the myth that is Dublin," the author demonstrates the degree to which both are figments of the imagination.

Throughout these richly illustrated pages, Fire-Eyes and Water Monsters abound. Pagan and Christian become kin. St. Brigid's benevolence is met and matched by Etain, loveliest of pagan women, whose name is translated as "Brow of Poetry." With deceptive ease Dames moves from these vivid images to passages of philosophical dissertation, buttressing his contention of "the underlying unity of Christian, pagan, and scientific myth." He offers one provocative statement after another. For example, in the chapter on Munster, he says, "The effect of a sacred centre is not complete until it has driven the pilgrim away." He also points out that in Old and Middle Irish, there was no word for superstition. "Whether embraced or not," he tells us, "*all* matters of belief were to be treated seriously."

Dames has produced an enormously thought-provoking book that works on many levels. Even the most rational and scientific-minded Americans will find themselves looking not only at Ireland but at their own land with new eyes after reading *Mythic Ireland*.

EICKHOFF, RANDY LEE

The Raid

Tor Books, St. Martin's Press, New York, 1996

he Raid is a new examination of the *Táin Bo Cúailnge*, the most
famous of all Irish mythic sagas. The Germans had Siegfried and
the Greeks Ulysses; Ireland had Cúchulainn (there are many different
spellings for his name in literature). With his "hero light" and divine
madness, he was the equal of any national hero.

The book quotes original passages from this epic tale of jealousy,
retribution, and heroism, together with a highly readable modern version
of the text. Set in Ireland over two thousand years ago, the story takes
place during the Irish Iron Age, a time of intense tribalism and warrior
kings. It opens with Ailill, the king of Connacht, and his wife, Maeve,
arguing over who is the wealthiest. This tale has been a mainstay of Irish
storytelling for centuries, yet their competitive marital discord sounds
as fresh as tomorrow.

Maeve loftily tells her husband, "I am too full of grace and giving
for one man. I have never slept with one man without another waiting
in the shadows to take his place." A quick comparison of their material
possessions shows them to be entirely equal, with the exception of a
magnificent white bull owned by the king. The jealous Maeve, who is
determined not to let her husband be her superior in any way, learns of
a brown bull in Ulster that is as good as Ailill's white bull. When her
attempts to purchase the brown bull fail, she declares war on the province of Ulster in an attempt to bring the Brown Bull of Cooley back to

Connacht. Personally led by their fierce queen, the Connachtmen set off on the greatest of all cattle raids.

Meanwhile, the warrior elite of Ulster, who are known as the knights of the Red Branch, have had a terrible curse placed upon them. In time of danger they find themselves going through all the pains of a woman in labor. Only Cúchulainn, the king's personal champion, is exempt. He is left to alone against Maeve's invading army.

Cúchulainn is a multidimensional character; a man's man, a woman's man, a loving friend, a monstrous enemy. His paternity is questionable from the start. He may be the son of Lugh, the Sun God— or the product of incest. This confusion of identity is often central to Celtic literature. He is supported by the Morrigan, the goddess of war, as he undertakes a reign of terror upon the Connacht warriors.

Cúchulainn prepared for battle is a spectacular figure. The bulk of his hair is drawn back into three loops, while "a hundred tight red-gold ringlets shone darkly on his temples." Four dimples are on his cheeks; he has seven fingers on each hand and seven toes on each foot. Dressed in "royal clothes he had earned with the strength of his warrior's hand," Cúchulainn is the personal champion of the king of Ulster. He also is a man possessed of a magical madness. We are told that the Ulster women, upon seeing him, "sighed and felt their hearts hammer in their breasts and their loins grow moist with desire." The original *Táin* was no gentle fairy tale, but a full-blooded portrait of a lusty age.

The saga includes a cast of characters any modern screenwriter would envy, and a number of sophisticated plot twists. When Cúchulainn finds himself committed to a fight to the death against his dearest friend, Ferdiad, we observe the agonies of a man betrayed by his own honor. Subsequently, Cúchulainn mourns his friend: "It seemed our friendship would be remaining forever between you and me. I loved the noble way you blushed, and loved your perfect form's finesse. And now I have this brooch only to mourn you with. Shameful that such a thing has befallen me."

In Cúchulainn's last stand at the conclusion of the story the reader will find a powerful metaphor for the determination of the Irish people to stand against oppression. Today, a magnificent bronze sculpture of the dying Cúchulainn, tied to a tree so he can meet his enemies on his feet, and with the Morrigan, the Crow Goddess and goddess of war, perched on his shoulder, adorns the General Post Office in Dublin—where the Easter Rising was fought in 1916.

The Raid describes one of the oldest epics in the world, predating Beowulf and the *Song of Roland*. The *Táin Bó Cúailnge* has long been central to Irish culture. Eickhoff's careful translation from the original Irish keeps the flavor of the ancient language while making the work accessible to modern, English-speaking readers.

GANTZ, JEFFREY, TRANSLATOR

Early Irish Myths and Sagas

Dorset House, New York, 1985

I n this book Jeffrey Gantz has translated some of the most representative tales from the Irish mythological cycle, providing a valuable
starting point for exploring Ireland's rich mythic heritage. The introduction discusses Ireland's early myths and sagas in general, the Celtic
culture that inspired them, the traditions of Irish storytelling, and the
manuscripts and related material which have preserved these stories
down to the present day.

Adopting an unusual format, Gantz next presents his bibliography,
followed by a most useful explanation of the pronunciation of Irish
words and names and a note on Irish geography. Thus he gives the
readers the material they will need for an appreciation of the text that
follows.

The translator accompanies each of the stories with a brief introduction that tells something of the tale's history and gives a précis of
the plot. The stories themselves include the romantic *Wooing of Etain*,
the hilarious *Destruction of Da Derga's Hostel*, and the unforgettable *Tale
of Macc Da Thó's Pig*. Others are *The Dream of Oengus, The Labour Pains
of the Ulaid* (Ulstermen), *The Birth of Cú Chulaind, The Only Jealousy of
Emer, The Intoxication of the Ulaid, Bricriu's Feast,* and *The Exile of the
Sons of Uisliu*.

Gantz describes *Bricriu's Feast* as the most characteristic story, with
"a mythic subtext, a heroic competition, visits to and from the other-

world, elements of humour and parody and a rambling, patchwork struc-ture." Quoting a passage from *The Exile of the Sons of Uisliu*, he comments, "This passage, from one of the finest stories ever written in Ireland, evinces much of what Irish literature is: romantic, idealistic, stylized and yet vividly, even appallingly concrete. Most of all, it ex-emplifies the tension between reality and fantasy that characterizes all Celtic art."

Gantz's scholarly work stays close to the original Irish. Unlike W. B. Yeats's friend and patron Lady Gregory, Gantz does not invent a "new" version of language to give an archaic flavor to the stories. Instead, he provides as literal a translation as is possible, catching ancient echoes. In *The Tale of Macc Da Thó's Pig*, we read: "Sleeplessness has come to Macc Da Thó's house. He turns away to the wall, a warrior in fierce combat. His clever wife observes that her husband cannot sleep. Tell no secret to a woman. A woman's secret is not kept; jewels are not given to slaves."

Early Irish Myths and Sagas provides a window onto a lost world, one that continues to hold a powerful fascination for Irish and Ameri-cans alike.

GLASSIE, HENRY

Irish Folk History: Texts from the North

University of Pennsylvania Press, Philadelphia, 1982

Henry Glassie has served as chairman of the department of folklore and folklife at the University of Pennsylvania, and has written several books on folkloric subjects. *Irish Folk History* is my favorite, not least because it gives us a view of the traditions of Northern Ireland as distinct from the island as a whole. The North has its own voice. To some extent, that was true long before partition; even before Elizabethan times. Ancient Ulster was a separate and distinct kingdom from those of Munster, Leinster, Connacht, and Meath. Some would say it was the most Gaelic part of Ireland.

The tribes that settled in the northern part of the island some three thousand years ago spoke a unique variant of the common Indo-European root language. They also brought with them traditions that were different from the tribes of western and southern Ireland. Some of the northern tribes subsequently crossed the sea to settle the highlands of Scotland and become the Scots. There was considerable cultural hybridization between the two cultures thereafter.

The introduction of Protestant settlers into the North three hundred years ago brought yet another element into the region commonly called Ulster. These settlers were both English and Scottish. While the Scots Presbyterian colonists shared an ancient heritage with the Irish natives, their culture had changed in many ways. The English colonists had hardly anything in common with the Irish. These newcomers would have a profound influence on the way the people of the North perceived themselves.

In this slim but beautifully written book, Glassie has assembled a potpourri of indigenous northern folk tales, stories, and songs. He collected the material from a community of active storytellers in County Fermanagh, and presents them to us still warm with living breath.

Consider the tale of a man called John Brodison from County Cavan. The countryside was beset with a plague of rabbits—except for Brodison's cabbage patch. Let him tell you the secret as Glassie reports it: "I went down to the quarry, he says, and I riz a wee cart of stones, and I put the stones around them [the cabbages], and I bought a pound of pepper, and I dusted the stones, he says, with the pepper, and the rabbits came and the pepper went up their noses and they started to sneeze, and they knocked their brains out against the stones, sneezin'." Such ingenuity is the delight of the northerner.

The art of the born storyteller, the seanchai, is one of the most highly respected in Ireland. Tales told by the crackling fireside have shaped the people's image of themselves for millennia. The Seanchai memorized the stories of the race, which contained the weight of cultural education as well as endless entertainment. For this reason the storyteller was always welcome, a meal put into his hand and a drink poured into his cup as soon as he came in the door.

Read Glassie's description of the value of the storyteller as artist: "From a distance little communities seem homogeneous, even bland, but from the inside they feel diverse and exciting. As stars glitter against the night sky, the community's artists burn away from their darkening contexts. They light the way for their neighbours, making life tolerable for their hardworking fellows."

I never tire of authentic folk tales. The richness of language beguiles. Irony, satire, and surprise are a constant delight. So much "shamroguery"—the pejorative the Irish themselves apply to imitation Irishness—is on the market today that books like Glassie's stand out like diamonds. In its pages the American reader will gain a new appreciation for the diversity that this small island contains.

REYNOLDS, JAMES

Ghosts in Irish Houses

Farrar, Straus & Cudahy, New York, 1947; Bonanza Books, New York, 1984

James Reynolds's depictions of the supernatural are unique both for their imaginative quality and for their compelling illustrations. A number of Americans have told me that their first experience of Ireland came from reading *Ghosts in Irish Houses*.

Reynolds, an Irish-born painter, traveled throughout the island collecting ghostly folk tales to illustrate with pen and palette. When published, the success of *Ghosts in Irish Houses* was such that he followed it up with *Ghosts in American Houses* and *Gallery of Ghosts*. But this one remains special. Eschewing standard tales, the author has dug out the marvelous and strange, stories with a peculiarly Irish flavor. Reynolds's ghosts are eccentric; he brings them to life with memorable word portraits that are as visual as his beautifully painted illustrations.

Take *The Headless Rider of Castle Sheela*. In 1739, Galty Mallory, whose family had been prominent Irish landowners since the Battle of Clontarf in 1014, set off on the Grand Tour of Europe. He returned with a bride, the beautiful Countess Hoja of Hungary: "There was a look of not-too-well-controlled wildness about the mouth of this arresting face." The daughter of a Tartar noble, Hoja possessed a heritage of hot blood which she passed on to her son, Ormond.

Ormond Mallory grew up to be an insolent ne'er-do-well. When he inherited the family stronghold at Castle Sheela, he promptly installed a buxom local widow, Moira Carmichael, as his mistress. Then he set about abusing her and indulging his true passion, which was horses. His favorite mount was a young hunter he called Follow. Ormond Mallory even encouraged Follow to enter the house and come up the stairs into the Great Hall.

Through his cruelty and vices Mallory made a lot of enemies in the neighborhood, so it is not surprising that eventually he failed to return alive from the traditional Christmas Day hunt. Follow brought back his decapitated body instead, firmly tied to the saddle. People said Ormond had got what he richly deserved. It is not his fate that lingers in the mind, however, but the sound of ghostly hooves as his faithful horse, Follow, still carries his decapitated body up the echoing stone staircase of a house long since deserted.

In another story, Reynolds tells of having himself seen the *Bridal Barge* of Aran Roe, a ghostly vessel dating from the eleventh century. He writes, "A full moon bathed Clew Bay in luminous light. Suddenly I stood spellbound, for into my line of vision, about a mile out to sea, sped the dazzling gold and red of the Bridal Barge. The moon pointed up the gilded shields on the prow and turned into fiery streamers the crimson pall flung across the bier high in the stern. Then, silently gliding into the middle-mist whence it had come, the phantom ship passed into the night."

In the moving tale of *Mickey Filler and the Tansey Wreath*, Reynolds tells us that his hero was "a more gentle, certainly a more vague version of Puck." Mickey Filler from County Clare was also the grandson of a notorious County Clare witch, Biddy Early. This simple-minded young man lived in the last century, collecting wild herbs which he peddled in the village. But his was a lonely existence. Then during the height of the Great Famine a small, lost girl wandered into his cottage while he was away and fell asleep. By the time Mickey discovered her, she had suffocated in the mattress of mandrake and verbena that formed his bed.

Sadly, Mickey buried the dead child, who seemed as beautiful to him as a doll. His last act was to place a wreath of tansey leaves on her golden hair. Then, a few weeks later, another starving child appeared. This one was dark-haired and still alive, though very weak. Mickey nursed her tenderly, innocently, eager for the companionship of another human being. He wove another wreath of tansey for her brow and cradled her in his arms to keep her warm. This was how the pair of them were found later, dead of hunger and frozen by winter's chill.

The ghost of Mickey Filler still haunts a remote glen in County Clare—but he is no longer lonely. Two beautiful little girls dance around him, one fair, one dark. Reynolds tells us they move "as if their feet scorned the grassy turf."

Then there is the story of Red Eva MacMurrough and her super-human leap from the battlements of her husband's castle; her husband Strongbow, who first brought conquest to Ireland. Or the tale of the exotic Princess Orloff and her sister Rosaleen, and the terrible hatred that festered between them, leaving scorching heat in the handle of a riding whip many years later.

Story after story captures the imagination with titles like *The Weeping Wall, Mrs. O'Moyne and the Fatal Slap, The Four Terrors, The Bloody Stones of Kerrigan's Keep, Badminton in Bloomers, The Cerements on the Stairs, The Drums of Rathmoy* . . .

If some of these tales have been heavily embroidered by the author, they are all the better for it. They introduce Americans to an unfamiliar Ireland, but one authentic in tone and flavor. Over the years since I first read Reynolds's book, I have made a point of hunting out the sites he wrote about, trying to verify the stories. I have not always been successful, nor would I want to be.

Mystery is better . . .

SCOTT, MICHAEL

Irish Folk and Fairy Tales Omnibus

Sphere Books London, 1989; Barnes & Noble, New York, 1993

Here are forty-two original stories collected into one huge book, combining three previously published volumes. The majority of the tales are built, in a fresh and imaginative way, upon traditional myth and legend. But Michael Scott has the ability to see the old afresh and create new plot twists and motivations.

Vol. One focuses on the faerie tradition. The first stories Scott relates are together known as "The Three Sorrows of Irish Storytelling": *The Sons of Tuireen, The Children of Lir, and Deirdre and the Sons of Usnach.* Of these, the story of the Children of Lir is perhaps the best known. Today, Celtic jewelers in both Ireland and America produce beautiful images of swans in gold and silver, inspired by this ancient tale.

Scott's version of the tale opens with the births of twin boys to King Lir of the Tuatha de Danann (the "magical people" of pagan Ireland). But the children have cost their mother her life. Lir has another son and a small daughter, however; a lovely miniature of her mother. Scott goes beneath the surface of the story to let us share the emotions of the characters. He writes of the widowed king, "He found it hard to accept that she was dead and would wander the lonely corridors half expecting to hear her laughter behind him or her light footfall on the stair. He saw her in every corner, smelled her scent in every room, heard her voice by his side, felt her presence in his bed."

In time the king marries his dead wife's half sister. In best fairy-tale fashion, she proves to be an evil stepmother. She is jealous of the four children and longs to kill them, but dare not go that far. In a scene of spellbinding sorcery, she transforms them into swans instead: "The water suddenly blazed about the children of Lir, a chilling blue-white fire which blinded without burning. Fionuala lost sight of Aedan and Conn and even Fiachra seemed thin and insubstantial in her arms. The light dazzled her eyes, bringing tears and causing spots to dance wildly on her retina. The world lurched; the dark sky and burning water losing definition and depth whilst the colours shook and vibrated."

In its original pagan form, *The Children of Lir* was a tale of unrelieved tragedy. The Christian monks who transcribed the story from the oral tradition changed the ending, incorporating a message of Christian redemption. Scott opts for the earlier version, but retains an ending that suits both traditions.

Other stories in Vol. One introduce us to faerie maids and leprechauns, to elvish folk and sea folk and the mysterious birth of the Shannon River. Thus the book is reminiscent of the first opera of Wagner's Ring cycle, the magical *Das Rheingold*, which prepares the audience for wonder.

Vol. Two takes us a step further, drawing for its inspiration partly upon the "Heroic Cycle" of Irish myth. The first story, *The Dawn*, is straight out of the oldest of all Irish tales, that of the first settlers on the island. With this beginning Scott sets the stage for the warriors and battles to follow. The second volume also contains stories developed from the rare Irish legends of were-creatures, tales that helped inspire Bram Stoker's *Dracula* (see p. 248). In some of the stories Scott introduces a character of his own creation: Father Morand, the Witchfinder. Always aware of the need to retain the human element, Scott gradually develops the Witchfinder into a portrait of a complex and intriguing personality.

Vol. Three returns to a sense of mystery and magic, with stories that move back and forth through time. Like a Celtic shapechanger, the author takes different forms to present different images. He presents us with mermaids and wolf-maids, harpers and card players. And in the final story, fittingly entitled *The Last Outpost*, he depicts the end of the faerie kingdom. Except that it isn't dead. Not in Ireland.

Irish mythology is a springboard for many writers these days, incorporated into everything from terror to science fiction. For those of us who love to read stories with an Irish flavor, there is a bewildering array to choose from. But it takes a special writer to be able to draw upon traditional sources and create something of his own, while still being true to the feeling and intent of the original. Dublin-born Scott has this talent. Americans reading his work will be able to see how strong the ancient influences are on modern writers—including many American fantasy writers.

STEPHENS, JAMES

The Crock of Gold

Macmillan & Co., London, 1912; Gill & Macmillan, Dublin, 1995

The Crock of Gold is widely acknowledged as one of the greatest
novels in the Irish comic tradition. An elaborate construction of
fantasy, satire, and humor propels the narrative through a cosmos peopled by pagan gods, human philosophers, policemen, tinkers, and leprechauns. Stephens's creation is an earthy Never-Never-Land filled with
frolic. Yet the intent of it all is serious. In calling attention to an Ireland
that never was, the author encourages the reader to juxtapose this against
the real Ireland, observing how much the reality owes to the fiction. He
also has a great deal to say about the nature of religion and belief.

Although I knew that *The Crock of Gold* was something everyone
with the slightest drop of Irish blood should read, I found it hard to decide how to categorize the books for the purposes of this list. Stephens's
masterpiece belongs equally with Novels and Humor. Divided into six
books, it comprises a colloquy between mankind and the gods.

Book One tells of *The Coming of Pan*, introducing a deity from
classical mythology into a pagan Celtic world peopled by an assortment
of colorful characters. Book Two, *The Philosopher's Journey*, focuses on
one of these characters, a man ostensibly in search of the Great God
Pan. However, his journey is actually an opportunity for the author
continually to introduce yet more characters who look at life—and the
soul—from every conceivable angle. This element reminds one of John
Bunyan's masterpiece, *Pilgrim's Progress.*

It is also full of fun. Talking with his friend Meehawl, the Philosopher comments: "Certain trades and professions, it is curious to note, tend to be perpetuated in the female line. The sovereign profession among bees and ants is always female, and publicans also descend on the distaff side. You will have noticed that every publican has three daughters of extraordinary charms. Lacking these signs we would do well to look askance at such a man's liquor, divining that in his brew there will be an undue percentage of water. If his primogeniture is infected how shall his honesty escape?" When the Philosopher encounters a woman on the road, he offers her a bite of the cake he has with him, volunteering the information that his wife made it. The woman responds that she doesn't believe he's married. When the Philosopher insists he has been married for ten years, she asks:

"And how many children would you have, mister?"

"I never had more than one."

"Ten years married and only one child? Why, man dear, you're not a married man. What were you doing at all, at all. I wouldn't like to be telling you the children I have living and dead. But what I say is that married or not, you're a bachelor man."

From this earthy platform we are launched into a very short Book Three, *The Two Gods*, where the purely pagan Pan dances through a Celtic paradise like a beam of sunlight. Encountering a Celtic deity with Christian overtones, Angus Óg, he engages in a dialogue that delineates the differences between the two cultures. Pan claims to embody Infinite Love and Joy, implying that nothing else matters. Angus Óg replies that the greatest thing in the world is the Divine Imagination. "The Divine Imagination may only be known through the thoughts of His creatures," he tells Pan.

The Philosopher makes his way home again in *The Philosopher's Return*, Book Four. He is both transformed and baffled by his experiences on the road, which have been influenced by the spirits who infest the atmosphere. He ponders: "We might ask, is the Earth anything more than an extension of our human consciousness, or are we, moving creatures, only projections of the Earth's antennae?" This same question would be asked generations later by Richard Lovelock and the proponents of the Gaia theory. Stephens was ahead of his time. And like the even earlier Dean Swift, he knew that the most profound philosophies can successfully be couched in humor.

In Book Five, *The Policemen*, the Philosopher's noblest impulses are misunderstood. Eventually he runs afoul of a wild assortment of be-whiskered policemen and lunatic laws. This book ends with: "When the morning came the Philosopher was taken on a car to the big City in order that he might be put on trial and hanged. It was the custom."

Book Six, *The Thin Woman's Journey and the Happy March,* moves us out of a world of tangible pain and back into the realm of the gods—and the fairies, and the leprechauns, and deep thoughts and great joy. And yet . . . there are the spires of Dublin in the distance. Reality and fantasy are interlocked as Stephens forces us to consider whether or not happy endings are within our own control.

The Crock of Gold is a book for everyone, Irish or not. When I first read it in my twenties, I thought I understood it. Each time I go back and reread it, I am forced to a new and different understanding, based on my own experiences until that reading. The book's special value to Americans is its ability to guide them into Irish thought processes: those marvelous mental circumlocutions peculiar to the natives of Erin.

YEATS, W. B., AND LADY GREGORY

A Treasury of Irish Myth, Legend, and Folklore

Avenel Books, New York, 1986

Here in one massive volume are both William Butler Yeats and Lady Gregory on the subject of the Irish supernatural. Thus are united two classic works that were both first published near the turn of the century and became the pillars of modern Irish mythology.

Yeats had a lifelong fascination with the supernatural. As editor of *Fairy and Folk Tales of the Irish Peasantry*, he brings us tales from Ireland's past together with much work of his own. Many of the translations from the Irish are by Douglas Hyde, founder of the Gaelic League. In his introduction, Yeats tells us: "As to my own part in this book, I have tried to make it representative of every kind of Irish folk-faith." He has succeeded admirably.

In the first section, "The Trooping Fairies," Yeats begins by telling us that the peasantry believed fairies were "Fallen angels who were not good enough to be saved, nor bad enough to be lost." Then he points out that Irish antiquarians had a different view, believing the so-called Little People to be "The gods of pagan Ireland, the Tuatha de Danann, who, when no longer worshipped, dwindled away in the popular imagination and now are only a few spans high." There follow stories of troops of magical beings possessed of unearthly beauty, tinkling laughter, and a strong streak of malice. Subheadings tell tales of Changelings and The Merrow, the Irish version of the mermaid.

"The Solitary Fairies" introduces Lepracauns, Cluricauns, and the

Far Darrig, all spelled according to the fashion of the early twentieth century. Here are found the Pooka, the Banshee, and the Leanhaun Shee, or Fairy Mistress, who seeks the love of mortals. The section is further enriched by the inclusion of William Allingham's poem, "The Fairy Shoemaker," and Samuel Ferguson's beloved "The Fairy Well of Lagnanay."

Next comes "Ghosts," a subject that reflects Yeats's interest in spiritualism. Poetry to chill the bone is interspersed with tales such as *The Black Lamb*, recounted by Lady Wilde, the mother of Oscar Wilde. The stories demonstrate how much a part of Irish life were the visitants from beyond the grave.

"Witches and Fairy Doctors" contains a sampling of tales from every corner of the country, but the section that follows, "T'Yeer-Na-N-Oge" (an idiosyncratic spelling of Tir Na n'Og), concentrates on one magical, vanishing island depicted in several permutations. Subsequent sections deal with Saints and Priests, The Devil, Giants, and the last, "Kings, Queens, Princesses, Earls and Robbers." Yeats concludes with notes that give his sources for various stories and beliefs, and lists authorities as well as related reading.

The second half of this volume is devoted to *Cuchulain of Muirthemne*, Lady Gregory's own version of the great saga of Ulster (see *The Raid*, p. 169). In addition to being the patron of the Irish literary renaissance, Isabella Augusta, Lady Gregory, was also an avid collector of folklore. Together with her books *Gods and Fighting Men* and *Visions and Beliefs in the West of Ireland,* the work reprinted here played a large part in rekindling Irish interest in the ancient tales early in the present century.

The original bardic tales that had descended through the oral tradition from an era predating Christianity were extremely earthy, bawdy, and violent. They were also an accurate depiction of the culture of their time. One of the classic examples is a spontaneous contest between Cuchuláin's wife Emer and some other women. They urinated into the snow and measured the size of the holes. The woman who proved she had the greatest bladder capacity won.

The monks who transcribed these tales in the sixth to twelfth centuries carefully expunged the more "pagan" elements, as well as those that contradicted Christian doctrine. Lady Gregory further sanitized the tales to make them more acceptable to post-Victorian sensibilities. In addition she created a high-flown, archaic style of writing intended to give a feeling of greater antiquity to the work. However, this actually tells the reader much more about Lady Gregory's own era than about ancient Ireland. A comparison of her work with modern, less squeamish translators reveals the cultural gulf that separates our time from hers— and hers from pagan Ireland.

But her books are well worth reading. They inform and entertain. Every Irish American should have a familiarity both with Yeats and with Lady Gregory. The golden era of the Gael that they sought to restore helped inspire the men who fought the Easter Rising in 1916.

NOVELS

BINCHY, MAEVE

Light a Penny Candle

Century Publishers, London, 1982; Signet Books, New York, paperback, 1997

Maeve Binchy's novels are beloved around the world and have earned an enviable place on American best-seller lists. Binchy is also the author of a number of stage plays, a television play, and three volumes of short stories. She writes from the heart: warm, gentle stories of friendship and love and discovery.

In *Light a Penny Candle*, a genteel British girl called Elizabeth White is evacuated from Blitz-battered London and sent to stay with the boisterous, very Irish O'Connor family. It is the beginning of an unshakable bond between Elizabeth and Aisling O'Connor; a friendship that will survive twenty turbulent years. The novel is as intimate as a TV soap but with much more depth and compassion.

After she is returned home to England, Elizabeth writes her friend Aisling:

> Could you pray that it will be all right? I suppose you must know I sort of gave up my faith. . . . Just pray that Mother won't go away with Mr. Elton, please Aisling, and ask people at school to pray for a special intention. Mr. Elton's very nice, it was he who took that silly picture, and he's always laughing and making jokes. And now that Mother's better and everything, she meets him a lot, and I'm so afraid he and she might be thinking of going off together. Sometimes when I come in from school and

there's a note from Mother on the table saying she'll be late, I'm almost afraid to read it in case it's saying more than that.

I may be wrong. Remember the time we all thought that Eamonn was drowned in the river, and he'd just gone home the other way? Well, that's the kind of fear I have now.

Most children have at some time or the other been afraid of losing a parent to fate or circumstance. Maeve Binchy has the gift for recalling such youthful terrors and bringing them back in vivid color. But more adult problems lie ahead for her characters. Elizabeth falls in love . . . and it is not all music and moonbeams. When she confesses to Aisling that she is pregnant, her friend responds breathlessly, "You mean, you mean you had intercourse with him? . . . What was it like?"

"Aisling O'Connor, I can't believe you. I've told you the most terrible tragedy, the worst bit of bad news anyone could have, and you ask me what it's like having sex . . . !"

Then the truth comes out. Although Elizabeth is pregnant, she won't be getting married. Instead, she intends to have an abortion—an act that shocks her friend to the core. Their differing backgrounds are thrown into sharp relief as the two young women struggle to come to terms with a moral dilemma as well as a physical crisis. The sixties Irish Catholicism of Aisling is clearly drawn, but Elizabeth's character is just as comprehensible. The strain on their friendship is evident. Yet the ultimate solution of one problem only opens the door to another.

Elizabeth's worries with her mother are far from over. Aisling is also struggling, both with the complexities of a rowdy Irish family and with her desire to create a life of her own. When she marries Tony Murray, she is proud that she is still a virgin, but a little frightened, too. Her honeymoon leaves something to be desired: The groom falls asleep, drunk, on their wedding night. It is merely a portent of worse to come. This time it will be Aisling's turn to appeal to Elizabeth for understanding and support. Somehow the two are always there for one another when the rest of the world lets them down. Life and death, marital breakup and new hope; they share it all.

In Maeve Binchy's books, no great dramas on an operatic scale take place. She writes of ordinary people leading ordinary lives. But she makes her characters very real, and through them presents a remarkably observant view of the society in which they live.

Dublin-born Binchy began her writing career as a journalist, producing a chatty, humorous column for the *Irish Times*. Her column was the first thing many people turned to when they opened the newspaper. Next day we would be asking one another, "Did you read Maeve Binchy yesterday, when she was telling about the two women she overheard talking on the train? Wasn't she *brilliant*?"

Binchy has perfect pitch when it comes to reproducing dialogue. The gift made her columns memorable and stands her in good stead as a novelist. If you have read Maeve Binchy, you are prepared for an Irish conversation over a pot of tea and some buttered scones.

With *Light a Penny Candle*, Binchy graduated to the larger canvas of the novel and has since gone from strength to strength. I include this, her first novel, in *The Essential Library* because it offers a view of Irish life as seen from the outside, the way many Americans would see it.

Across the Bitter Sea

Hodder & Stoughton, London, 1973; Coronet, paperback, New York, 1995

A*cross the Bitter Sea* is set against the turbulent background of Ireland after the Great Famine. The plot is constructed around the classic triangle: Samuel Flaherty, a generous landlord who runs counter to the stereotype of his class; the rebel Morgan Connolly, whose life is consumed by the struggle for survival; and Alice MacDonagh, who loves one and marries the other.

Like such historical novelists as Walter Macken, Eilís Dillon chose to view Ireland through the somewhat narrowed focus of an Irish family saga. Although she concentrated more on personal relationships than on events, from her own experiences she was able to present a vivid picture of Ireland during the nineteenth and early twentieth centuries.

With sure skill, the author evokes time and place from the very beginning:

> On a warm June day in 1851, a week before her eldest son's wedding, Mary MacDonagh was out in the far potato field. She moved slowly along the edge by the wall, looking at the ground as if she were searching for the nest of a renegade hen. The hen was dead and gone; ten days ago she had found the carcass in a field, but she provided an alibi for those terrible compulsive trips to the potato field by asking the neighbors if they had seen the

brown one laying out. She was entitled to search the fields for her while she eyed the crop of potatoes. The flowers were fine and white. The leaves were glossy and thick. There was no sign of the withering, no brown spot, no smell of rot, that ghastly smell that all Ireland had breathed in with death.

From this opening, still fraught with the underlying tensions of the Great Famine, the novel sweeps forward into a huge panorama of suffering, frustration, and bitterness. The Ireland in which it takes place is no gentle green land, but a ravaged country occupied by ravaged people.

Dillon also allows the reader glimpses of life as it was lived by those whom the famine did not—could not—touch. Her scenes of glittering ascendancy balls ring true; when she tells the reader that "Six million acres of land were owned by three hundred people. Five million people owned nothing," we feel the residual bitterness that still haunts Ireland one hundred and fifty years later.

The names of major figures of the period appear throughout the book, men such as Daniel O'Connell, who won Catholic emancipation for Ireland, and Charles Stewart Parnell, who almost won Home Rule. Dillon's fictional characters remain firmly at center stage, however, demonstrating how the events of history affect the lives of ordinary people. *Across the Bitter Sea* is first and foremost a love story. Yet its inherent tragedy holds true right down to the final drama: the surrender of the Irish Volunteers at the end of the Easter Rising.

This richly detailed historical novel was written by a niece of Joseph Mary Plunkett, one of the signatories of the Proclamation—Ireland's Declaration of Independence. Plunkett was executed on May 4, 1916, with the other leaders of the rising. His legacy to his Galway-born niece Eilís Dillon was a lifelong interest in history. She also had a reverence for good writing and no patience with carelessness. A kindly, soft-spoken woman, Dillon made no secret of the fact that she was infuriated by the inaccuracies in certain best-selling "Irish" novels written by people with no real knowledge of the culture.

Although Dillon died several years ago, both her adult novels and numerous books for children remain very popular in Ireland. I had the privilege of knowing her personally, as she and I worked together for a time on the Irish Children's Book Trust. Sometimes I take one of her books down from the shelf just for the pleasure of hearing her voice again. Dillon's work is valuable for Americans not only for its historical accuracy but, more importantly, because it gives an honest picture of the Ireland which sent so many men and women to American shores.

Doyle, Roddy

Paddy Clarke Ha Ha Ha

Secker & Warburg, London, 1993; Penguin USA, 1995

Winner of the prestigious Booker Prize for Fiction in Britain, this book has been described as "an absurd comedy of the common-place." The hero is ten-year-old Patrick Clarke, who hates zoos, kissing, and his little brother; wants to be a missionary like Father Damien and coerces his friends into pretending to be lepers; never picks the scabs off his knees before they're ready. He wants to have fun. He wants to stop his parents arguing. And he's confused about life in general; the more he sees, the less he understands.

The year is 1968, the scene is Dublin. In Roddy Doyle's brilliant first novel, Paddy Clarke is every little boy who grew up in that place and era. The dialogue rings absolutely true. This is English as spoken by the working-class Dublin Irish. Roddy Doyle's great gift, as proved in subsequent highly successful novels such as *The Van*, or *The Woman Who Walked into Doors*, is perfect pitch when it comes to reproducing contemporary speech patterns.

Listen to Paddy describing a painful episode following a boyish mis-demeanor:

> She told my da and I got killed. He didn't give me a chance to deny it. It was just as well. I would have denied it and have got into even bigger trouble. He used his belt. He didn't wear a belt. He kept it just for this. The back of my legs. The outside of my

hand that was trying to cover my legs. The arm that he held onto was sore for days after. Round in a circle in the living room. Trying to get well in front of the sweep of the belt so it wouldn't hurt as much. I should have done it the other way, backed into the belt, given him less room to swing.

Doyle also has a gift for depicting the often-hidden complexities of family relationships. Paddy Clarke lives in a normal family, meaning one beset by tribulations. Some of them are hilarious and the little boy's responses to them add to the fun. There is a serious undercurrent, however; a real story being told here. The marriage is breaking up and Paddy Clarke is caught in the middle. The focus of the book is not the disintegration of a family but the survival of one small human spirit. Triumph and bewilderment, warmth, cruelty, love, and slaps across the face are part of this child's world, and the reader is swept along with him as he tries to make sense of it all.

Again, Paddy is speaking of his father:

> I looked at him for a long time, trying to see what was different. There was something. He'd just come home, late, just before my bedtime. His face was different, browner, shinier. He picked up his knife slowly and then looked as if he'd just discovered the fork on the other side of the plate, and he picked it up like he wasn't sure what it was. He was telling himself to do everything he did, I could see that, concentrating. His face was tight on one side and loose on the other.

Paddy tells us, "My da had more wrong with him than my ma. There was nothing wrong with my ma except sometimes she was too busy."

The marriage is at an end, and so is Paddy Clarke's childhood. The moment when we know he has grown up comes, appropriately, at the very end of the book, and is both triumphant and painfully poignant.

Of all Roddy Doyle's books, I have chosen *Paddy Clarke Ha Ha Ha* for this collection because any American boy will find something of himself here; if not his personal experiences, at least his reactions to them. The raw nerves of the youthful male psyche are fully exposed in Doyle's tender, funny, moving novel.

DU MAURIER, DAPHNE

Hungry Hill

Victor Gollancz, London, 1943

Daphne du Maurier is perhaps best known for her classic novel of romantic suspense, *Rebecca*. Most of her novels and short stories were built around actual places or events, and that unforgettable story of thwarted passion and vengeful murder was no exception. Du Maurier modeled Manderley in *Rebecca* on the beautiful Cornish country house of Menabilly. Menabilly was truly the house of her dreams; but although she lived there for years, du Maurier was never able to purchase the property.

Hungry Hill is based on the true story of the Puxley family, Cornish landowners who held copper mines in West Cork in the last century. The Puxleys were notorious for their treatment of the miners in their employ. They demolished what was left of the ancient stronghold of the last of the Gaelic princes, O'Sullivan Beare, to build a pretentious Gothic mansion they called Dunboy Castle, thus appropriating the name of O'Sullivan's home as well as its stones. According to local folklore, "Copper John" Puxley also shot the last breeding pair of golden eagles in Ireland to take home to his wife, simply because she complained she had never seen an eagle.

During the Irish Civil War, when the homes of many wealthy crown sympathizers were being destroyed, the Puxleys abandoned their mansion. The Irish promptly crossed the lake and put the palace of "Copper John" to the torch.

Du Maurier calls her mineowners the Brodricks, but bestows the name of Copper John on its grim patriarch. In true saga fashion, she follows the fortunes of various Brodricks and also of the native Irish whose livelihood depends upon them. *Hungry Hill* unfolds its dramatic tale of intertwined lives and destinies in the shadow of the mountain from which the real-life Copper John took his wealth. The book itself is a work of fiction, but like all great novels it is also about truth. Du Maurier was a fine novelist; even a figure as dark as her Copper John has more than one dimension. When his hound is poisoned, he sadly muses, "There had been beauty in that dog, and a soul too." His impoverished neighbors the Donovan family are suspected of the crime.

Copper John recalls old Morty Donovan "cursing him that night in the rain on Hungry Hill. Clonmere had been theirs before a Brodrick set foot on the place. And then, like so many other families, the land had been taken away from them after the rebellion and given to some peer or other, and so to the first Brodrick. It was natural that they show resentment, and natural enough that they detest the duty-loving, law-abiding John Brodrick, who stopped them smuggling and took away the only chance they had of making a bit of money on the sly."

Hungry Hill is a story of ceaseless motion: the roiling emotions within its principal characters and the restless, purposeless traveling that seems to occupy their lives. Nothing stays the same. Yet everything stays the same. The land and the people who occupy it are cursed: "The moon rose over the shoulder of Hungry Hill, he could feel the light of it, in his blindness, and he thought it was the lamp she had lit for him, and that she stood waiting for him by the open door. He turned to go to her, and the black shaft yawned at him as he went. . . ."

Although du Maurier's writing style is lucid and lyrical, this is not an easy book to read. It is too painful. When I visit the haunted landscape from which it sprang, I am unable to separate du Maurier's characters from reality in my own mind. American readers will find, in *Hungry Hill,* some of the darkness that is an inseparable part of Ireland's beautiful face.

EDGEWORTH, MARIA

Castle Rackrent

First published 1800; Oxford University Press, 1964; World's Classics, paperback, 1995

Castle Rackrent is at once Gothic melodrama and a scathing social satire on the evils of seventeenth-and eighteenth-century land-lordism in Ireland. The book's subtitle is *An Hibernian Tale, Taken from Facts, and from the Manners of the Irish Squires Before the Year 1782.* The narrator, Thady Quirk, presents the reader with four generations of Rackrent heirs: Sir Patrick, the dissipated spendthrift; Sir Murtagh, the litigious fiend; Sir Kit, the brutal husband; and Sir Condy, the lovable, improvident dupe of Thady's own son, Jason Quirk. These almost archetypal beings represent the entire class against which Ireland would one day rebel. Yet the author came from that class herself.

In her long life (1767–1849), Maria Edgeworth received only one proposal of marriage, from Chevalier Edelcrantz of the court of Sweden. She refused, unable to consider leaving her beloved father and the family seat at Edgeworthstown in County Longford. Maria's life was dominated by her father, Richard Lovell Edgeworth, to whom she was devoted. He in turn treated her as almost an equal and involved her in every aspect of daily life, including the running of the Edgeworthstown estate.

Her father also encouraged Maria to write, and her early stories for children are full of the theories and morals in which he had instructed her. She was an extraordinary woman, who acted as both mother and tutor to her twenty-eight brothers and sisters by her father's four wives.

She wrote surrounded by the bustle of this enormous household, which also included various aunts and cousins. Her writing is characterized by humor and her attention to detail and character. Sir Walter Scott cited her work as one of his own major influences.

Edgeworth labored unceasingly to highlight the problems of the peasantry and to implement her father's sometimes revolutionary ideas. In advanced years when Ireland was devastated by the Great Famine, she worked tirelessly on behalf of the poor—exertions that led directly to her death on May 22, 1849.

Castle Rackrent was a great social force in its time, proving the power of the novel to affect the real world. Edgeworth's book is as outdated now as Harriet Beecher Stowe's *Uncle Tom's Cabin*, but in the nineteenth century this novel had a similar power to influence and inflame its audience.

ELLIS, PETER BERESFORD

The Rising of the Moon

Methuen, London, 1987

This thoroughly researched historical novel is based on one of the strangest incidents in the joint histories of Ireland and America. In 1866, a band of the American-founded Irish Republican Brotherhood, known as the "Fenians," invaded Canada in an attempt to force war in one British colony in order to free another—Ireland. The Fenians hoped to establish an Irish republic-in-exile, and to use this as a base to command international recognition for their cause.

The American Civil War was not long over; among the Fenian ranks was a sizable contingent of Civil War veterans. Swelled by their numbers, the "army of invasion" encamped near Buffalo, New York, and prepared to cross the Niagara River. Once on the Canadian side of the border, their first objective was the capture of Fort Erie. Their sheer effrontery left the British flabbergasted.

The Rising of the Moon is a vast, sprawling war story, an adventure tale, a romantic novel. Some of the most colorful personalities of the era, such as Thomas Meagher, John O'Mahony, and Thomas D'Arcy McGee, figure prominently in the story, together with a host of fictional characters. The author has woven his massive novel around the numerous plots and counterplots, the politics, spying, treachery, foolhardy courage, and sheer glorious madness of the Fenian campaign.

Ellis opens the book in New York City, with two young men in Union uniform watching the parade of the Irish Brigade. The time is May 1865, a month after Abraham Lincoln's assassination. The two men are brothers Gavin and John-Joe Devlin. Of Gavin, the author writes, "Manhood had come too quickly and the harsh experience had left its scars in the deep etched lines which creased his eyes and mouth." The younger man, John-Joe, displays an innocence his brother lacks, one that will follow him throughout the book. He is still excited by the perceived romanticism of battle; but Gavin has a different opinion, based on all-too-painful memories:

> The earth was wet, an icy, clinging mud in which he had lain for what seemed an eternity. It was cold and soft like the bodies of the dead among which he had taken shelter. . . . It was quiet. Deathly quiet. The only sound was that of the stertorous breathing of the men who lay in the icy mud with him; who crouched among the barren waste of leafless trees; who, unseen, peopled the formless, desolate landscape. . . . Far off a bugle sounded. Then it began. The end of the world.

The Rising of the Moon follows the fortunes of the two men as they become involved with the Fenian movement. Afire with nostalgia, John-Joe makes his way to Ireland—an Ireland he has never seen. There he meets rebels such as the passionate, dedicated Dualta Hanrahan and begins to realize the vast differences in understanding between the Irish Americans and the native Irish. Ultimately he returns to America, where both he and Gavin play their parts in the Fenian invasion of Canada, the climax of an unforgettable story.

Ellis employs considerable political philosophy throughout the book, as in this telling exchange:

> A voice cried, "To free Ireland! That's the only principle, isn't it?" Roberts stood, hands on hips, nodding his head and smiling. "Indeed, my friends. But I must say something further. It has been the misfortune of our people that our conquerors have transmitted to the world nearly all that the world knows of our history and character."

The author is a prolific writer who has published both fiction and nonfiction of Irish interest, including such works as *The Boyne Water* and *The Druids*. *The Rising of the Moon* is perhaps his most ambitious work to date; but more than that, it provides a valuable piece of the complex jigsaw that is the Irish-American relationship.

FLANAGAN, THOMAS

The Year of the French

Holt, Rinehart, Winston, New York, 1979; Henry Holt, paperback, 1989

Thomas Flanagan's highly acclaimed novel has won many awards, including the National Book Award. It tells the heartbreaking story of the failed French invasion of Ireland upon which so many Irish pinned their hopes for freedom. Coming from an academic background, Flanagan immersed himself in various contemporary accounts of the 1798 rebellion in Mayo, and his painstaking historical and cultural research shows in every aspect of the book.

The action in Mayo was part of a larger undertaking that would become known as the Rising of '98, one fueled by the winds of revolution sweeping across Europe and America. Fired by the writings of Tom Paine, thrilled by the success of America's War of Independence, thousands of Irish people—Catholic and Protestant alike—united to fight off British domination. As always, they had too few weapons and too many forces assembled against them. Their one hope lay in outside help—a help the rebels hoped the sympathetic French would provide. France had a long history of war against England, and Ireland was acknowledged to be "the back door into England," an excellent staging post for any future campaigns.

The Mayo incident is hardly more than a footnote in Irish history, yet from this the author has woven a complex tapestry of people, places, and events. Perhaps the most colorful character among a vast array is the poet Owen MacCarthy, a "hedge schoolmaster" who instructs children both in the classics and the language of the Gael. The role of the itinerant schoolmaster, forced to teach in hiding because an education was forbidden to the native Irish by English law, sets the tone and helps to demonstrate the issues at stake.

Flanagan uses MacCarthy to open and close the book with a circularity a Gaelic poet would appreciate. A hard-drinking libertine, MacCarthy loves many things not wisely but too well. He says of himself, "I have never broken the law when sober." Under his influence, the style of the novel sometimes achieves a lyrical quality that is a joy to read.

The Year of the French is not about poetry, however. It is primarily a novel of large battles and small faction fights, of the impulses that drive men to try to kill one another. There are few women, and when they appear, it is the war that defines them. The men they love are soldiers, rebels, purveyors of a reckless dream their wives and sweethearts do not understand. But characters like Lord Cornwallis understand all too well, and Flanagan's sharply etched portraits of fighting men are compelling. The portrait of the young Protestant, Wolfe Tone, founder of the Society of United Irishmen, is particularly engaging. Tone has just spent three years in France, attempting to enlist French aid for the Irish cause. The author describes him as "bouncing from hope to despair to hope, drafting memorials, sitting long hours in the anterooms of ministers, flattering politicians and wishing that he had the money to bribe them." At last he is overjoyed to make an ally of a young French officer, Gen. Jean-Joseph Humbert.

It is Humbert who sails into Mayo's Kilcummin Bay in August 1798. His arrival and initial military success is greeted with rapture by some and fury by others. As Irish rebels rush to join with the French, the Reverend Broome, resolutely Anglican, Protestant, and British, states: "The plain fact of the present is that a wily and unscrupulous French general has seduced the people of this barony from their proper allegiance."

When Broome refers to the Irish rebels as "barbarians," he elicits a furious response from an Irishman called O'Donnell: "Barbarians, do you say? And what are the lobsterback soldiers with their gibbets at every crossroads? I wonder at you, the way you make every man with a pike a barbarian, and every man with a bloody English bayonet an angel of justice."

But success does not last. All too soon the French surrender, and with them the Irish hope of freedom is surrendered as well. In the aftermath, one of the female characters says bitterly of the French: "They have risen up like a wave, and like a wave they are falling back to the sea. The English have retaken all of Connaught from Athlone to Ballina. Castlebar lay empty before them, and they have filled its gaol with rebels. And there is your republic for you and your proclamation and your army of the Gael. It is your English that you should be practising at now, for it is English that will give out the rules and laws and regulations in Connaught."

The author has taken the risk of using multiple first person narrators. This device is at once the novel's strength and its greatest weakness. Presenting historical events from several points of view allows for panoramic scope. Flanagan does not always make clear just who is speaking, however. Also, his principal narrators are literate and predominantly upper-class, leaving the vast peasantry for whom freedom was being sought poorly represented. Even MacCarthy, a peasant by origin, is an educated man who scorns "poor cowherds with matted hair."

But these are small criticisms of a novel that attempts so much and succeeds so well. The story builds relentlessly from one shining victory to a series of devastating defeats, creating a growing despair which is the novel's central theme. The author has stated, "I'm American, not an Irishman . . . but *The Year of the French* is an Irish novel, not an American novel." It is also a great novel.

GODWIN, PARKE

The Last Rainbow

Avon Books, New York, 1995

This touching novel is an example of how well an American writer can capture the spirit of the ancient past in that part of the world known as the British Isles. Parke Godwin has written a number of novels built around such subjects as the Battle of Hastings, the Arthurian legends, and Robin Hood. But with *The Last Rainbow* he strayed into my territory, so I was anxious to see how he handled one of the icons of Ireland. I was not disappointed.

In presenting a fantasy version of the life of Patrick long before he became the patron saint of Erin, Godwin opens his story with Earth Mother and her husband Lugh Sun. Thus he draws on the pagan Celtic pantheon that the real-life Patrick would one day confront. The author also introduces their "children," the Prydn, a mysterious, quasi-Pictish race roughly akin to the legendary Tuatha de Danann. From the realist's point of view, they may be holdovers from the Neolithic era. But to Patrick—whom Godwin calls "Padrec"—they will be the embodiment of ancient magic.

A young priest burning with the fire of his Christian faith, Padrec of the Britons comes willingly to the pagan isles to spread the word that will save men's souls. He soon finds himself wandering a breathtaking realm filled with wonder and danger. In this twilight land of powerful sorceries Padrec meets Dorelei, the beautiful leader of the mystical folk.

Her culture is depicted with the consummate skill of a historian, drawing together the many threads that shaped early life in these islands:

> In old times a person was chosen as Barley King for the year and scythed with the harvest at the end of it. Prydn once sacrificed for the same reasons, for the prosperity of the herds. . . . Now it was all pretend, although the devotion and the serious meaning remained. . . . There was feasting and much making of child-wealth, as was fitting. As man sowed wealth in woman, hay and cabbage and other crops could now be sown in the ground. All their magic had to do with crops and staying in one place.

The book is written with a light hand, to be taken as a fairy tale, a prequel to reality, or even a cautionary tale about the fragility of magic. But it is also thought-provoking, a philosophical discourse upon the merits of relative belief structures. Toward the end of the novel, Dorelei addresses the Earth Mother whose image has grown dim under Padrec's influence, even as Dorelei's folk have made him question his Christian god: "I am not a girl anymore, Mother, but a woman with the marks of bearing on my belly, and a fool who can no longer hear your voice. Padrec and I are a braw pair, lost to his god and you alike. We have a word for faith and magic, no more. When the magic was with us the word was not needed."

The Last Rainbow is that most challenging of novels to write, a fantasy which is also a form of speculative history. St. Patrick is so interwoven with the culture of Ireland, and thus by extension with Irish America, that any fresh look at him is interesting. But Godwin's book is fascinating in its own right, a tale to lose oneself in.

GREELEY, ANDREW M.

Irish Gold; Irish Lace; Irish Whiskey

Forge Books, St. Martin's Press, New York, 1994–98

Andrew M. Greeley, best-selling Irish-American author, has written a number of novels that he describes as "parables for our time." With *Irish Gold*, the first in the above trilogy, he moves the setting of one of his books to Ireland.

The hero is another Irish American, Dermot Coyne: young, brash, and very wealthy. Coyne returns to his ancestral home to find out why his maternal grandparents left their village during the time of the Troubles in 1922. When three men attack Dermot, warning him to "let the dead sleep in peace," he becomes more determined than ever to solve the puzzle.

Nuala McGrail, a student at Trinity College, joins Dermot's search, bringing her own mysterious talents to the job. Together, they discover a secret cabal, American spies, £20 million in gold, and the love of their lives. Along the way they find a solution to one of Ireland's most enduring mysteries—who really killed Michael Collins?

Irish Gold was followed in 1996 by *Irish Lace*, reuniting Dermot and Nuala in the United States for a new adventure, and then by *Irish Whiskey*, published in 1998. All contain fast-paced action, an interweaving of philosophy that does not intrude on the plot, and a considerable dollop of romance. Their Irish-American viewpoint is as revealing in its own way as the British viewpoint, presenting another perception of this land and its people.

Rev. Andrew M. Greeley has had an extraordinary career. He is not only an ordained priest in the Roman Catholic Church but also a distinguished sociologist and journalist, as well as program director of the National Opinion Research Center at the University of Chicago. Greeley's energy is tremendous. He has published more than seventy nonfiction books on history, sociology, politics, theology, and education, and a volume of poetry entitled *Women I've Met*.

Greeley's very first novel, published in 1979, was *The Magic Cup*, which reflected his lifelong interest in Celtic lore by telling an Irish version of the quest for the Holy Grail. His subsequent, hugely popular novels include mainstream contemporary fiction, detective stories, and what may best be described as theological fantasies.

HOLLAND, JACK

The Prisoner's Wife

Dodd, Mead & Co., New York, 1981; Poolbeg Press, Dublin, paperback, 1995

J ack Holland was raised in a Belfast ghetto. A journalist by profession, for many years he wrote a weekly column for the *Irish Echo*. His nonfiction work, *Too Long a Sacrifice: Life and Death in Ireland Since 1969*, showed a depth of knowledge and understanding that impressed readers on both sides of the border in Ireland. With *The Prisoner's Wife*, Holland moved into the realm of fiction to present an intimate, painful look at reality.

Nora Costello is a creature of the tortured Belfast Catholic ghetto in which she has spent her life. Her husband Johnny, a member of the IRA, has been arrested for bank robbery and sentenced to spend the rest of his life in prison. Their contact is limited to weekly, closely watched visits in a tiny wooden cubicle, where they are separated at all times by a table. But just as restrictive is the moral code to which Nora must conform outside the prison. Prisoners' wives who are unfaithful to their husbands—seen as heroes in an age-old conflict—are subjected to merciless, humiliating treatment by their peers. Yet love does find Nora, and she must face up to its challenge.

In the person of Michael Boyd, a Belfast-born reporter who now works and lives in New York, Nora sees a chance for escape. America has long represented "the land of the free" for Irish people suffering from oppression. This use of America as icon gives *The Prisoner's Wife* particular interest for readers across the Atlantic.

Holland has drawn a vivid portrait of a passionate woman who challenges the puritanical assumptions of the world in which she lives as she tries to reconcile her futile love for her husband with the possibility of a new life. The drama inherent in the Northern Ireland situation has spawned a number of novels and movies of varying quality. As a trained observer who has lived at the heart of the scene, Holland is uniquely qualified to write on the subject. *The Prisoner's Wife* has the sharp edge of truth.

Americans who have never lived under similar circumstances find it hard to comprehend the intractable hatreds and the raw bigotry of Northern Ireland. Through the medium of Holland's novel, these emotions are laid painfully bare.

JOYCE, JAMES

A Portrait of the Artist as a Young Man

First published in London and New York, Random House, Modern Library, New York, 1996
First published in Serial Form in 'The Egoist;' published in New York in Dec. 1916, London, Jan. 1917.

The hero of Joyce's early semi-autobiographical novel is called Stephen Dedalus—reminding us that it is Stephen Dedalus whom Joyce later uses as his alter ego in *Ulysses.*

This is a less complex, more accessible book than *Ulysses,* but forms a good introduction to Joyce's other work. It begins at that most basic of human beginnings, a small boy first responding to his senses. Joyce writes, "When you wet the bed, first it is warm than it gets cold. His mother put on the oilsheet. That had the queer smell."

The child Stephen is at once innocent and precocious. The language the author employs in the early chapters is made up of simple sentences in keeping with his youth, yet it tells us that he observes keenly. On some deep level he is already aware of hidden significances in the events of childhood. From the beginning, Joyce weaves the complex pattern which will emerge as the character of an adult human being.

As we are told of his youth and schooling we are also told, almost peripherally, of the history of Ireland during that era. Names like Parnell and Michael Davitt are the currency of everyday speech. The background which develops behind the central figure is built up of a series of swift, impressionist flashes, so that its shadows serve as counterpoint to the brilliantly lit protagonist. Always, we are with Stephen and our sympathies are engaged on his behalf.

More than any of Joyce's other work, *Portrait of the Artist* concentrates on clerical influences. This was the principal control system in the life of any young man growing up in Ireland early in this century. Joyce views Catholicism simultaneously with a certain nostalgic glow and an almost tangible repugnance.

At first, young Stephen is enraptured with theology. It becomes part of the sensual landscape of his spirit. A priest tells him that "The devil, once a shining angel, a son of the morning, now a foul fiend came in the shape of a serpent, the subtlest of all the beasts of the field." In a subsequent interior monologue, Stephen at age sixteen finds himself tormented by his awakening sexuality and equating it with the foulness of the serpent. This inculcation of guilt will become a central theme in all Joyce's work, one that is common to the Irish Catholic experience.

The introduction of human love, in the form of a girl standing pensive in a stream, presents the second major thread of the story. "She seemed like one whom magic had changed into the likeness of a strange and beautiful seabird.... She was alone and still, gazing out to sea; and when she felt his presence and the worship of his eyes her eyes turned to him in quiet sufferance of his gaze, without shame or wantonness.... Heavenly God! cried Stephen's soul, in an outburst of profane joy."

Most of the action takes place in the mind rather than on the physical plane, but the result is the same: growth. By the end of the book— which is quite short compared to *Ulysses* or *Finnegan's Wake*—Stephen Dedalus has matured emotionally and intellectually. In a philosophical conversation with the medical student, Cranly, Stephen is surely speaking for James Joyce.

The subject has been religion. Cranly asks, "Do you fear that the God of the Roman catholics would strike you dead and damn you if you made a sacrilegious communion?" To which Stephen replies, "I fear more than that the chemical action which would be set up in my soul by a false homage to a symbol behind which are massed twenty centuries of authority and veneration."

After a subsequent conversation with his mother concerning the Blessed Virgin Mary, Stephen comments that he is handicapped by his sex and youth. To him, woman has come to represent something very different. His youthful need to worship is revealed as already torn into two halves, a problem that will follow him all his life . . . and shape every aspect of James Joyce, the writer.

In *Portrait of the Artist*, Joyce seeks to trace the causative factors by which he himself developed both as an artist and as a human being. He also presents us with an integral part of his larger body of work.

JOYCE, JAMES

Ulysses

First published in Paris, 1922; by Sylvia Beach, Shakespeare & Co. Random House, New York, 1934 according to p. 667 of Ellman biography; complete annotated edition, Lilliput Press, Dublin, 1997

Asked to name one Irish novel, more Americans would say *Ulysses* than any other. With its vivid characterizations and stream-of-consciousness writing, Joyce's masterpiece burst on the world literary scene like a skyrocket.

James Augustine Joyce was born in Dublin in 1882, and died in Zurich, Switzerland, in 1941. A description of his life may be found in the entry for James Ellman's excellent biography, *James Joyce* (p. 48). Writing was Joyce's passion, but Ireland was the wellspring of his art. Although circumstances eventually resulted in his leaving Ireland permanently, his birthplace never left him. He was later to claim that if Dublin were destroyed, the city could be rebuilt from his description in *Ulysses*.

While Joyce was working on what would become his most famous novel, he encountered a friend on the street one day and the friend asked if Joyce had been "seeking the right words." Joyce replied, "No, I have the words already. What I'm seeking is the perfect order of words in the sentences I have."

Ulysses is one long riotous tumble of words, of images layered upon images to produce a feast for the senses as well as the mind. The entire novel takes place within one day as Leopold Bloom strolls around Dublin, meeting friends and acquaintances, musing on life, death, sex, food, and the city. He pauses for a glass of wine at Davy Byrnes's public house:

> Mild fire of wine kindled his veins. I wanted that badly. Felt so off colour. His eyes unhungrily saw shelves of tins, sardines, gaudy lobsters' claws. All the odd things people pick up for food. Out of shells, periwinkles with a pin, off trees, snails out of the ground the French eat, out of the sea with bait on a hook. Silly fish learn nothing in a thousand years.

Everything is grist to Bloom's mill, from macabre speculations about death and cemeteries to lecherous imaginings about women. Layer upon seemingly random layer builds up a portrait of him both as a Jew and an outsider, and as an Everyman who is baffled by existence and buffeted by circumstance.

Meanwhile, Stephen Dedalus—who serves as James Joyce's alter ego—and "stately, plump Buck Mulligan"—who was modeled on Oliver St. John Gogarty—are setting out for themselves. Their lives intersect with that of Bloom throughout the day, and their conversations reveal yet more aspects of Dublin life.

Ulysses is not difficult to understand if, as the author intended, you allow the words to flow unedited through your mind just as you do your own fragmented thoughts. The climax of the book is unquestionably the last chapter: one long, unpunctuated soliloquoy by Molly Bloom. An earthy woman who loves to laugh, she surrenders to a torrent of racy memories and adulterous passions:

> . . . O Lord I must stretch myself I wished he was here or somebody to let myself go with and come again like that I feel all fire inside me or if I could dream it when he made me spend the 2nd time tickling me behind with his finger I was coming for about 5 minutes with my legs around him I had to hug him after O Lord I wanted to shout out all sorts of things. . . . I gave my eyes that look with my hair a bit loose from the tumbling and my tongue between my lips up to him the savage brute Thursday Friday one Saturday two Sunday three O Lord I cant wait till Monday. . . .

At the time the book was published, in February of 1922, no one had ever read anything like it.

Bawdy, ironic, and witty, *Ulysses* was banned in both America and England for some years and ultimately resulted in a redefinition of the obscenity laws. But it was never banned in Ireland. The Irish recognized themselves in Joyce's portrait of rakish, shabby-genteel Dublin, and they loved the word games he played with the language. In time the whole world came to appreciate the author's genius.

In the years since Joyce's death a veritable army of scholars have made his writing their life's work, guaranteeing that he is never out of print. Subsequent works such as *Finnegan's Wake* (1939) were critically acclaimed, but *Ulysses,* more than any other Irish novel, has assured Dublin's fame as a literary capital.

Llywelyn, Morgan

1916

Forge Books, St. Martin's Press, New York, 1998

When asked to compile this list, I had no intention of including one of my own books. But I could find no other novel in print that explored the American associations behind Ireland's 1916 rebellion against British rule; a rebellion that became famous as the Easter Rising.

For almost eight centuries a dream of restored freedom and self-determination had fueled the Irish struggle against English/British domination. *1916* reveals how the Irish Republic was little more than a noble ideal espoused by intellectuals until the Irish Volunteer Corps became its physical expression and the Easter Rising its bloody birth. In the same way the American Revolution was inspired by the writings of Tom Paine, leading in turn to the battlefields of 1776. The book also shows how the Volunteers came to be known as the Irish Republican Army, and the way in which the violent seeds of the IRA's subsequent evolution were sown by the actions of the British government itself.

Through the everyday lives of its characters, *1916* describes the social and political situation in Ireland in the early part of the twentieth century. The historical focus is upon three of the most extraordinary leaders of the Easter Rising, all poets—Pádraic Pearse, Thomas MacDonagh, and Joseph Plunkett. Access to these real people is through the eyes of a fictional protagonist, Ned Halloran. As the son of a relatively prosperous farmer in County Clare, Ned represents the Irish middle class that had begun to develop since the Famine; a group seldom examined in fiction.

Ned's sister Kathleen allows the reader to observe events in Ireland as seen from the American side. As the novel opens, she has already gone to America. There she has become engaged to marry an official with the White Star Line. Her parents, and Ned, set out for the wedding—aboard the *Titanic*. When Ned's parents go down with the ship and he himself barely survives, Kathleen urges him to make a new life in America. But he insists on going home.

There a kind patron sends him to St. Enda's, the boys' school outside Dublin. The headmaster is Pádraic Pearse. Ned's education in what was surely one of the most progressive schools ever founded, and his resultant membership in the Irish Volunteers—which would become the Irish Republican Army—form a fictional counterpoint to the real history.

Ned is befriended by a journalist, Henry Mooney, who gets him involved in the newspaper business just as Pádraic Pearse gets him involved in revolution. Ned also falls in love with a defiant prostitute named Síle who has taken control of her own destiny and is spying for the rebels. He rescues a tiny orphan girl—who insists she is called Precious—from the horror of the Bachelor's Walk Massacre when British soldiers fire on unarmed civilians at the conclusion of a Volunteers' march. Thus, step by step, Ned's personal life becomes inextricably involved with the larger struggle for Irish freedom.

Meanwhile, Kathleen in America is undergoing her own increasingly desperate search for independence. Married to the wrong man, she finds the right one—perhaps too late. Her sympathies are still with Ireland, and she avidly follows the gathering storm of revolution as told in letters from her brother. Against her husband's wishes, Kathleen also gets involved with Irish-American organizations devoted to the cause.

Generations of Irish emigrants had fled across the Atlantic; it was inevitable that eventually their eyes would turn homeward again. Early in this century, American-based sympathizers encouraged a resurgence of Irish nationalism. It was America, through the Irish Republican Brotherhood, which largely funded the Easter Rising. Many native Irish people had lost any hope of freedom; after so many failed rebellions, the country was sinking into apathy.

The novel accompanies Ned Halloran as he marches through Dub-

lin with the Irish Volunteers on Easter Monday. They are on their way
to seize the General Post Office and make it the headquarters of a new
Irish republic. Due to a confusion of orders that would be farcical if it
were not so tragic, the band of men who have come out on the chosen
day is lamentably small. They already know they have little chance of
winning. But it is too late to turn back. They have openly challenged
the British Empire; they must see it through to the end.

The column stepped out briskly, moving with certainty of purpose as they proceeded from Liberty Hall down Lower Abbey
Street. There were no British soldiers in evidence. A few civilians stopped to watch the march go by, but most were as indifferent as always. It did not matter. Nothing mattered but the
doing of it. In the middle of the column, Ned walked with his
shoulders back and his chin held high. *Marching in the company
of men, with the golden sunshine pouring over them like a blessing.*
After the Great Famine the political theoretician James Fintan
Lalor had written, "Somewhere and somehow, and by someone,
a beginning must be made, and the first act of armed resistance
is always premature, imprudent, and foolish." *Sometimes you
have to make things come right or die trying!*

The week that was to follow would shake Ireland to the core. Like
so many rebellions before it, the Rising at first seemed a failure. But in
its failure lay the seeds of triumph. Twenty-six counties of Ireland today
comprise the free, sovereign Republic of Ireland, as a result of the sacrifices made in 1916.

With the outbreak of IRA violence in Northern Ireland some thirty
years ago, it became unfashionable to acknowledge the gallantry of the
original Irish Republican Army. The characters of the executed leaders
of the Easter Rising were distorted and maligned by revisionist historians. *1916* is an effort to recover that neglected heritage and commemorate those heroes. It also is the first broad-spectrum account of the
Easter Rising told both from the Irish and the Irish-American points
of view.

McCann, Colum

This Side of Brightness

Metropolitan Books, New York, 1998

Dublin-born Colum McCann is an outstanding example of the new generation of Irish writers who are making a mark for themselves internationally. In Europe McCann's collection of short stories, *Fishing The Sloe Black River,* was nominated for the highly prestigious Aristeion Prize, and won both the Rooney Award for Irish Literature and the Hennessey Award for Best First Fiction.

This Side Of Brightness is an astonishing leap of the imagination that spans decades and distances and digs below the surface of the earth, as well as into the depths of the human soul. It has been described as the first authentic novel about homelessness in this era.

The novel opens in 1991, introducing a character memorably named Treefrog who is attempting to help a half-frozen crane break free from the ice in the Hudson River. His good deed done—although the bird's ultimate fate is surely death—Treefrog makes his way back to his home in one of the warren of subway tunnels beneath Manhattan. There his pitiful, sometimes laughable strategies for survival bring to life the details of a bleak existence lived beneath the surface of the world's richest city.

The reader is then transported back to 1916 and life among the sandhogs, the nickname given to the men who dug those tunnels. Nathan Walker has come up from the swamplands of his native Georgia to undertake one of the most dangerous jobs in America. The subterranean world he has entered is filled with extremes. Its bitter cold is a shocking contrast to the muggy heat of the American South; the sudden, brutal accidents that can snuff out life are a strange counterpoint to the almost brutal grace of the sandhogs themselves.

As they labor belowground the men form a brotherhood; black, white, Italian, and Irish working together. Once they return to the surface, however, an ethnic isolation separates them. In effect they occupy two worlds, as this remarkable book takes place in two worlds.

When a blowout sends three of the sandhogs erupting through the surface of the East River—"blown upward like gods"—Nathan Walker survives. A second blowout kills an Irish sandhog, Con O'Leary, leaving him sealed in a tunnel "like a fossil." These images are typical of the author's simultaneously spare and rich style, which burns itself into the reader's consciousness.

The accident results in a bond forming among the sandhogs that will continue to affect three generations, down to the era of Treefrog himself. The novel proceeds by moving back and forth between one view of New York and the other, between a past rich in hope and energy and a present devoid of either. Seventy years of doomed loves, accidental crimes, and scarring social taboos weave together into a complex tapestry that is both unique and unforgettable.

A book so totally American in topic deserves a place in this collection for one special reason: *This Side of Brightness* demonstrates how brilliantly the best Irish writers can utilize sensitivity and mastery of language to depict other cultures.

MACKEN, WALTER

Seek the Fair Land Trilogy, *comprising* Seek the Fair Land; The Silent People; *and* The Scorching Wind

Macmillan, London and New York, 1959; Pan Books, paperback, 1988; Brandon Books, Cork, Ireland, 1994

Although it consists of three separate volumes, I am listing this trilogy as one book. The three novels together create a historical panorama that will both entertain and inform Irish Americans. *Seek the Fair Land* is set in the Cromwellian period in the 1650s; *The Silent People* tells of the years of O'Connell and the Great Famine, 1826–47; and *The Scorching Wind* concerns the Easter Rising, the War of Independence, and the Irish Civil War, 1915–22.

These novels deal with three distinct periods and thus do not tell a single, unified story, but they are linked thematically. This is a shared world; even the same names are used by the leading characters. Each novel presents a reluctant rebel on the run, and each offers a powerful evocation of history on a personal level.

A strongly pacifist theme runs through all of Walter Macken's work. He refuses to glorify violence. His heroes tend to be schoolteachers, or at least educated men. But his villains are true villains; there is no more demonic image than that of Oliver Cromwell's follower Sir Charles Coote in *Seek the Fair Land*.

Characterization is Macken's strength. Whether fleshing out actual figures from history or bringing his own creations to life, he provides a wealth of the small detail that goes to make up a complete picture. The following passage from *Seek the Fair Land* provides one example. It takes place in 1649 in the doomed city of Drogheda, at the height of Cromwell's assault. While fleeing for his life, the hero, Dominick MacMahon, has just stumbled over the body of a woman:

> He knew before he got to his knees beside her. O God no, he said, but his prayer was in vain because Eibhlin was lying there on the street, her face to the sky, her black curly hair loosed and lying in the dust. Her breast and stomach had been pierced again and again with the blade of a heavy sword. Her eyes were open. He felt her face. It was warm, only cooling. If I had only been here earlier, just a little earlier. Just a little bit. He could see her face in the light of the fires and the ascending moon. Maybe it wasn't she at all. But it was. Her nose turned up a bit at the tip. Calm she seemed, almost a smile on her face, the small teeth showing. They hadn't done anything else to her, only killed her. But what did they do to my children?

Leaving this tragic scene behind him, Dominick spends the rest of the novel in search of someplace where there is peace and safety. This is Ireland in a bloody era, however, and for an Irishman there is no peace or safety. But as a skilled dramatist, Macken interjects moments of joy and humor into his books so they are not unrelievedly grim: "Peter and Mary Ann had come laughing across the hills. Peter was riding the horse and Mary Ann was holding on tightly to him. You get hiccups when you laugh on the back of a trotting horse. . . ."

The plot of *The Silent People* revolves around Dualta Duane, a young Irishman in the first half of the nineteenth century. The landlords have ground down his people, who are tenant farmers; injustice is rife and starvation stalks the land. Dualta is incapable of giving in. He battles tyranny while struggling to survive hunger, poverty, and disease, always believing there must be something better. He finds love with a young schoolteacher, Una MacMahon, but taking a wife makes his struggle against the oppressors much more difficult. When their children are born, it seems as if emigration offers the only hope. At the book's end, Dualta buys four tickets for passage on a ship to America. But he is an Irishman to the core, as the climax of the novel movingly attests.

The hero of *The Scorching Wind* is once again an Irishman named Dominic, who has a brother called Dualta. Galway-born, they are as different as night and day. One is fair, one is dark; one is sensible, one is wild. This final novel in Macken's trilogy, set in the early 1920s, tells the story of the bitter split in the ranks of Sinn Féin caused by the Anglo-Irish Treaty of 1921. With the outbreak of civil war in Ireland it seems inevitable that the brothers will wind up on opposite sides.

Born in Galway in the momentous year of 1916, Macken was the son of a carpenter who was killed in France in World War I. Walter Macken began acting in the Galway Gaelic Theatre at the age of seventeen; he worked his way up to producer and stage manager before marrying and going to London, where he found more remunerative employment as an insurance salesman. Yet his heart was always in Ireland.

He returned in the 1940s, to act and to write. His first published work was a play in the Irish language. This was followed by plays and then novels in English, interspersed with a theatrical career that included performing on the London stage, with the Abbey Theatre in Dublin, and on Broadway. He also took a leading part in the film (1962) of Brendan Behan's *The Quare Fellow*. But Macken's greatest and most lasting success came with his historical trilogy.

Macken's style is, at times, almost American, leaving no doubt that he wrote his books for an international audience. Adults and children alike have learned much of what they know of Irish history from Walter Macken and he is still widely read.

MacLaverty, Bernard

Grace Notes

Jonathan Cape, London, 1997; W. W. Norton & Co., New York, 1997

Bernard MacLaverty is one of the most exciting of the new Irish writers. His collection of short stories, *Walking the Dog*, received high praise. *Grace Notes* confirms the author as a major literary talent; the book was shortlisted for the prestigious Booker Prize in England.

The pain of loss and the agony of creation are the themes of this beautifully written novel. Whether coming to terms with death or facing up to the responsibilities of giving birth, his heroine is totally believable. A man writing from the woman's viewpoint is not always successful, as far too often the writer assumes that the two sexes feel the same about everything and have similar responses. MacLaverty knows better.

Catherine McKenna is a gifted composer and music teacher, but her talents and her freedom come at a price. Her music takes her from her home in Derry, Ireland, to Scotland. In making this step, this expression of independence, Catherine alienates her father. He forbids her to come home again once she leaves. Ireland is embedded in her soul, but so is music—and she must choose.

She does not return home until her father's funeral. There the pain of the past is revisited in the sorrow of the present. Catherine has secretly borne a child; a child which, like her musical compositions, she could not share with her family. This hidden human creation merely reinforces the divisions between herself and them. Catherine's life is composed of unbridgeable gulfs, for she is also emotionally separated from the father of her child. No one understands her, yet Catherine's spirit is incapable of surrender. Throughout her story she continues to compose her music, sometimes clinging to it as to a life raft, at other times soaring as if on wings. In the most banal of situations she searches for rhythms to bend to her purpose, while simultaneously struggling to find her personal voice.

Grace Notes is a sensitive, measured novel, which gives a revealing picture of one aspect of life in modern Ireland. The emotional situations are handled with an admirable restraint that gives them even more poignancy. An acute sense of place and a hunger for belonging will strike responsive chords in many American readers. This could be a real life being lived in Ireland today, and I am happy to recommend the author as one to watch for the future.

MacMahon, Bryan

The Honey Spike

Dufour Editions, Chester Springs, Pennsylvania, 1967; Poolbeg Press, Dublin, paperback, 1994

Americans visiting Ireland are always curious about the tinkers. These are the native gypsies, whose brightly painted, horse-drawn wooden caravans were once such a feature of the local landscape. Entire families of itinerants traveled the roads of Ireland year in and year out, never staying in one place for long, making their living by mending tin pots and pans for thrifty housewives—hence, "tinkers."

Now the colorful caravans have been replaced by aluminum housetrailers, which run the gamut from rusting wrecks to well-equipped luxury homes sporting the latest in television aerials and satellite dishes. No one needs household tinware mended any more; today's housewives simply go to the nearest shop and buy new. The itinerants have had to find other ways to support themselves.

The term "gypsy" may evoke a romantic image, but the reality is far different. In modern Ireland, the tinkers are known as "travelers," and are on the receiving end of racial discrimination. Yet they are as Irish as anyone; perhaps more so. They claim to be directly descended from the native, Gaelic Irish who were displaced by Cromwell's "plantation" of English and Scottish colonists three hundred years ago. While this is debatable, nevertheless they maintain a tightly knit community that rarely if ever marries beyond its own members. Travelers are readily identified by their distinctive accent and determinedly nomadic lifestyle.

It is their lifestyle which has earned them the vilification they suffer.

Charges of theft and violence against travelers are common. Though they no longer use horses to pull their caravans, many of them still keep and trade horses, which they feed for free by staking them out on the side of public highways. Some men send their women and children out to beg on city streets; others make their living selling scrap and used household goods of dubious provenance. The rubbish the travelers accumulate and the filth they leave behind when they move on scandalize the "settled" community.

In *The Honey Spike*, one of Ireland's most accomplished writers gives us a vivid picture of the life of the travelers: despised, illiterate, living by their wits. The work is also performed as a play, offering rich roles for the actors.

Martin Claffey has fulfilled his ambition to travel the length of Ireland. Now, just days before she is to give birth, his wife Breda insists on returning to County Kerry so her child will be born in the Honey Spike—known to her family as a lucky place. With considerable grumbling, Martin reluctantly agrees. His worst fears are soon confirmed. On their journey southward they encounter an IRA raid, a countryside hostile with suspicion, and the Puck Fair where a male goat is crowned as the only true king of Ireland.

MacMahon gets under the skin of his characters. The reader feels nose-to-nose with them, crowded together in the chaotic intimacy of their home on wheels. The author reveals the private longings of a woman whose pregnancy makes her question her way of life; the strutting machismo of a man whose manhood is defined by his "freedom." They are shown in constant, often unspoken conflict with a society that rejects them; a rejection in which they take a perverse pride. The people depicted in *The Honey Spike* are simultaneously pathetic and infuriating—and worthy of understanding.

Bryan MacMahon, who died in February 1998, was also a poet, playwright, and critically acclaimed short story writer. His last book was an autobiography entitled *The Master*, a reference to his long career as a schoolteacher.

MARCUS, DAVID

A Land Not Theirs

Transworld Publishers, New York, 1986; Poolbeg Press, Dublin, paperback, 1993

C ork in 1920—rebel Cork, fighting Cork, suffering Cork. The Irish War for Independence is exploding and the Black and Tans are running amok. No one can be neutral in this ultimate struggle for Irish freedom—not even the men and women of the tiny Jewish community in Cork City. Are they to fight for a land not theirs? Or should they go to rebuild their promised land in the Palestine territory so reluctantly ceded to them by the British? What is their future to be?

David Marcus uses a broad canvas. His epic novel presents a totally different perspective of the Irish fight to become a nation. By writing from the Jewish viewpoint, Marcus gives us yet another aspect of the Irish experience. Those who are unaware of the existence of minority religions in Ireland will find this book an eye-opener. It corrects the customary image of Ireland as a tight little island inhabited only by the Gael. A number of different peoples have contributed to create the Ireland of today; their story is important.

The plot of *A Land Not Theirs* revolves around the family of Joshua Cohen. Marcus has a gift for creating unforgettable female characters, and both Bertha Cohen and her daughter Judith are compelling figures. The names of Marcus's principal characters are biblical: Joshua, Jacob, Judith. While remaining true to the Irish context, the author perfectly captures the warmth and closeness of the Jewish community:

There was nobody in the assembled congregation at the Shabbos-morning service who didn't already know the date Rabbi Moishe would be leaving for Palestine, yet when he faced them and announced that his group would be parting on 12 December people turned to each other with raised eyebrows, confirmatory nods, grunts of satisfaction. . . . Abie Klugman, sitting in his usual seat at the back of the synagogue, felt only bliss and gratitude. His eyes were closed tight to keep in his tears, and his two arms were wrapped across his chest to contain the surge of ecstasy that pushed like a tide through his body.

As the conflict between the IRA and the Black and Tans escalates, the Jewish enclave known as the Celtic Crescent is torn apart. Choices have to be made. To the Cohen patriarch, the traditions of centuries are sacrosanct, to be protected above all else. He is a Jew, blood and bone. For his son Jacob, however—equally Jewish—Ireland exerts a powerful force. Musing on Cork City's origins, in his mind's eye Jacob sees not only the hallowed stones and primitive cells of the monastery at Gilabbey Rock but also "time's transformation of the first settlements into the elegant storied city that he loved. He had been born here, he had grown up here, it was a part of him, almost physically, certainly spiritually."

The effort to establish one's personal identity within the larger framework of a land at war forms the core of this intensely passionate and fast-paced novel. In writing of his people, the author also manages to write of all people everywhere. *A Land Not Theirs* is an excellent example of the way in which a historical novel can make the past accessible and illuminate the present. David Marcus is one of Ireland's outstanding men of letters and this is arguably his finest work.

O'BRIEN, EDNA

The Country Girls Trilogy and Epilogue

Hutchinson, London, 1960; New American Library, New York, 1990

This is the daring (for its time) fiction that shocked and scandalized Ireland, and made its author an expatriate. While still in her twenties, red-haired, green-eyed Edna O'Brien from County Clare launched her career in 1960 as a novelist by publishing *The Country Girls*. Written during what the author recalls as "Twelve weeks of London fog," the book tells the story of two young women: quiet, brooding Caithleen, and her happy-go-lucky friend, Baba. From their rural childhood and convent education, the story follows the pair to Dublin in search of life and love. They want to know what men are; they want to know what sex is. They want to be wanton.

> "Tell us everything," Cynthia said to us. Cynthia was gay and secretive and full of spirit. "Have you boy friends?"
>
> "Have *you*?" Baba asked.
>
> "Oh yeh. He's terrific. He's nineteen and he works in a garage. He has his own motor-bicycle. We go to dances and everything."
>
> "Are you fast?" Baba asked bluntly.
>
> "What's fast?" I [Caithleen] interrupted.
>
> "It's a woman who has a baby quicker than another woman."
>
> "Is it, Cynthia?"
>
> "In a way." Cynthia smiled. Her smile was for the motor-

bicycle, riding with a red kerchief round her hair, over a country road with fuchsia hedges on either side; her arms clasped round his waist. Her ear-rings dangling like fuchsia flowers.

Skittish and cunning and full of hope, O'Brien's young women are vividly drawn. Walk down any Dublin street and you might meet them still. They carry with them a lingering hint of the Irish countryside from which they sprang, a blurred melancholy they are determined to escape. During the sixties, "nice" Irish girls were not supposed to act or speak or even think as O'Brien's heroines do. Her novels brought a breath of much-needed realism to the stifling prudery of de Valera's Ireland.

O'Brien was just beginning what would prove to be a distinguished career as a novelist. *The Country Girls* is the first part of a trilogy that includes *The Girl with Green Eyes* and *Girls in Their Married Bliss*, all three reprinted here as one volume. O'Brien would go on to write a number of other works. But the simplicity and art of her first novel, with its seemingly casual sentences and fresh, immediate style, has never been bettered.

O'BRIEN, KATE

The Ante-Room

William Heinemann, London, 1934; Virago Classics, paperback, 1991

Kate O'Brien was the consummate geographer of Irish society; the iconoclast who blasted its most hallowed traditions. Her analytical voice cut through "nice" pretensions. She was described as both a sexual and a creative dissident in a country and at a period of the utmost conservatism—the early part of this century.

Born in Limerick in 1897, Kate O'Brien produced a body of work that included award-winning novels as well as plays, journalistic articles, biography, and travel writing. She lived for years in Spain, which she loved, but her Irish roots remained deep and she was elected to the Irish Academy of Letters in 1947.

O'Brien's novel *The Ante-Room*, written during the 1930s, tells of the decline of the great merchant fortunes of Ireland. The culture depicted is a long way from the "pig in the parlor." This is middle-class Ireland, where women had their clothes made by Dublin dressmakers and surrounded themselves with all the luxury they could afford in an effort to forget the poverty of their grandparents.

The time is 1880; the principal characters are members of a prosperous provincial family. As Teresa Mulqueen lies dying, her relatives gather around her; but beneath this drama another, no less poignant, unfolds. Unmarried daughter Agnes awaits the return of her sister and brother-in-law. She loves her sister, but she passionately adores the sister's husband. Their marriage, she knows, is unhappy. Ahead lies a terrible battle between her rigid and uncompromising Catholicism and the intensity of her love.

Agnes struggles with the agonies of the confessional:

> For her final fear was of words. When she was a schoolgirl once or twice she had to accuse herself of vague curiosities and stirrings of her sensual imagination—matters which she had not understood, but which she knew to wear the look of sins against the sixth commandment. . . . Must she say that since she had last seen him her defenses had grown less and less against definite adulterous longings? Must she tell of nights when sleep would not come because of his mad haunting, or of other nights when she would hold sleep off, the longer to delight in him?

Agnes's dilemma may seem ridiculously old-fashioned to modern Americans, but it was an intrinsic part of Irish life right up to the midpoint of the present century. To understand anything of Ireland, one must come to grips with its repressions.

Kate O'Brien knew well the world she depicts in *The Ante-Room*. Her grandfather was one of those who had been evicted in the aftermath of the famine, but he did not give up. He drove an asscart to Limerick and managed to establish himself in trade there. In time the family prospered, but their security was undermined by the unlaid ghosts of their ancestors, walking again in hunger and anger. Out of this cauldron Kate O'Brien has created some of Ireland's most memorable writing.

O'CONNOR, EDWIN

The Last Hurrah

Random House, New York, 1956; Little, Brown, Boston, 1985

A winner of the Pulitzer Prize, *The Last Hurrah* tells of the passing of an era personified by Frank Skeffington, Irish-American mayor of a big, powerful city on the eastern American seaboard. Skeffington's last campaign, and his death after losing the election, are observed by his nephew, Adam Caulfield. Skeffington has treated Caulfield almost like a son because his own son has been something of a disappointment.

Skeffington is a charming demagogue: witty, calculating, seedy, and grand at the same time. Throughout his long career he has remained a man of the people. "Every once in a while," he remarks, "I see where some advanced young public servant, who still has the ring of the pot on his seat, publicly applauds the passing of 'that cruel and barbarous custom, the wake.' Whenever I see that I take down my little book and chalk up a new name in the boob section. The man who said it obviously hasn't the remotest understanding of the times, the circumstances, of our people, the way they feel and the way they regard death."

Edwin O'Connor does have that understanding, however. His genetic heritage informs and illumines his writing, giving an essentially American story a very Irish flavor. Invoking an image out of *Gulliver's Travels*—another famous novel with an Irish connection (see p. 250)—Skeffington at one point says he is fighting to keep his city from "reverting to government by pygmies." But expert politician though he is, ultimately he loses to a more modern campaigner. His victorious opponent is the puppet of a cabal that includes a newspaper publisher who is infuriated by Skeffington's nonchalant extravagance; the Cardinal, enraged by Skeffington's exploitation of the church; the WASPs who control most of the city's wealth and resent his Catholic background; disgruntled rival politicians who resent his success; and the reformers of a younger generation. There is something poignant in Skeffington's final battle against such formidable forces, and the baffled gallantry with which he faces defeat.

O'Connor describes the twists and turns of political machination with consummate skill. His underlying irony is always subtle, never intrusive. The characters are so thoroughly developed that each of them seems a personal acquaintance. The book was called a *roman à clef* at the time, something the author never denied. Its portrait of an old-fashioned Irish Catholic ward heeler still rings with a recognizable truth. This was a substantial part of the Irish-American experience as immigrants rose to power through the political ranks. Skeffington is a wily old fox, yet very human, and his ultimate downfall is extremely moving. It is not surprising that a fine motion picture was made of *The Last Hurrah* (1958), with Spencer Tracy as Skeffington.

Jawaharlal Nehru, the first prime minister of India, cited *The Last Hurrah* as his favorite novel in the English language, a book he read again and again.

O'FLAHERTY, LIAM

The Black Soul

First published in London, 1924; Wolfhound Press, Dublin, 1981

Liam O'Flaherty is a master storyteller, called "the finest writer of his generation" by no less an authority than John Banville. Masterpieces such as *Famine* and *Insurrection* are found on many Irish bookshelves, for good reason. Both are definitive novels of turbulent times which many other writers have addressed as well.

The Black Soul was chosen for this list because it is unique. Intense, compelling, eerily atmospheric—as *Wuthering Heights* is to the Yorkshire moors, so *The Black Soul* is to the Aran Islands. O'Flaherty manages to capture a romantic atmosphere as feverish as that of Emily Brontë or Thomas Hardy, rendering some modern "romance" novels pallid by comparison.

The Black Soul is the story of Little Mary and her husband Red John, whose entire lives have been circumscribed by the narrow mores of island life. Little Mary is said to be the illegitimate daughter of a nobleman. Red John is a coarse-fibered peasant who salvages shipwrecks. He secretly worships his wife for her beauty while hating her for the vast gulf that separates them. To add to the problem, Red John is unable to get his wife pregnant. Trapped together in a cottage exposed to the wildest elements of the Atlantic, their marriage has become a battleground where silent, cruel wars are fought between an inarticulate man and an increasingly unhappy woman.

Into this overwrought atmosphere comes a Stranger, a man with

great black eyes that pierce Mary's like a wolfhound's. When he becomes
a boarder in their house, she is fascinated by him. He is educated, elegant, everything her husband is not. "And what a mouth he had! O God
of the thousand battles, it was the kind of mouth she had kissed in her
dreams, kissed until her lips were bruised." Tragedy is implicit in their
coming together, yet no power on earth is strong enough to keep Little
Mary and the man called Fergus O'Connor apart.

The tragedy is not theirs alone, however, but also that of Red John.
With consummate skill, the author gradually reveals him as a victim of
circumstance just as much as the lovers are. "And all the while his passion for Little Mary, fanned by the lustful spirit of spring, maddened
him. But her glance terrified him. He saw that she was lost to him.
Drear phanthoms pursued one another through his savage unreasoning
mind that brought his breath from his lungs in gasps. So he worked
furiously without purpose to keep himself from going mad."

The Black Soul is written on one unbroken note of tightly sustained
tension. Every paragraph propels the protagonists toward something
huge and inevitable, while holding the reader captive with the power of
language. The novel is simultaneously pure Irish and universal, an emotional experience as elemental as the sea.

O'GRADY, STANDISH

The Bog of Stars

T. Fisher Unwin, London, 1926

M ona-Reulta; or, *The Bog of Stars* is actually the opening story in a collection of Standish O'Grady's short fiction entitled *The Bog of Stars and Other Stories and Sketches of Elizabethan Ireland*. This allegory, elegant in its simplicity, contains some of the most poignant writing in the English language. Within some twenty pages the author captures the entire tragedy of the Elizabethan wars in Ireland, when the Irish were bribed and coerced into turning against each other. He begins with a discourse on the nature of bogs, that most despised feature of the Irish landscape. Yet within them O'Grady finds a peculiar sort of glory—that of the reflected heavens. He tells us that *Mona-Reulta* translates as the Bog of Stars.

The story begins in the dusk of a January evening sometime in the late sixteenth century. The subject of the tale is a young drummer boy who is in the employ of the British queen's armies. Their mission is to seek out and destroy one of the rebellious Irish chieftains, a notorious robber known to his enemies as the Raven. But embedded in the drummer boy's memory is an image of himself as a child, an orphan from a once proud line, being given hospitality by that same Irish chieftain. In his innocence he had thought the Raven and his men to be quite splendid, supernatural heroes of olden time. He recalls too an Irish lass who gave him a gift, and told him that one day he would do a great deed.

The Queen's men pass the Bog of Stars. The gayest, brightest moments of the boy's lost childhood flash before his eyes like the twinkling lights on the surface of the dark water. The attacking force stealthily approaches the town where the Raven sleeps unawares. Suddenly, the rattle of drums sounds a warning. Within minutes the Irish chieftain and his people have escaped, and the English find nothing but an evacuated town.

The traitor is hauled up before them for a court-martial. "Why, being man to the Queen, didst thou play traitor?" the Lord Deputy demands of the drummer boy. But the lad offers no defense except to say that he saw a star shining on the bog pool.

Furious, the Lord Deputy orders him executed. That evening, tied hand and foot, the drummer boy is taken to the pool and a stone is fastened to his ankles. O'Grady tells us, "He was perfectly still and composed; there was even an expression of quiet pride in his countenance. He was to die a dog's death, but he had been true to his star."

The Irish poet George Russell, known as "A E.," wrote in the introduction to O'Grady's trilogy, *The Coming of Cuculain*, that "His sentences are charged with a heroic energy, and when he is telling a great tale, their rise and fall are like the flashing and falling of the bright sword of some great champion in battle."

Standish O'Grady was a member of the landed gentry and a grandnephew of one of Lord Nelson's captains, Admiral Hayes O'Grady. His uncle had served with distinction at Waterloo and his father was both a landlord and rector of Bearhaven, in County Cork. A handsome man, with his dark hair and brilliantly fair complexion O'Grady looked more Gaelic than Anglo-Irish. His roguish eye and musical Cork accent were a magnet for the ladies. But most of all he had a romantic heart. It was this heart that led him to supplement his barrister's income by writing fiction. Over the years he turned out a number of works based on both Irish history and mythology. *The Flight of the Eagle*, the story of the sixteenth-century Irish prince Red Hugh O'Donnell, inspired a movie by Walt Disney.

O'Grady's work also served as inspiration for a whole generation of writers. No less a talent than W. B. Yeats paid him tribute by saying, "Whatever is Irish in me he kindled to life . . . to him every Irish imaginative writer owes a portion of his soul."

Finding books by O'Grady is not difficult, even today. They were printed in their thousands; some became classics. American stores that specialize in Irish material and/or used books often will have one or more. I urge you to seek them out. To read them is to acquire a deeper understanding of the romance of Gaelic Ireland.

PLUNKETT, JAMES

Strumpet City

Delacorte Press, New York, 1969

This novel grew out of the author's personal involvement with the labor movement and the Workers' Union of Ireland. He joined the union at the age of eighteen and eventually became a union secretary, working under "Big Jim" Larkin.

Strumpet City was inspired by the Great Strike of 1913, when Larkin was at the zenith of a career that would make him famous throughout the international trade union movement as one of its most charismatic figures. Although James Plunkett was born shortly after the Great Strike, of which his own father was a victim, from earliest childhood the author had heard accounts of the strike and the devastating lockout that followed. They were events that played a crucial role in creating the Easter Rising of 1916.

Jim Larkin himself became Plunkett's best source, informing his writing on labor movement topics with the incisive clarity of a good documentary. Before writing *Strumpet City* as a novel, Plunkett developed the material through several permutations. First was a highly successful radio play, *Big Jim*; this was later expanded and adapted for the stage as *The Risen People*. As the process evolved, Plunkett gradually changed the focus of the story from Jim Larkin to a celebration of the innate dignity—and the emerging revolutionary spirit—of the Dublin working class. *Strumpet City* dramatically contrasts the extremes of Irish society of the time while introducing some vivid characters—such as the complex priest Father O'Connor and the proud tramp Rashers Tierney—that linger long in the mind. The novel is vigorous, exciting, and emotive, while its political subtext gives it an intellectual weight many historical novels lack.

Take Plunkett's description of the crowd at a protest march in Dublin: "They jammed the street in front of the station, a jumble of torches and banners, a tightly packed array that had generated a soul and mind of its own, capable of response only to simple impulses, able to move itself, to emit a cry, to swing right or left, to stop altogether. They had come out en masse from the hovels and tenements, disrupting traffic, driving the respectable off the sidewalks. Their sudden arrogance was astonishing."

In 1955, Plunkett visited the Soviet Union as part of a delegation of writers and artists. This was the peak era of anticommunism in Ireland, inspired in part by the wave of rabid McCarthyism in the United States. As a result, James Plunkett's pro-labor writings were soundly condemned by such conservative publications as the *Catholic Standard*. A demand was made for Plunkett to be dismissed from his position of trust with the union, but the union refused to bow to the pressure. When Plunkett eventually did resign his union office, it was at his own instigation and for a much better reason: he was offered the position of drama assistant with the national radio, Radio Éireann. Since then Plunkett has continued to be a major creative force and has several other novels to his credit, including the brilliant *Farewell Companions* with its mythic overtones.

A gifted storyteller, he immerses himself in the atmosphere of his work and writes from the heart. If I were stranded on the proverbial desert island and told I could take just one Irish historical novel, I think it would be *Strumpet City*.

STOKER, BRAM

Dracula

First published in London, 1897; Penguin USA, paperback, 1993

D *racula* is a story with which every schoolchild is familiar. The
bloodthirsty Transylvanian count who journeys—coffin and all—
to England to prey upon beautiful young women has provided chills and
thrills to generations of horror story aficionados. Long-dead Count Dracula sustains himself by drinking the blood of the living and feeding off
their life force. Jonathan Harker's desperate struggle to rescue the
woman he loves from this monstrous vampire is a classic example of the
struggle between good and evil, and the mingled images of eroticism
and immortality exert a peculiar fascination.

For purposes of inclusion in this collection, however, the focus is
on the author rather than the book. Even people who never read have
heard of *Dracula*, but few are aware of the profound influence Ireland
and its folklore had on the author.

Abraham Stoker was born in Dublin in 1847. From earliest childhood he was entertained by the tales his Irish mother told him. A gifted
storyteller herself, she stimulated the young boy's mind with stories of
the banshee, or female Irish fairy, whose wild wail presaged imminent
death. She also vividly recounted the cholera epidemic that had killed
thousands when she was a child. That description is virtually the first
draft for a story Stoker subsequently wrote as part of a collection of
bizarre fairy tales. And there can be little doubt that the stories he heard
of the horrors of the Great Famine, together with tales of the vampiric

Boban Sith and Dearg Dubh of Irish legend, provided the inspiration that would one day produce *Dracula*.

Today, Stoker's reputation rests upon that one work. Yet throughout his life he was a prolific and dedicated writer who took his craft seriously. He was producing both short stories and essays by the time he was seventeen. He subsequently penned *The Personal Reminiscences of Henry Irving*, a prominent actor of the time, and the two became lifelong friends.

Stoker also admired Walt Whitman, and during his youth he wrote the American poet a number of fervid letters. They were to meet years later, when Stoker was touring America with Henry Irving. Of that meeting, Whitman remarked, "Best of all was meeting Bram Stoker, the Irish boy who wrote so uninhibitedly."

Uninhibited Stoker certainly was. He swept young Florence Balcomb off her feet with a passionate courtship, ignoring the fact that she had been the sweetheart of another Irish writer and fantasist—Oscar Wilde. This was before Wilde's own marriage, or his subsequent admission to being a homosexual.

In 1878, Abraham Stoker and Florence Balcomb were married. That same year, Henry Irving leased the Lyceum Theatre in Dublin and gave Stoker a job as acting manager. This position helped support Stoker, his wife, and their only son, Noel, for twenty-seven years.

During all this time Stoker continued to write, creating a sizable body of work. With the exception of a series of children's stories, all of his novels are morality plays that entail the winning and threatened loss of a woman's love. Several were critically acclaimed at the time. But following the success of *Dracula* he began to focus increasingly on the supernatural. Thus Bram Stoker returned to the roots his Irish mother had planted in his childhood.

SWIFT, JONATHAN

Gulliver's Travels

First published in London, 1726; Longman Classics, paperback, 1988;
Barnes & Nobel, Rockleigh, New Jersey, 1997

Today, Swift's masterpiece has been expurgated and condensed until it is perceived as a children's book; but it was written for adults as a devastating political satire. His thinly veiled portraits of societal mores and the politics of the time were sharply drawn, readily identifiable to his readers. When the book first appeared in 1726, it was read from the council cabinet to the country cottage and took the English-speaking world by storm.

Ostensibly the story of a dedicated voyager who repeatedly finds himself among alien cultures, *Gulliver's Travels* holds up a dark mirror to human nature. The tiny people of Lilliput with their shrunken view of the world are no less absurd than the all-powerful giants of Brobdingnag, to whom Gulliver is no more than an exotic toy. The gentle, horselike Houyhnhnms represent the innocence of the animal kingdom as compared to the barbarities of mankind.

Like *Dracula* and *The Picture of Dorian Gray*, two other immortal fantasies, *Gulliver's Travels* is included in this list because it was written by an Irishman and influenced by Irish experience. Swift is best remembered as dean of St. Patrick's Cathedral, Dublin, and for his rather curious relationships with two women.

Jonathan Swift was born in Dublin in 1667 and educated at Trinity College, Dublin. In 1689 he received an appointment as secretary to the statesman Sir William Temple at Moor Park, Surrey, in England. Having taken holy orders, in 1694 Swift became prebend of Kilroot in County Antrim, Ireland. But he soon tired of the isolation he found there. Returning to Moor Park, he served for a time as tutor to the young and beautiful Hester Johnson who was the daughter of a companion of Temple's sister.

Swift did not publish his first two books, *A Tale of a Tub* and *The Battle of the Books*, until 1704. By this time he was vicar of Laracor in County Meath, and for this reason both works were published together anonymously. While his career as a churchman grew, he led a second life with his pen. In 1701–10, Swift divided his time between Dublin and London, where he represented the archbishop of Dublin and also gained a considerable reputation as a wit and raconteur. Giving his support to the Tory Party, he lambasted the Whigs in print.

On the advice of Swift, Hester Johnson settled in Dublin. Swift's political and social activities during this period are described in *Journal to Stella* (publisher posthumously, 1766–68), a collection of letters that he wrote to Hester, whom he affectionately called "Stella." Some believe they were married, but there is no conclusive proof.

Swift had hoped for a bishopric, so he was disappointed to be named dean of St. Patrick's Cathedral, Dublin, in 1713. He resented being banished from the intellectual stimulation of London. A young woman named Esther Vanhomrigh—he called her "Vanessa"—had fallen in love with him and followed him to Ireland. When she took a house near the cathedral, her presence eventually became an embarrassment to Swift and caused a strain in his relationship with Stella. Vanessa died of consumption in 1723; Stella five years later. Her skull is entombed with his.

After the publication of *Gulliver's Travels*, Dean Swift became famous. The book was inspired by the disillusion of his maturity and uses fiction to condemn, among other things, the ill-treatment of the Irish. Satire, the preeminent form of Irish humor, was always his weapon. In the ironic tract entitled *A Modest Proposal* (1729), Swift once suggested that poor families should ease their burden by selling their excess children as food for the wealthy.

Swift who died in 1745, possessed a towering intellect and was one of the greatest writers of his day. His prose was unmatched for strength and clarity and is still a delight to read, assuring him of literary immortality. Modern admirers, many Americans among them, continue to make their way to St. Patrick's Cathedral to pay homage at his tomb.

The Picture of Dorian Gray

Rockleigh, First published in Lippincott's Monthly Magazine, London, 1890; The Modern Library, New York, 1992

D ublin-born Oscar Wilde's biography is discussed at length elsewhere in this book. While he is almost as famous for the scandal that destroyed him as for his writing, his creative work has an enduring life of its own. *The Picture of Dorian Gray* was his only novel, but Wilde is also remembered for his heartbreaking short story, *The Happy Prince;* for *The Canterville Ghost*, twice made into a feature-length film; for a number of ultra-sophisticated plays, including *Lady Windermere's Fan* (1892), *An Ideal Husband* (1895), and *The Importance of Being Earnest* (1895); and for the intensely moving autobiographical poem, *The Ballad of Reading Gaol* (1898).

Wilde's 1882 lecture tour in America was a tour de force marked by witty epigrams that are still widely quoted. Americans appreciate his humor, which is neither provincial nor dated. Every time a Customs inspector at an airport asks me if I have anything to declare, I recall Wilde's classic retort, "I have nothing to declare except my genius." And I smile.

But *The Picture of Dorian Gray* is not funny. Like Stoker's *Dracula*, Wilde's novel is a tale of the supernatural—and also a morality play, the form that was preeminent at the time. In this novel, Wilde created a unique image that has come to be almost a catchword. If you ask someone who seems ageless, "Do you have a picture in the attic?" you are referring to the magical portrait which enabled Dorian Gray to retain his youthful freshness through decades of dissipation.

Originally modest and gentle, the eponymous protagonist of the novel has been blessed with an extraordinary beauty of which he is quite unaware. Wilde describes him as "wonderfully handsome, with his finely-curved scarlet lips, his frank blue eyes, his crisp gold hair. There was something in his face that made one trust him at once. All the candour of youth was there, as well as all youth's passionate purity. One felt that he kept himself unspotted from the world." The novel reveals the dichotomy of Wilde's nature by both worshipping and warning against the dangers of physical beauty. The physical beauty of Lord Alfred Douglas would one day lead to the author's own downfall, eerily foreshadowed in this novel.

Early in the story, Lord Henry Wotton tells Dorian Gray, "Youth is the one thing worth having."

"I don't feel that, Lord Henry."

"No, you don't feel it now. Some day, when you are old and wrinkled and ugly, when thought has seared your forehead with its lines, and passion branded your lips with its hideous fires . . . you will feel it terribly."

The warning bears strange fruit. Gazing on his just-completed portrait by the artist Basil Hallward, Dorian has a sense of his own beauty for the first time. He also imagines the face ravaged by age and experience, and feels "as if a hand of ice had been laid upon his heart."

In an agony of regret for the future, Dorian cries, "How sad it is! I shall grow old, and horrible, and dreadful. But this picture will remain always young. It will never be older than this particular day in June . . . If only it were the other way! If it were I who was to be always young, and the picture that was to grow old! . . . I would give my soul for that!"

Which, of course, is just what happens.

Wilde's masterly skill controls the novel from the "Artist's Preface," a brief collection of aphorisms designed to counter hostile criticism, to the inevitable, tragic dénouement. We do not like Dorian; we are not meant to. Wilde is too clever a writer for that. Through Dorian's character, he intends to show us aspects of human nature that are hard to face even in ourselves.

The Picture of Dorian Gray might have been written specifically for today's America with its passion for physical perfection. As a cautionary tale the story is unsurpassed, and also supremely entertaining. Wilde's sophisticated style is that of an Oxford man, but his Irish love of the fantastic is evident on every page.

POETRY

CLARKE, AUSTIN (EDITED BY HUGH MAXTON)

Selected Poems

Lilliput Press, Dublin, 1992

M any critics consider Austin Clarke second only to Yeats among
the Irish poets. Born in Dublin in 1896, he died in 1974, his life
thus encompassing the end of colonial Ireland and the birth of an independent Irish state. Perhaps this is why Clarke dedicated himself in
his writing to an excavation of personal, historical, political, and spiritual
repression. He began by producing some of the most anguished and
beautifully fashioned lyrics in the English language. He evolved to a
sardonic voice distinguished by its questioning of authority and its sexual
frankness.

Writing as a man who has been changed into a woman in the poem
Tiresias, he says:

Lightly I fingered the nipples
And as they cherried, I felt below the burning answer.

Clarke's poetry combines the classical Irish poetic elements: love of
nature, love of country, sensuality, bitterness. He takes risks and justifies
them by finding new pathways of expression. His poems expressing religious doubts lead into poems about women, and they in turn to questions of nationalism. Thus he ultimately questions the roles of Nation
and Woman as Saviour and Sinner, roles that have been ascribed to
them in other lands as well as Ireland.

Clarke became a lecturer at University College, Dublin, but in 1921 he went to London to write reviews for *The Times, The Observer,* and *The Times Literary Supplement.* He returned to Ireland in 1937, determined not to become an exile, and entered wholeheartedly into the arts community of his native land. He formed the Dublin Verse Speaking Society, which produced verse plays at the Abbey and the Peacock, and broadcast a weekly program of poetry on Radio Éireann. In all, he published more than thirty works of poetry, drama, fiction, and autobiography, as well as a number of critical essays.

Clarke is an intellectual's poet, but he can be read with the heart. His work introduces an American audience to the philosophical Irish mind.

COADY, MICHAEL

Oven Lane

Gallery Press, Dublin, 1987

Michael Coady, of Carrick-on-Suir, County Tipperary, is a critically acclaimed poet who won the prestigious Patrick Kavanagh Award in 1979. *Oven Lane* is something very special, with unique meaning for Irish Americans. The work grew out of an obsession for finding out what happened to his grandfather's father. James Coady had abruptly abandoned his family and gone to America in the last century. There he seemed to vanish off the face of the earth. Then, many years later, a mysterious letter arrived from Philadelphia . . .

In 1982, Michael Coady made a pilgrimage to America to try to discover this missing piece of his heritage. The poems that resulted from his odyssey are preoccupied with the mystery of human destiny through choice and chance. Using the magic of language, Coady shows us Ireland and America as if superimposed upon one another. In phrases sculpted within the intimacy of the heart, he creates vignettes that allow us to observe the world from which the emigrant fled and to glimpse the one he found.

One of the most moving poems is ostensibly a letter written to James Coady, the "lost father of my grandfather." The poet shifts from voice to voice, sometimes reflecting that of the middle-aged Irish schoolteacher who is Michael Coady today, at other times speaking for that long-lost immigrant in an attempt to understand and forgive. It is a long work, singularly moving. I once heard the poet read it aloud at a Writers'

Symposium in County Tipperary, and the image he invoked was so powerful that his ancestor became part of my own past.

Oven Lane is a reverse image of the voyage of discovery many Americans take to Ireland, looking for their roots. As someone with Irish roots who was born in America and has since come home, I believe Coady's work will touch a chord within many Irish Americans. This is one book that will be difficult to find in the United States and may have to be ordered from a bookshop in Ireland; it is worth the effort.

FAOLAIN, TURLOUGH

Blood on the Harp: Irish Rebel History in Ballad

Whitson Publishing Co., Troy, New York, 1983

Music and lyric together tell a story, and nowhere as vividly as in Irish ballads. Students of Irish history are sometimes advised by natives to jettison the dry prose of scholarship and listen instead to the music of the people. But Turlough Faolain's obvious respect for both the scholar and the poet makes it clear that the study of Irish history need not be an "either-or" undertaking. He demonstrates that it is a great deal more fun to learn from the historian and the bard at the same time.

Blood on the Harp traces the compelling story of the Irish resistance to domination from its roots in the pre-Christian past up to the time modern Irish nationalism found its republican identity. The chapter headings set out the chronology: "The Coming of the Stranger," "Assimilation of the Sassenach," "The Twilight of the Gael," "The Desmond Wars," "The Nine Years War," "Plantation," "The Great Rebellion," "The War of the Two Kings," "Ascendancy and Wild Geese," "Peasants and Patriots," "The United Irishmen," "The Eve of Rebellion," "Explosion in Leinster," "The Boys of Wexford," "Ulster Also Rises," "Reprisal," "The Year of the French," and "Bold Robert Emmet."

Throughout the book over one hundred thirty rebel ballads are interspersed with historical narrative. Each song is given an introduction that tells the story behind it and establishes its place in Ireland's struggle for freedom. Verses puzzling to readers not familiar with the nationalist tradition are clearly explained—a great help for many Irish Americans. *Blood on the Harp* even includes such helpful items as a day-by-day calendar of the Rising of '98.

Although highly informative, Faolain's painstaking research never gets in the way of enjoyment. These are ballads that were meant to be sung lustily by real people. Many of them are still sung in just that way. The haunting "Boulavogue," perhaps the most vocally demanding of all, was a great favorite of the late John Fitzgerald Kennedy.

> At Boulavogue, as the sun was setting
> O'er soft May meadows of Shelmalier,
> A rebel hand set the heather blazing
> And brought the neighbors from far and near.
> Then Father Murphy from old Kilcormuck
> Spurred up the rocks with a warning cry:
> "Arm, arm!" he cried, "For I come to lead you,
> For Ireland's freedom we fight or die!
>
> He led us on against the coming soldiers,
> The cowardly yeomen we put to fight
> 'Twas at The Harrow that the Boys of Wexford
> Showed Bookey's regiment how men could fight.
> Look out for hirelings, King George of England,
> Search every kingdom that breeds a slave,
> For Father Murphy of the County Wexford
> Sweeps o'er the land like a mighty wave.
>
> At Vinegar Hill o'er the pleasant Slaney,
> Our heroes vainly stood back-to-back;
> And the yeos at Tullow took Father Murphy
> And burned his body upon the rack.
> God grant you glory, brave Father Murphy,
> And open heaven to all your men;
> For the cause that called you may call tomorrow
> In another fight for the Green again.

The Spirit Level

Faber & Faber, Boston, 1996; Noonday Press, paperback, 1997

The Spirit Level is Séamus Heaney's first book of poems since he was awarded the Nobel Prize for Literature in 1995. As with all Heaney's poetry, the collection chronicles the evolution of the poet against the background of his Irishness as well as universal experience.

Heaney was born in County Derry in Northern Ireland, a fact that gives his work a special flavor and poignancy. His first book of poems, *Death of a Naturalist*, published in 1966, established him almost immediately as a writer with something new to say. But Heaney has never settled for the easy option of writing about the Troubles; instead, his work is involved with all humankind. He had been praised both for his alert response to new political realities and for his ongoing concern with family history and spiritual well-being.

Sometimes the language sings and soars, the compelling work of a mature poet at the height of his powers. Elsewhere it brims with the youthful exuberance of a little boy playing with his siblings as he tells us,

> We entered history and ignorance
> Under the wireless shelf.

When Séamus Heaney was a boy, everyone in Ireland called the radio "the wireless"; many still do. It is that quality for observing the commonplace and commenting upon it with startling freshness which has won Heaney his enviable place in the international world of letters.

Poetry is to be savored like sips of wine, and this man's special gift is that each sip is different. One of my favorite Heaney poems, "A Dog Was Crying Tonight in Wicklow Also," is a powerful mystical experience that somehow bridges the distance between anthropomorphic pantheism and Christian theology. But every poem he writes goes straight to the heart of someone.

Séamus Heaney provides a reason to rejoice in being Irish, from whichever side of the border.

HOAGLAND, KATHLEEN, EDITOR

1,000 Years of Irish Poetry

Devin-Adair, Connecticut, 1957

I rish poetry is central to the Irish experience. As diverse as the people themselves, it runs the gamut from the pure, evocative prose of the ancient bards to the overblown sentimentality of the nineteenth century and the gritty realism of the twentieth. Each in turn speaks for Ireland. None gives the total picture. For that you really need an anthology.

Personally, I like poetry anthologies. They give me a chance to sample the work of poets I may not know and to rediscover others I may have forgotten. This book is a highly readable sampling of the sweep of Irish poetry across the centuries. Chronologically arranged, it begins with the greatest of all bards, Amergin of the Milesians. His three surviving poems date from as early as 500 B.C. Hoagland opens the collection with the best known and most frequently quoted of Amergin's compositions, as translated by Douglas Hyde:

I am the wind which breathes upon the sea,
I am the wave of the ocean,
I am the murmur of the billows,
I am the ox of the seven combats,
I am the vulture upon the rocks,
I am a beam of the sun,
I am the fairest of plants,
I am a wild boar in valour,

I am a salmon in the water,
I am a lake in the plain,
I am a word of science,
I am the point of a lance of battle,
I am the God who created in the head the fire.
Who is it who throws light into the meeting on the mountain?
Who announces the ages of the moon?
Who teaches the place where couches the sun?—

                                       If not I.

Of this ancient poem with its mystery and power, Robert Graves wrote in *The White Goddess*, "English poetic education should, really, begin not with the *Canterbury Tales*, not with the *Odyssey*, not even with *Genesis*, but with the *Song of Amergin*."

Monastic poetry from the early Christian era focuses on a love of nature that predates Christianity. One of the most beloved is "Pangur Bán," about a white cat of the eighth or ninth century and the scribe with whom he lived.

I and Pangur Bán, my cat
'Tis a like task we are at;
Hunting mice is his delight,
Hunting words I sit all night.

'Tis a merry thing to see
At our tasks how glad are we,
When at home we sit and find
Entertainment to our mind.

'Gainst the wall he sets his eye
Full and fierce and sharp and sly;
'Gainst the wall of knowledge I
All my little wisdom try.

So in peace our tasks we ply,
Pangur Bán, my cat, and I;
In our arts we find our bliss,
I have mine and he has his.

By the twelfth century, mythological and heroic poetry is making its influence felt. "The Story of Macha," and "Kincora," MacLiag's lament for Brian Bóru, are two outstanding examples. Powerful epics tell the tale of great warrior kings; vivid verses bewail their passing. A thread of surviving antiquity runs like a ribbon through historic time, as in "The Song of Finn."

The sixteenth century marks the beginning of what is characterized as "Modern Irish Poetry." Stirring patriotic poems and tender odes of love are joined by verses such as "On the Prospect of Planting Arts and Learning in America." Many names familiar to American readers will be found here: Oliver Goldsmith, Thomas Moore, and William Butler Yeats keep company with Patrick Pearse, Francis Ledwidge, and Austin Clarke. Some of the poets whose work is included have gained international fame; others are little known outside their native land.

At the end of the book are Notes on the Poets, the Translators and the Great Books. Thumbnail biographies of the poets include much material that is hard to find elsewhere. There is also an index of poets, an index of poems, and an index of first lines. *1,000 Years of Irish Poetry* is a wonderful way to acquaint yourself with the bardic soul of Ireland.

KENNELLY, BRENDÁN, TRANSLATOR AND EDITOR

Love of Ireland: Poems from the Irish

Mercier Press, Cork and Dublin, 1989; Irish-American Book Co., New York, 1990

A compilation that captures the freshness, spontaneity, candor, and emotional intensity of poetry written in the Irish language. Brendán Kennelly has translated a number of well-known and beloved poems such as "A Cry for Art O'Leary" from the original Irish, making them accessible to a whole new audience. One might ask, "When so many translations of Irish poetry already exist in print, why bother with another?" The answer is simple. Language changes drastically over the years; the English translation of a poem dating from fifty years ago is now less true to its Gaelic original. Kennelly set himself the task of bringing forward the flavor and cadences of the language from its original era; he has succeeded admirably.

"The Old Woman of Beare," for example, is part of Ireland's folkloric heritage. Like Caithleen ni Houlihan or Roisín Dubh, she is one of the female symbols of Ireland—an Ireland that began in radiant beauty and has suffered terribly. Most modern translations lose the stark pain that Kennelly restores here:

The sea crawls from the shore, leaving there
The despicable weed, a corpse's hair . . .

The poet tells of a woman who once was beautiful but has become a tormented hag. She bemoans her lost youth, the kings who have kissed her lips, the wine that has sung through her veins. Like so much ancient Irish poetry, the words speak to things in modern souls as well. The language becomes not a barrier but an enlargement.

A deep understanding of both Irish and poetry allows Kennelly to bring us startlingly fresh readings of dozens of short lyrics. The voice he uses, though modern in diction, is true to the creation of each poet. This book will enable the Irish-American reader who does not speak Gaelic to appreciate the power and the nuances of that language.

Brendán Kennelly was born in Ballylongford, Company Kerry, in 1936. He was educated at St. Ita's College, Tarbert; Trinity College, Dublin; and Leeds University. Kennelly's published works include *My Dark Fathers, Dream of a Black Fox, Cromwell*, and *Moloney Up and At It*. He also introduced and edited *The Penguin Book of Irish Verse*, and is Professor of Modern Literature at Trinity College, Dublin.

MONTAGUE, JOHN

Collected Poems of John Montague

Gallery Press, Loughcrew, Ireland, 1995

Perhaps my favorite poem in all the Irish pantheon is the one entitled "Like Dolmens Round My Childhood, the Old People . . ." John Montague proceeds to tell in verse the stories of a variety of elderly local characters: a kindly man who fed the birds and was robbed as he lay dead; a gossip who was the "fanged chronicler of a whole countryside" but derided others out of loneliness; a fierce woman living in a crumbling gatehouse, dreaming of gypsy love rites. The poem concludes:

> . . . once, in a standing circle of stones
> I felt their shadows pass into that dark permanence of ancient
> forms.

John Montague writes of enduring themes clothed in unforgettable images. We consider him an outstanding Irish poet, yet actually Montague was born in Brooklyn, New York, in 1929. He grew up on a farm in County Tyrone, however, and eventually moved to County Cork. He has taught in France, Canada, and the United States, and has been poet-in-residence at the New York State Writers' Institute and recipient of the American Ireland Fund Literary Award. Yet Montague remains as he was, a voice for the Irish people and for all people.

MERRIMAN, BRIAN (TRANSLATED BY COSSLETT
O CUINN)

The Midnight Court

Written in 1780; Dolmen Press, Dublin, 1973; Poolbeg Press, Dublin, 1989

Brian Merriman, reputedly the illegitimate son of a "country gentleman," was actually born to the wife of an itinerant stonemason
in Ennistymon, County Clare, in 1749. Soon afterward the family
moved to Feakle in the east of the county. Brian Merriman's education
may have been no more than that of a "hedge school," but he picked up
other scraps of education from wandering scholars and poets and eventually became a schoolteacher himself. He also had a small farm near
Feakle that he cultivated for many years, winning two prizes from the
Dublin Society in 1797 for his crop of flax.

East Clare abounds in legends. One of the most striking is the story
of the great *bean sidhe* (banshee), or fairy woman, named Aoibheall, who
lives atop Crag Liath overlooking Lough Derg. Perhaps the banshee
whispered into Merriman's ear as he tilled his fields. Something remarkable must have inspired a simple schoolteacher to write an epic
satire of 1,206 lines, *Cúirt an Mheán Oíche* or *The Midnight Court*.

It was to be the masterwork of his life. Only two other poems,
neither of them of any importance, have been credited to him. A bawdy
saga of gargantuan comic eloquence and energy, *The Midnight Court*
was composed in 1780 and has since been described as the first statement
in Ireland of women's liberation.

The plot is ready-made for humor. Within the precincts of a magical
court, the behavior of men is judged by Aoibheall's kin, the fairy folk.

The plight of young women who lack husbands; clerical celibacy; free
love; the misery of a young woman married to an old man; and the right
of all women to healthy sex and pleasure in marriage are the subjects
under discussion. The poem was long considered shocking and subver-
sive by the Roman Catholic Church, whose priestly celibacy it derides.
But for many, *The Midnight Court* came as a breath of fresh air, an Irish
Canterbury Tales.

It is also remarkably clever. Americans who think of eighteenth-
century Ireland country folk as thick-witted should read this:

> Nice girls in such a situation
> Find remedies for much frustration
> In realms of imagination
> If overwhelmed by temptation
> Thoughts grow too vividly conjunctive
> They're only pluperfect subjunctive,
> While happy married people live
> With them in the indicative.

In tribute to Brian Merriman, a society devoted to the history and
literature of ancient Thomond—now County Clare—was founded by
Con Howard in 1967 and named Cumann Merriman. The society has
since undertaken a number of important cultural projects (see *America
and Ireland, 1776–1976*, edited by David Noel Doyle and Owen Dudley
Edwards, at p. 147). Once more the American connection surfaces.
Some years ago Con Howard served as Irish consul in Boston, and then
as cultural attaché to the Irish ambassador in Washington, D.C.

RYAN, DESMOND, EDITOR

The 1916 Poets: Pearse, Plunkett, MacDonagh

Gill & Macmillan, Dublin, 1995

Poems by three leaders of the Easter Rising who were subsequently executed by the British. At once moving, passionate, innocent, and deeply devout, these are works of love and faith. They speak more clearly than any history book could of the quality of the men who led Ireland's most desperate bid for independence.

Patrick Henry Pearse was born in Dublin in 1879. His father, James, was a sculptor specializing in religious themes. Pearse trained for the law, but instead of practicing he founded and became headmaster of St. Enda's College. St. Enda's was devoted to the principle of teaching Irish boys their heritage. Pearse joined the Irish Republican Brotherhood in 1913, subsequently becoming one of the founders of the Irish Volunteers. He acted as commander in chief of the republican forces during the Easter Rising of 1916, and was executed by the British on May 3 of that year.

Thomas MacDonagh was born in 1878 in County Tipperary. His mother was an Englishwoman who converted to Catholicism; his father was a schoolteacher. MacDonagh followed in his father's footsteps by becoming a university professor, teaching at Trinity College, among other places. By 1915, MacDonagh was also a member of the General Council of the Irish Volunteers, as well as director of training for the country and commandant of the Second Battalion of the Dublin Brigade. He commanded the garrison at Jacobs' Biscuit Factory during the Easter Rising, and was executed on May 3.

Joseph Mary Plunkett was born in Dublin in 1887, one of seven children. His father, George Noble Plunkett, was a papal count and director of the Museum of Science and Art. Joe Plunkett was educated at Belvedere College and then at Stoneyhurst, in England. Pale, delicate, with weak eyes, a poet and a mystic, he was co-founder of the Irish Theatre. Joe Plunkett was slowly dying of glandular tuberculosis of the throat when he joined Pearse and MacDonagh in the Easter Rising and fought in the General Post Office. He was executed on May 4—hours after marrying his sweetheart, Grace Gifford, in Kilmainham Jail.

What united these three men was their love of Ireland—and their devotion to poetry. Each has left words of enduring beauty. Thomas MacDonagh wrote:

A half of pathos is the past we know,
A half the future into which we go;
Or present joy broken with old regret,
Or sorrow saved from hell by one hope yet.

Joseph Plunkett is perhaps best remembered for:

I see His blood upon the rose
And in the stars the glory of His eyes
. . . His cross is every tree.

The last word should go to Pádraic Pearse, who wrote poetry in his cell in Kilmainham Jail the night before his execution. "The Wayfarer" has the power to break your heart:

The beauty of the world hath made me sad,
This beauty that will pass;
Sometimes my heart hath shaken with great joy
To see a leaping squirrel in a tree;
Or little rabbits in a field at evening,
Lit by a slanting sun . . .

YEATS, WILLIAM BUTLER (EDITED BY RICHARD J. FINNERAN)

Collected Poems of W. B. Yeats

Scribner's, New York, 1997

There are so many collections of Yeats's poetry that almost any will do. The important thing is to discover the poet for oneself. Master craftsman and romantic visionary, William Butler Yeats played with all the masks of poet, playwright, philosopher, and politician in his search for an ideal life where all masks blend into one. His poems are witness to and metaphor of that lifelong quest.

Yeats's poetry is crowded with symbol and image, with sensuous music and the play of intellect. His work had extraordinary range. Yeats found inspiration in the ancient bards and heroes, in the beauty of nature, in the motives and affairs of men, in youth and in old age. Everything touched him, and he touched on everything in turn. Because he became almost *the* ubiquitous Irish poet, there are those who denigrate Yeats, just as there are those who sneer at Tchaikovsky simply because his music is so popular. Popularity has a reason, however. Words and music that touch people's souls acquire not only popularity but immortality. W. B. Yeats has both. The titles of the poems in this collection comprise a roll call of favorites: "Down by the Salley Gardens," "The Lake Isle of Innisfree," "When You Are Old," "The Hosting of the Sidhe," "The Song of Wandering Aengus," "The Wild Swans at Coole," "In Tara's Halls," "I Am of Ireland," "Under Ben Bulben."

Yeats's poetry is not all romance, however, nor serious and solemn. Consider "On Hearing That the Students of Our New University Have

Joined the Agitation Against Immoral Literature," or "To a Poet Who Would Have Me Praise Certain Bad Poets, Imitators of His and Mine," or "To a Wealthy Man Who Promised a Second Subscription to the Dublin Municipal Gallery If It Were Proved the People Wanted Pictures."

One of the most powerful and poignant of Yeats's poems tells of an Irish pilot who knows he will be killed fighting for the British in World War I: *"An Irish Airman Foresees His Death."* The most revealing lines in the poem are these:

> Those that I fight I do not hate,
> Those that I guard I do not love.

REFERENCE BOOKS

GRENHAM, JOHN

Tracing Your Irish Ancestors

Gill & Macmillan, Dublin, 1992

Every year, countless Americans attempt to trace their Irish roots. Some work from home, often starting from scratch with no idea of what to do first. I have received hundreds of letters from readers who want to learn more about their families, and hope I can answer them simply because I make my living writing about Irish history. Others actually come to Ireland with a vague idea of a grandfather's parish, the name of a townland, or a clue from the family Bible. Physically being present in Ireland makes it easier, but not much. Genealogical research is a long, painstaking, often frustrating procedure. A cross between solving a whodunit and putting together a jigsaw puzzle, it can be a daunting undertaking. Most people need help.

American-published books on researching your family history are not necessarily helpful enough. Historical situations have made Ireland a unique problem. Tribes and septs, land divisions and the ravages of war, have all played their part in creating confusion. Records have been lost, burned—or were simply never kept. But anyone who ever lived in Ireland, small as it is, has left some clue somewhere. John Grenham is dedicated to helping their descendants find them.

Tracing Your Irish Ancestors is a comprehensive and authoritative guide for people who are willing to take the time to research their genealogy. Recognizing that the circumstances of each individual family are different, Grenham has structured his book to reflect those differences. In his introduction he tells you where to start, what you can expect to find, and the names of U.S., Canadian, and Australian sources that may be helpful. He assumes that the amateur genealogist is embarking on the undertaking for the first time and provides a thoughtful and sympathetic guide.

In Part One, Major Sources, the author goes into specifies. He explains civil records, telling the reader what information they may give and what genealogical relevance they have. He also discusses research techniques. From there he moves to the important Irish census records, church records, and land records. Part Two, Other Sources, goes into detail about wills, the Irish Genealogical Office, passenger and emigrant lists and published works on emigration, the Registry of Deeds, newspapers, and directories. Part Three, A Reference Guide, examines the problem through the medium of known ancestral occupations. Next come county source lists such as local history, local journals, gravestone records, estate records, and place names.

The book concludes with family histories, parish records held in Dublin repositories, and a list of available research services and societies. Grenham also has thoughtfully provided county maps divided by diocese, which alone are almost worth the price of the book for Americans trying to trace their families.

John Grenham is a professional genealogist formerly attached to the Genealogical Office in Dublin. He is now project manager with the Irish Genealogical Project, which is charged with compiling a broad database of all Irish family records.

KELLY, FERGUS

Guide to Early Irish Law

Dublin Institute for Advanced Studies, Dublin, 1988

This fascinating book gives details of the ancient Irish law, the second oldest codified law in the world—and probably the most humane. Predating Christianity, Brehon Law evolved in Ireland over a number of centuries and was probably based on even older Celtic tribal law. It recognized the rights of women; controlled through pride and prestige rather than through force; provided means of compensation for every form of offense; and considered its principal function to be restoring the offender and the offended to amity.

Originally Brehon Law was passed on through the oral tradition, as pre-Christian Ireland was not a literate society. That does not mean the early Irish were uneducated; quite the contrary. Education was always highly prized. The Druids were the intellectual class of the Irish culture as they had been of the Continental Celts. Far from being the bizarre "priests" beloved of modern horror writers, the Druids in actuality were teachers, healers, diviners, historians, genealogists, poets—and judges.

Wisdom was passed down through various druidic schools, and taught by rote over a number of years to apprentices. In County Clare the ruins of one of the greatest of the Brehon law schools still exists. As a result of the coming of Christianity to Ireland in the fifth century A.D., these early law texts began to be transcribed by monks. Fergus Kelly's guide to early Irish law is based on texts that originated in the seventh and eighth centuries and survive—although often incompletely or in a corrupt form—in manuscripts of the fourteenth to sixteenth centuries.

Kelly begins his study of this ancient legal system by examining the society in which it developed. Quoting a lecture delivered by a legal expert, D. A. Binchy, in 1953, he tells us that early Irish society was "tribal, rural, hierarchical, and familiar—using 'familiar' in its oldest sense, to mean a society in which the family, not the individual, is the unit." Upon this family-based culture, Brehon Law was predicated. It was up to the family to be responsible for and control its members. If one of them transgressed, the entire family was assessed fines, and, even more tellingly, disgraced. In a society that placed prestige at the top of its requirements, this was a powerful control mechanism.

Kelly's introduction explains the complex degrees of family relationships within the *Tuath*, or tribe. Chapter 1 discusses the Law of Persons, insofar as it pertains to tribal kings and their responsibilities to their people. Chapter 2 elaborates on the same law in relation to clerics, poets, satirists (the satirist was highly feared in ancient Ireland, for a great satire could bring down a king), lawyers, physicians, Druids, craftsmen, manufacturers, entertainers, and servants. Chapter 3 deals with the law as it specifically pertains to women: marriage, divorce (there was divorce in ancient Ireland!), separation, the legal capacity of women, offenses both by women and against women, and the law covering children and fosterage. Chapter 4 moves into the extremely complicated area of property, proving that what appears to be a simple, pastoral tribal culture required as many legal protections against property disputes as our own. Chapter 5 covers offenses beginning with the first and most serious: killing. Subtopics include lawful and unlawful injury, abandonment of sick maintenance, rape, sexual harassment, the refusal of hospitality—and satire, defined as "verbal assault on a person." Even a person's liability after death for offenses committed while living is set out. Chapter 6 deals with contracts, pledges, and sureties. This is followed by chapters on distraint, procedure, and punishment. Interestingly, there is no record of mutilation as a form of judicial punishment until A.D. 1224. One could however be put to death, flogged, or outlawed.

These chapters are followed by reproductions of some of the legal texts in the original monastic Latin, together with a detailed list of the texts. There is also an extensive bibliography and a very helpful index of Irish terms.

This examination of early Irish law is enlightening. No other social document gives such a thorough look at the forces that shaped us as Brehon Law. The breadth, wisdom, and antiquity of the Irish culture will amaze many Americans.

KENNER, HUGH

A Colder Eye: The Modern Irish Writers

Johns Hopkins University Press, Baltimore, 1989

The international reputation the Irish have achieved in the field of literature is sometimes exaggerated, a case in point being the recent visit of the Taoiseach, or Irish prime minister, to China. His welcoming committee assured him they knew all about Ireland: it is full of writers and they have all won Nobel prizes, he was told quite seriously.

This name for excellence makes Irish literary criticism a field unto itself. Kenner's thoughtful and intensely researched book does not quite live up to its full title, as it is hardly a broad-spectrum examination of modern Irish writers. Instead he focuses on those identified with the Irish Revival at the turn of the century and shortly thereafter. But within these parameters he does a superb job of acquainting the reader with important Irish writers in a way that is both informative and highly entertaining.

Literary criticism can be as dry as dust. *A Colder Eye* is as pungent as an Irish woodland on a May morning. The author's Irish credentials are scanty, for which he makes no apologies. It is actually an advantage. He approaches his work not as an Irishman writing from the inside, but as an objective outsider. Oliver Cromwell wanted to have his portrait painted "warts and all," and Kenner looks at his chosen Irish writers in the same way. He makes us appreciate the warts for the character they add to the whole.

A Colder Eye takes W. B. Yeats as its springboard, then goes on to examine the works of James Joyce, Flann O'Brien, Samuel Beckett, Sean O'Casey, J. M. Synge, Lady Gregory, and others of the period. Kenner sets each in its broader context. Thus we are given a thumbnail lesson in Irish history, both social and political, replete with countless anecdotes that serve to illuminate the creator as well as the creation.

As an example, in describing the play called *A Pot of Broth,* Kenner tells us it was "written more or less by W. B. Yeats though most of its talk has the cadence of Lady Gregory." This witty story of the Little People has been described as the first story in the Irish dialect written during the Irish Literary Revival. As such it is dated, but its cleverness transcends its limitations.

In Kenner's writing there is an underlying tone of satire, at which the Irish themselves are past masters. The Irish, he points out, are unintimidated by literary pretensions—possibly because they are so accustomed to rubbing elbows with the greats of literature in Grafton Street or the local pub. He also rightly observes that the Irish can be a touchy people. That touchiness, and the way the author dealt with it when researching this book, add greatly to the charm of *A Colder Eye.* Here we have the voice of Ireland as heard by a foreign ear, then meticulously reproduced with all its color and vigor but without condescension.

A Colder Eye is the perfect introduction to the Irish Revival and explains its enduring importance. Literally hundreds of books have been written examining this period and these authors, but to my mind none of them are as eminently satisfactory as Kenner's little gem.

MacLysaght, Edward

Irish Families, Their Names, Arms and Origins

Allen Figgis & Co., London, and Towato, New Jersey, 1978

In this first of what would prove to be several volumes on the subject, Edward MacLysaght gives the names, origin, thumbnail history, and coats of arms of most of the major Irish families. His work is invaluable for acquiring a broad view of these families, as many Americans wish to do in tracing their own family histories.

Part One includes an introduction that explains why the author undertook this work. He elaborates on many common misapprehensions relating to genealogical studies and to heraldry. For example, he says, "It is a common popular error to speak of coats of arms as 'crests.' Many of the oldest armorial bearings have no crests. In some cases different crests were in use by several branches (septs) of a family, while the arms were common to all. A crest on the other hand cannot exist except as an apanage of a coat of arms." He also explains the differences between Mac and O, pointing out that *Mac*, which means son, indicated that the surname was formed from the personal name of the father. O names are derived from a grandfather or even earlier ancestor. In the Irish language, *ó* or *ua* denotes grandson, or male descendant.

MacLysaght goes on to describe how and why surnames have become distorted, and then to identify the most numerous as distributed by county. He also similarly examines the distribution of male Christian names—though not female.

Part Two lists Irish family names themselves, with their history and that of some of the most prominent members of the family. A number of these listings are extensive and filled with history in their own right. They also give the reader an idea of the vast difference between the Irish version of a name and its Anglicized counterpart. For example, "Kavanagh is one of the very few ancient Gaelic Irish names which has neither the prefix Mac or O. It is wrong to call it Ó Caomhánach in Irish as is sometimes erroneously done. In Irish it is simply Caomhánach which is an adjective denoting association with St. Caomhán, the first Kavanagh having been fostered by that saint."

Where there are genealogies tracing back to ancient times, as many of them do, the author cites folkloric history. Thus, in discussing the clan O'Connell, he tells us that "Traditionally the genealogy is traced back to Eremonian Aengus Tuirmeach, who was said to have been the High King of Ireland about 280 B.C." These sorts of details are fascinating to the family researcher. MacLysaght also clarifies the matter of tribes, family branches, and unrelated clans that have the same surname.

The book differentiates between the ancient Gaelic names and those of other origin. Many names we now commonly think of as Irish are of English—or Welsh, Flemish, Norman, or even Scandinavian—derivation. The author explains when and how the family first became connected with Ireland.

Part Three consists of a barony map and illustrations of the individual Irish family arms. These are very well produced, in accurate color, with a textual description on the facing page. Some American readers with Irish surnames may be delighted to discover their own arms represented.

Part Four contains a treatise on Anglo-Irish surnames, including the anglicized forms of Gaelic Irish surnames. Here again, brief historical sketches are given of the families named. This is followed by Appendix A: Surnames Indigenous and Common in Britain Which Are Used as the Anglicized Form of Gaelic Irish Surnames. Appendix B contains Surnames Commonly and Correctly Regarded as Gaelic Irish Which Are Nevertheless Found Indigenous Outside Ireland. Appendix C lists Gaelic Irish Surnames Which Have an English Appearance But Are Rarely Found Indigenous in Britain. Appendix D consists of Gaelic Irish Surnames Which Have a Foreign Appearance But Are Rarely Found Indigenous Outside Ireland. Appendix E lists The Best Known Norse, Norman and English Names Which Have Become "Naturalized" by Long Association with Ireland. The final appendix lists Irish Surnames Rarely Found Outside Particular Counties or Baronies.

The book concludes with a bibliography, index, and a handsome fold-out map of Ireland 1300–1600, the era of peak heraldic development.

TRAVEL AND PICTURE BOOKS

AALEN, F. H. A., KEVIN WHELAN, AND MATTHEW
STOUT, EDITORS

Atlas of the Irish Rural Landscape

Cork University Press, Cork, Ireland, 1997

Massive size, quality production, and substantial essays by twenty-one experts recommend this work both to the casual reader for dipping into and to the serious Hibernophile for detailed study. This interdisciplinary atlas draws on archeology, ethnology, and history in all its forms. A wide range of illustrative material, including maps, photographs, paintings, and remote sensing data, is supported by a sensitive and clearly written text.

The book opens with a quote from the French geographer Vidal de la Blache, who observed that "man and his environment are more intimate than a snail and his shell." This sets the theme for the entire atlas.

The first section is entitled "Synthesis of Habitat and History." As F. H. A. Aalen points out, "In increasingly urbanised societies, there is a misplaced view of the countryside as 'natural.' But like cities, the real landscape is artificial, skilfully contrived through time to meet social and economic ends." Using state-of-the-art computer cartography, the atlas then proceeds to explore the features that give the Irish countryside its unique character.

The island is divided into nine physical regions: the northwest, the northeast, the igneous uplands, the "drumlin" belt (named for its drumlin hills, which in turn refer to the characteristic shape of a hog's back), the central bogland and moraine, the southern hills and valleys, the southeast, the southwest, and the extreme west. Illustrations, graphs, and maps work together to present an excellent picture of the underlying Irish geology, giving a clear view of the dramatic differences to be found within what is essentially a very small island.

The next section is devoted to *"Early Landscapes: From Prehistory to Plantation."* Here the introduction of man-made elements is examined, from the evocative remains of stone sites of the Mesolithic (Middle Stone Age) to deserted villages dating from the medieval period, and plantation-era castles. The patterns established as human beings developed varying degrees of agricultural skill, and of civilization, are discussed. In conclusion, as one contributor points out:

"As the landscape was gradually modernized and transformed during the last three centuries, the evidence of thousands of years of prior human occupation persisted. Certain monuments were protected by local respect and by the limits of technology. In recent decades, however, with the implementation of state and European policies of agricultural development, there has been an accelerated rate of destruction. In some parts of Ireland one-third of all earthworks marked on the Ordnance Survey maps of the nineteenth century have disappeared. An increased awareness of Ireland's surviving field monuments will help guarantee the preservation of this extraordinary landscape legacy.

Following on this comes "The Modern Landscape: From Plantation to Present." Here we see the evolution of rural Ireland from a lightly settled, pastoral, heavily wooded countryside to its present form. One of the principal factors was the subjugation, colonization, and eventual integration of Ireland into the expanding British Empire. Equally important was the fact that after 1685, transatlantic shipping was of increasing importance to Britain: "From being an island behind an island on the rainy rim of Western Europe, Ireland now became the last European stepping-stone to America, tightly tied to Britain and its Atlantic colonies."

Those landscape elements that had particular influence on the history of this period are highlighted. With the destruction of native timber, peat bogs came to be the principal source of fuel in the countryside. Ireland was forced to burn its own ancient earth to keep warm. The importance of the potato, and its devastating cycle of disease in the middle of the nineteenth century, can hardly be overestimated.

The next section, "Components of the Irish Landscape," looks in turn at Bogs; Forests and Woodlands; Fields; Buildings; Towns and Villages; Demesnes (great private estates); Communications; Mining, Power, and Water. The part each of these plays in the whole is clearly explained, together with photographs and line drawings that bring the various elements to life.

This is followed by "The Challenge of Change." Here contributors discuss current issues such as housing pressures, landscape boundaries, the destruction of antiquities, and various environmental protection initiatives. Throughout the atlas there is keen concern for the future of the countryside, and an awareness of the threats posed by modern technology and new methods of agriculture.

The final section consists of six regional case studies concentrating on particular areas of interest both north and south of the border: the Hook in County Wexford; the Lecale Peninsula in County Down; the Burren in County Clare; the Boyne River Valley in County Meath; the Ring of Gullion in County Armagh; and Connemara in County Galway. Tim Robinson's study of Connemara in particular is so beautifully written that it could stand alone.

Step by step, the atlas builds up a multidimensional picture of Ireland's landscape and all of the elements involved over its long history. A wide range of distribution maps, many newly drawn, bring together data from the Ireland Archaeological Survey database. There is even a place-name index to guide the armchair traveler. Americans who have never visited Ireland can gain a good sense of the physical island in these pages. Those who know the land will learn still more.

The Book of Kells

HarperCollins, New York, 1995 (reproductions and text)

The Book of Kells has been described by many, connoisseur and layman alike, as the most beautiful book in the world. Now the premier manuscript in the library of Trinity College, Dublin, it was produced over twelve hundred years ago and has survived against all the odds.

The Book of Kells is the most spectacular of a group of illuminated manuscripts created in Ireland and northern Britain between the seventh and tenth centuries, a time when Irish monasticism was in the vanguard of Christian culture. The text of the four Gospels is a mixture, long retained by the Irish Church, of Vulgate Latin together with many words and phrases from earlier Old Latin translations of the Bible. This text is handwritten in exquisite medieval script and accompanied not only by lavish "illuminated" pages of Celtic artwork but also by stunning ornamentation within the lines of text itself.

The so-called carpet pages are world-famous. Some depict the writers of the four Gospels set in highly stylized Celtic frameworks; others create a universe of elegant abstract design around a single letter of the alphabet. Every page of the manuscript is richly ornamented; each qualifies as a work of art. The detail is lavish, much of it so minute that only a strong magnifying glass can reveal it. Yet this work was done long before eyeglasses, let alone electric light.

The origins of the Book of Kells are uncertain. We can be certain only that it was a labor of love undertaken by diverse hands in a Christian monastery somewhere in the British Isles, during the era Europe regarded as the Dark Ages. When and how the monastery at Kells in County Meath acquired the manuscript is not known. The monks there may have produced it, though some scholars believe the work was done in a monastery on the island of Iona in Scotland.

The earliest surviving reference to the Book occurs in an account in Irish of a theft from the monastery at Kells in 1006. The *Annals of Ulster* relate that "The Great Gospel of Colmcille, the chief relic of the western world, was wickedly stolen during the night from the western sacristy of the great stone church of Cennanus [Kells]." It was subsequently recovered and passed through a number of hands over the centuries before finding its final and proper resting place in Trinity College.

The bound manuscript is very large both in dimensions and in number of pages. It was not meant for daily use or study but was a sacred work of art, presumably intended to grace the altar on very special occasions. The pages are of vellum, which has stood the test of time; more remarkably, the colors of the artwork retain their brilliance to a degree that seems almost miraculous. The hundreds of thousands of visitors who have filed through the Trinity College library to see the Book of Kells comment on this one aspect more than any other.

There are many books about this masterpiece, including a large folio three-volume facsimile that sells for over $5,000. Over the years a number of firms have published reproductions, particularly of the spectacular "carpet pages," although nothing can equal the original.

No surviving artifact speaks more convincingly of the culture of early Ireland. The Book of Kells is a preeminent example of Irish art and as such a reproduction belongs in every Irish-American home. The HarperCollins edition is but one of many; I cite it in this collection because of its accessibility and the quality of the reproduction.

McNEILL, THOMAS

Castles in Ireland: Feudal Power in a Gaelic World

Routledge, New York, 1997

For the Irish castle enthusiast, this book is a must-have. The remains of several thousand castles representing various levels of Irish, Norman, and Anglo-Irish society still stand in Ireland today as an integral part of the landscape. Thomas McNeill gives the armchair traveler a guided tour of the most noteworthy, district by district.

Castles exert a strong influence on the imagination. A lord's power and prestige were displayed in the bold architecture and theoretically impregnable position of his stronghold. *Castles in Ireland* examines the society that produced these structures and traces the development of lordship and power in medieval Ireland.

The book opens with "Early Castles: To c. 1225." During the first millennium of the Christian era, the fortresses of Gaelic chieftains had largely followed the form of Iron Age ringforts. They employed earthen bank-and-ditch fortifications sometimes underlaid with stone. Within these might be artificially constructed mounds topped by buildings of timber and plastered wickerwork. The royal seat of the high kings at Tara; Emhain Macha in Ulster; and Rath Cruachan in Connacht all followed this design.

After Ireland's invasion by the Normans in the twelfth century, Gaelic chieftains began to build castles in imitation of feudal warlords. Meanwhile, the Normans were building castles to protect them from the hostile natives. The period was one of dynamic political change. It was inevitable that new types of construction appear, frequently rising upon older sites. MacNeill describes several examples and relates the archological work that has been done on them.

In Chapter 2, "Early Castles of Stone," the author examines the establishment of foreign lordships in Ireland from 1170 onward. In 1174 a destroyed Irish stronghold at Trim, on the Boyne River, was rebuilt in stone by the new Norman overlord of Meath. It was to be the largest of all Irish castles—a title it still retains. MacNeill's description of Trim Castle gives a vivid picture of this immense fortress, currently undergoing extensive scientific excavation and restoration:

> The great tower still dominates both castle and town by its height and unique design: a central block, to which were attached side towers. It was built in several stages, the first being the central block to the first-floor level, but with the walls carried up a floor higher, to support the side towers that rose to that level. This extraordinary structure was roofed, and recent examination of the fabric has shown that it had a wall-walk and parapet on top of the walls of the central block. Later the whole was raised a height of three floors in the central block, which also received a north-south dividing wall of stone internally, and four floors for the side towers. Its height was then further increased, incorporating the earlier wall-walk into a gallery level above the main third floor.

Chapter 3, "Early Castles of Earth and Timber," looks at those structures that continued to follow more traditional patterns. MacNeill points out that the difference between stone and timber castles was largely the difference in time, resources, and commitment necessary to construct them. Workmen had to be trained in the new architecture. Only the wealthy could afford to import skilled stonemasons from England and the continent. Chapter 4, "Castles and the Establishing of English Lordships in Ireland," discusses the important role of early castles in the administration of Ireland. They were not only defensive fortresses but also status symbols and centers of bureaucracy. Chapter 5, "The Central Period of English Lordship," focuses on the thirteenth century, the era in which most of Ireland's "classic" castles were constructed. MacNeill describes in some detail the life lived within those castles. They were not primarily residences; the builders had to accommodate the primary demands of armory and garrison. Thus, domestic provisions were the last consideration: "The great hall remained dominant as the venue for ceremonial and most public events, but increasingly as the pivot of a formal arrangement of the domestic rooms of the whole castle. At the 'low' end were the service rooms; at the other, the lord's. [These consisted of] an outer chamber for meeting his household, and an inner, private chamber for sleeping and confidential business."

Chapter 6, "Castles in the English Fashion," goes into considerably more detail as to architectural design, while Chapter 7, "Castles in a Divergent Tradition," looks at some of the more interesting variants, including Ferns Castle in County Wexford. Ferns was once the home of the notorious Dermot MacMurrough, who invited the Normans into Ireland in the first place.

The chapters that follow discuss lesser stone castles and enclosure castles of the late Middle Ages. Finally, the author looks at Gaelic tower-houses, concentrating primarily on those in the west of Ireland. He gives their dates, distribution, structure, and use, all items of interest as a number of these tower-houses have been purchased and restored as private homes today—many by Americans.

MARSDEN, SIMON, WITH TEXT BY DUNCAN MCLAREN

In Ruins: The Once Great Houses of Ireland

Alfred A. Knopf, New York, 1980; reprinted with additional material by Little, Brown, Boston, 1997

This is one of my very favorite books. Simon Marsden is a talented photographer with a deep appreciation for the ghostly and the mysterious. In this remarkable book he spans the centuries, photographing the beautiful and haunting ruins of Ireland, the once great houses, castles, Gothic and Palladian mansions designed by the most accomplished architects of their day. These were the principal seats of great families, the summer retreats of the rich and privileged, houses that were splendid in their prime and are magnificent in their ruin—victims of Oliver Cromwell, civil war, famine, land acts, private bankruptcy, and the passing of the ascendancy.

With a clever use of photographic technique and developing, Marsden succeeds in making his pictures look as ancient as their subjects while still preserving an astonishing clarity. His pictures give the impression of scenes glimpsed in a dream. Nothing seems quite real. The photographer's skill blurs the harsh realities of destruction, veiling decay with an aura of romance. The distance beckons; the clouds conceal.

Marsden's photographs are enhanced by a sympathetic text provided by Duncan McLaren. This weaves history together with folklore and gossip, surrounding each ruin with a swirl of tempting stories. The text accompanying a photo of thirteenth-century Castle Hackett in County Galway, for example, is taken from the writings of Speranza, Lady Wilde (Oscar Wilde's mother): "Finvarra, king of the fairies of the west, keeps up friendly relations with most of the best families of Galway, especially the Kirwans of Castle Hackett. Finvarra is a gentleman, every inch of him, and the Kirwans leave out each night for him kegs of the best Spanish wine. In return, it is said, the wine vaults of Castle Hackett are never empty, though the wine flows freely for all comers."

A portrait of Killua Castle, brooding against a dark sky in County Westmeath, is captioned: "An obelisk marks the alleged planting of Ireland's first potato by Sir Walter Releigh. No one remembers Lawrence of Arabia—the Chapmans' illegitimate son, owners of Killua's lost towers."

The gaping ruin of Castle Lyons in County Cork is that of the great house of the earls of Barrymore—a name famous in American theatrical circles of this century. Castle Lyons was built in the sixteenth century and burned down in 1771. We are told that from this house the family ruled over three hundred thousand acres. "The carelessness of a work-man finished its life, and the Earl died only two years after the fire. His first son, known as 'Hellgate,' married the heiress of the tragic Ardo Castle. He ultimately ruined his rich and powerful family by gambling."

Two photographs depict Dunboy Castle, the Gothic mansion of the Puxley family who served as inspiration for Daphne du Maurier's novel, *Hungry Hill* (see p. 199). During the Irish Civil War, guests were awak-ened by the rattle of chains in the night. The Puxley family left the house soon after. While they were away, members of the Free State army stole across the lake and put Dunboy to the torch. The civil war ended two days later.

One of the loveliest houses in the book speaks for all of them. At Mount Shannon in County Limerick, "Doric columns guard the en-trance to the once fine house of the Lord Chancellor of Ireland, John Fitzgibbon, the Earl of Clare. The drawing room no longer has silk on the walls or gilt furnishings; ivy hangs there now, and large brown cows move through the open walls."

O'BRIEN, JACQUELINE, WITH DESMOND GUINNESS

Dublin, A Grand Tour

Weidenfeld & Nicolson, London, 1994; Harry Abrams, New York, 1994

This is an elegant, stylish examination, tracing the city's history and architecture from earliest times. We are told that "The existence of Dublin as a trading port was known beyond the bounds of the Roman world, as the Greek cartographer, Ptolemy, marks it as 'Eblana' on a map drawn by him in the second century A.D." After landing at Skerries in northern County Dublin sometime in the fifth century, "legend avers that the national apostle [St. Patrick] passed through Dublin where he performed a miracle, striking his staff on the ground to reveal a well of pure spring water where he baptized converts."

The Vikings came next, turning the settlement at the mouth of the Liffey into a Scandinavian seaport. Knowledge of their tenure comes principally from archeological discoveries at Wood Quay on the south bank of the Liffey, where the finest intact Viking town in Western Europe was uncovered—only to have Dublin Corporation build their new office block on top of it.

Dublin has had a checkered history ever since. But its architecture remains one of its glories. The color photographs in this book were taken by Jacqueline O'Brien, a world-renowned photographer who also happens to be married to Vincent O'Brien, one of the most successful racehorse trainers in the history of Ireland. The text was written by the Hon. Desmond Guinness, a leading authority on Irish houses and castles and a pioneering force behind the Irish Georgian Society, dedicated to the preservation of Ireland's architectural heritage.

Dublin's finest surviving buildings are examined in detail, their beauty and history discussed in a crisp, informative style. Some of the gems included are Christ Church Cathedral, Drimnagh Castle, Newman House, Dublin Castle, Trinity College, the Royal Hospital Kilmainham, Freemasons' Hall, and the National Museum. The book also gives readers a knowledgeable look behind Dublin's famous Georgian facades, revealing an amazing variety of residential interiors. The exquisite plasterwork done by some of Europe's finest craftsmen still adorns such buildings as Newman House on St. Stephen's Green. The "saloon" is ornamented with allegorical figures in the plaster ceiling executed by Paul and Philip Lafranchini. The brothers created a larger version of this ceiling for Carton House, the magnificent Palladian mansion built in 1739 in County Kildare.

But as Desmond Guinness writes, "Of all the Georgian squares in Dublin, it is Merrion Square that stands supreme for the purity of its architecture, the excellent state of its preservation and the subtle variety of its fanlights and doorways." This image of Georgian Dublin is known worldwide, an image of grace and elegance.

Because the focus of the book is on decorative style, the picaresque elements that give Dublin its unique flavor are not included in the grand tour. There are no views of the Liberties or Temple Bar, no references to the infamous slums that were once considered the worst in Europe. However, the authors have compiled a tribute to the splendor that was also Dublin, and may still be seen and appreciated today.

O'BRIEN, JACQUELINE, AND PETER HARBISON

Ancient Ireland from Prehistory to the Middle Ages

Weidenfeld & Nicolson, London, 1996; Oxford University Press, New York, 1996

A sumptuous book, with spectacular photographs of historic sites, artifacts, jewelry. Even such old standards as Tara and the Rock of Cashel are treated to new and imaginative views.

Peter Harbison's credentials are impeccable. He has held a number of positions in Ireland connected with archeology and the environment, has written many books, and is a former editor of *Ireland of the Welcomes*, the magazine that has served as an introduction to Ireland for many Irish Americans. The text Harbison has written is perfectly integrated with O'Brien's photographs, many of which are breathtaking.

The first chapter of the book, "Ireland Before History," starts with the Stone Age, when Ireland's long history of human habitation began. Newgrange, in County Meath, the oldest *engineered* building on the planet—it predates both Stonehenge and the pyramids—receives loving attention. The sheer size of Newgrange dazzles the mind. Dazzling, too, is the facade of white quartz that fronts the huge man-made mound. A massive stone carved with mysterious symbols guards the entrance to a passageway leading into the heart of the structure. At sunrise during the winter solstice, and only then, a shaft of golden light follows that passageway to a trefoil chamber deep in the mound. There, for nineteen minutes, Father Sun brings the promise of life to the womb of Mother Earth. Every year—for almost six thousand years. Such is the amazing engineering of this Neolithic masterpiece.

Newgrange shares the spotlight with such evocative Bronze Age monuments as Poulnabrone Dolmen in the Burren, County Clare. Poulnabrone is surely the most photographed dolmen in Ireland, for good reason. O'Brien shows the upright stone walls of what was once a chieftain's tomb, gleaming in pale limestone and topped with a massive slab, set against a thunderously dark sky. Here is nothing but stone and sky and a feeling of incredible age. Farther on, the magnificent goldwork of Ireland's Bronze Age craftsmen fairly leaps off another page, demanding a sharp intake of breath in admiration.

Chronicling the arrival of the Celts between seven hundred and five hundred years before the birth of Christ, O'Brien shows us many of the structures attributed to these Iron Age people. The beautiful curvilinear designs carved upon the Turoe Stone in County Galway show the influence of La Tene artwork, which the Celts brought with them from Continental Europe.

In Chapter 2, the authors examine the early Middle Ages, discussing Patrick and the Christian movement in Ireland, and the various sites associated with it. Representative examples of both monastic round towers and Celtic high crosses are shown, each captured at their moment of greatest drama or beauty beneath Irish skies.

Chapter 3 deals with the eleventh and twelfth centuries. Harbison tells us: "One of the most appealing of all the smaller Irish Romanesque churches is that at Monaincha, not far from Roscrea, built on what was an island in a lake drained in the nineteenth century. The island was a hermitage of the ascetic Culdees and, according to Giraldus the Welsh historian, who visited Monaincha in 1185–86, no female—human or animal—could live on the island." Chapter 4 covers "The Anglo-Normans, 1169–1400." Harbison sets the political scene, then O'Brien shows us the physical results with such buildings as King John's Castle (actually built by Hugh de Lacy) in Carlingford, County Louth. The choir of St. Patrick's Cathedral, Dublin, makes a stunning photograph with the banners of the great families hanging in solemn rows above the choir stalls. This is the oldest part of the cathedral, built around 1254.

Late medieval Ireland, in the fifth chapter, includes Dunguaire Castle in County Galway, where many Americans have been entertained at medieval banquets in recent years. Another popular tourist destination is W. B. Yeats's restored tower-house, Thoor Ballylee, also in Galway.

The book concludes with a chapter devoted to Stuart, Tudor, and

Plantation architecture. With its romantic fairy-tale appearance, exqui-site Killyleagh Castle in County Down reminds one of a French château. By contrast, the massive fortification of Charles Fort at Kinsale, County Cork, brings to mind a more tragic image: the Battle of Kinsale that spelled the doom for ancient Gaelic Ireland.

In each chapter history goes hand-in-hand with stunning visual im-ages, so that one absorbs effortlessly. For quality of writing and beauty of illustration no book recently published on early Ireland can match this production.

O'DONNELL, E. E., COMPILER

Father Browne's Ireland

Wolfhound Press, Dublin, 1997

Father Frank Browne was a genius with a camera. Perhaps more important, he was in the right place at the right time. Over a number of years he documented every aspect of Ireland and Irish life as it evolved through the first half of this century.

Francis Mary Hegarty Browne was born in Cork in 1880, the youngest of eight children in a prosperous middle-class family. He took his first photographs at the age of seventeen when he was brought on a Grand Tour of Europe. In 1912 his uncle, the bishop of Cloyne, bought Frank a ticket for the first stage of a famous maiden voyage—that of the *Titanic*. Young Frank sailed from Southhampton to Queenstown (Cobh), where he disembarked with a remarkable set of photographs. The *Titanic* set off for New York without him. When the ship sank, Frank Browne became famous overnight. Many of his pictures appeared in newspapers worldwide.

Frank Browne was ordained in the Jesuit Order in 1915, and his subsequent work as a priest facilitated his photography by allowing him to travel extensively. He was a friend of James Joyce; they attended both school and university together, and Joyce refers to him in *Finnegan's Wake* as "Browne the Jesuit."

As an army chaplain during World War I, Father Browne earned both the Military Cross and the Belgian Croix de Guerre, yet it is his photographs that form his most lasting memorial. Books of his photos of

Dublin and Cork and even Australia, compiled by his fellow Jesuit, E. E. O'Donnell, recall a vanished way of life. But the first of the collections, *Father Browne's Ireland*, remains the definitive work of its type. The black-and-white images captured in the priest's camera show us Irish people at home in humble cottages and grand houses; Irish children at play, as innocent and as mischievous as children anywhere; Irish faces that capture the essence of youth and age, of beauty and endurance and grief. The photographer loved people and loved Ireland. Both are evident in his work.

Here we see a truly beautiful view of Derry's Bogside in more peaceful times; a dignified old lady in shawl and bonnet exchanging news with a friend in Castlewellan; a carefree young woman dancing with a goat in a rural setting; the elegant interior of Shelton Abbey; the thatched cottage of a tailor near Cloone; Shannon Airport when it was brand-new (and astonishingly empty); the horse fair at Kilrush with men and horses gathered together in the narrow street; a little girl swinging from the handle of the village pump; Sports Day at Ballydavid, with a man doing the high jump in the old way while Gaelic-speaking spectators watch; the idiosyncratic West Clare railway, immortalized by Percy French; "shawlies" in the Claddagh; a motor accident on the main Dublin-Cork road in 1932; a little boy sheltering under an overturned currach at Brandon Cove.

Nothing was staged. Father Browne never posed anyone to give a more dramatic effect; he simply photographed what he saw. But he saw everything, and his wonderful photographs comprise a unique social document. Here is Ireland as the country was in his lifetime; we shall never see her like again.

The twentieth century is about to give way to the twenty-first. Ireland is changing; has changed. It is now both a sovereign, independent republic and a full member of the European Community. As of this writing, it also boasts the fastest-growing economy in all of Europe (which would be a great surprise to the Irish of an earlier era). Many of our immigrants are returning home to share in the new prosperity. Dublin has taken its proper place as a world capital, with all the sophistication—and growing crime rate—that title implies. Even in rural areas, the breathtaking landscape is in danger of being submerged beneath a tidal wave of new residential construction.

But people still greet you warmly wherever you go, and a silvery silence still envelopes the Lake Isle of Innisfree.

SEVERIN, TIM

The Brendan Voyage

McGraw-Hill, New York, 1978

This is the ultimate travel book, about the most remarkable voyage in the joint history of America and Ireland.

In 1976, author and adventurer Tim Severin set out to reproduce the voyage of a sixth-century Irish monk, St. Brendan. It was claimed that Brendan had crossed the Atlantic in a curragh, or Irish boat, made of leather, and he and his fellow monks may been the first Europeans to set foot on American soil. Most dismissed the story as a myth. Yet some documentation did exist in the form of an ancient manuscript describing the voyage, and purporting to be written by Brendan himself. It was enough to make Severin wonder if he could duplicate the undertaking and thus prove its possibility, much as Thor Heyerdahl did to prove prehistoric Pacific voyaging with the *Kon-Tiki*.

Before Severin could begin, he researched the ancient writings thoroughly. First came the problem of determining whether leather would be strong enough and waterproof enough to use as the skin of an ocean-going boat. Every detail as described by Brendan had to be investigated; again and again, they were proved practical. A basketlike frame of ashwood strips was tied together with leather thongs. Then forty-nine oxhides, tanned in a solution of oak bark and steeped in wool grease, were hand-sewn over the frame, using more than twenty-three *miles* of waxed flax thread. The work was painstaking. New skills were being mastered—or rather, old skills were being relearned after many centuries. Every step had to be just right; lives would depend upon it.

When all was in readiness, Severin and his crew—an Irishman, a Cockney, a Norwegian, and an Englishman—set out from Ireland's Dingle peninsula, the traditional site of Brendan's own departure. The voyage that followed would be one of the world's great adventure stories, documented photographically by *National Geographic*.

Severin's descriptions of the hazards they encountered make for white-knuckle reading. At one stage they were caught in the North Atlantic pack ice:

> This can't go on for much longer . . . Either *Brendan* will be blown clear of the floe, or she will be smashed to smithereens. As I watched, *Brendan* jostled forward another six feet on the next wave, and there was a chance to gauge the rhythm of destruction. It was obvious that the next blow would strike the steering paddle and snap its shaft. That would be the final problem: to be adrift in the pack ice with our steering gear smashed. Now the great floe was level with me where I stood at the tiller bar. The face of the floe stood taller than I did and in the light cast by my torch, the ice gleamed and glowed deep within itself with an unearthly mixture of frost white, crystal, and emerald. From the water-line a fierce blue-white reflected up through the sea from the underwater ice ledge. And all the time, like some devouring beast, the floe never ceased its constant roar and grumble as the ocean swell boomed within its submarine hollows and beat against its sides.

In the end it was not the modern navigational aids they had brought along that saved them, nor the technology of the twentieth century. Their saviour was the seafaring wisdom of a sixth-century Irish monk, and the equipment that saw the adventurers at last make landfall in America was the equipment reproduced from his directions.

Suggested Sources for Irish-Interest Books

In North America:

Dufour Editions, Booksellers
P.O. Box 7
Chester Springs, PA 19425

Irish Books and Media
1433 Franklin Avenue East
Minneapolis, MN 55404-2135

The Irish Bookshop
580 Broadway, Room 11103
New York, NY 10012

Sandpiper Books
110 & 112 South Pacific Way
P.O. Box 1439
Long Beach, WA 98631

On the Internet:

Advanced Book Exchange—www.abebooks.com
Alt.bookstore—www.altbookstore.com
Amazon.com—www.Amazon.com
Barnes and Noble online—www.barnesandnoble.com
Bibliofind—www.bibliofind.com
Bookpages—www.bookpages.co.uk
Borders online—www.borders.com
The UK Internet bookshop—www.bookshop.co.uk

In Ireland:

De Burca Rare Books
"Cloonagashel"
27 Priory Drive
Blackrock
Co. Dublin

Genealogy Bookshop
3 Nassau Street
Dublin 2

Fred Hanna 27–29 Nassau Street
Dublin 2

Hodges-Figgis
56–58 Dawson Street
Dublin 2

Hughes & Hughes
St. Stephen's Green
Dublin 2

Kennys' Bookshop
High Street
Galway Co. Galway

Phibsboro Bookshop
342 North Circular Road
Dublin 7

Waterstones
7 Dawson Street
Dublin 2

INDEX